DISCOVER
YOURSELF

DISCOVER **YOURSELF**

Understand Your Mind

•

Know Your Body

•

Nurture Your Spirit

•

Realize Your Potential

LILLIAN TOO

Hay House, Inc.

Carlsbad, California • Sydney, Australia

Canada • Hong Kong • United Kingdom

I dedicate this very special and beautifully designed book to my husband, to our recently married daughter, Jennifer, and to her husband, our wonderful son-in-law, Chris.

She is a Snake lady and he is a gentleman Dragon—belonging to fire and earth elements—so I know they are well suited. They were married in April this year, a time of spring and of new beginnings. Gracing their wedding banquet were five auspicious lions to attract good fortune and happiness from the four directions, and blessings from heaven.

This book further commemorates this most joyous occasion in our lives. I pray they have wonderful times ahead, discovering and loving each other more deeply with each passing year.

Copyright © 2002 by Lillian Too

Published and distributed in the United States by: Hay House, Inc., P.O. Box 5100, Carlsbad, CA 92018–5100 • (800) 654-5126 • (800) 650-5115 (fax) • www.hayhouse.com
Distributed in Canada by: Raincoast, 9050 Shaughnessy St., Vancouver, B.C., Canada V6P 6E5

Designed and produced by The Bridgewater Book Company

Photography by Peter Webb
Illustrations by Coral Mula and Sarah Young

Library of Congress Control No.: 2002111138

ISBN 1-4019-0152-2

06 05 04 03   4 3 2 1
Ist printing, January 2003

Printed and bound in Singapore by Tien Wah Press

Contents

Part Two: DISCOVERING SECRETS OF YOUR BODY

Part Three: DISCOVERING YOUR SPIRIT

Part Four: DISCOVERING YOUR POTENTIAL

Introduction

How many of us can resist the seduction of getting to know ourselves? Once we step across the threshold of initial misgivings, scrutinize our bodies and our minds, examine the way we view ourselves in relation to others, explore how we interact with those we are intimate with, investigate the pathways of our intellect, and study the various dimensions of our spiritual aspirations, we will uncover new aspects about the self that will astound, delight, and perhaps even surprise us.

Many aspects of our personae will astonish us. As we move from the mental to the physical and the spiritual within us, the process of unlocking will cause magical realizations to surface. We begin to comprehend all the different aspects that impinge on the way we control and manipulate our destiny. So the investigation of everything we are holds clues to what we can be, what we are meant to be, and what we will ultimately be.

We are part of the diversity of peoples that make up the human race. It is impossible to examine oneself in isolation, separate from the rest of the world. We can really only understand ourselves fully when we accept that everything we are, and will be, has meaning only in relation to outside forces, to other people, to the rest of the world. There is interconnectivity between us and everyone else in the universe.

There are also many different dimensions to the perception of the physical self, the classification of mental states, and the appreciation of spiritual aspirations.

You will see your mind and your body from different perspectives and discover new ways of looking at the components that make up the self. Many aspects of your persona will astonish you.

Our existence and simply our being are best observed in terms of the aggregates that define the self. And so we look at the forms, shapes, and colors that identify us. When we investigate the way we interact with our sensory perceptions, we will get a feel of who we are in terms of what we like and dislike and how we react to the things we see, smell, taste, feel, and the sounds we hear.

Thousands of nuances shape our momentary likes and dislikes, our perceptions and reactions at all the three levels of "being," and these also change with the passage of time. It is not that we are fickle—only that each human person is an exciting object of numerous discoveries that transforms and changes continually. Understanding these things makes our awareness of people far more acute. It is when we start to live in this state of awareness that we are forced to confront the awesome labyrinth of choices, trade-offs, and differences that begin to reveal themselves. This is when we start to see the world with new, wider, brighter eyes.

You will discover that you are neither merely a "single type" nor a "single moment" person.

Within this book, then, are manifold ways to discover the self. We begin by examining the mental, physical, and spiritual dimensions of the human personality. Aspects of this trinity of self will merge to create each unique person. They combine the influence of perceptions, attitudes, emotions, thought processes, and spirit, and they impact on the way people live, react, and interact with others. Moreover, they create a view of self that produces a unique perception of reality that makes up each person's world. The last part of this book deals with destiny as we investigate different methods of foretelling the way life unfolds. In the process, we will find answers to unasked questions about our own immortal soul.

When we discover ourselves, complete with all our magnificent imperfections, hangups, myriad obsessions, and passions, we will find a tolerance that will eventually lead to real acceptance of all the people who make up our world—and herein lies the secret of happiness.

Part One

DISCOVERING YOUR MIND

How do our minds react to a broad range of stimuli? In this section, we will use alternative ways to probe the consciousness of the real self. Many of the approaches used here are based on the way the Chinese view the Universe and how they explain the world in terms of the cosmic breath—a life force that pervades all of our breathing and all of the environment's vigor. This cosmic life force is called chi, *which is the living energy of humankind's world.*

We will investigate the strength of our beliefs, the intensity of our purpose, and the depth of our emotions, obsessions, and passions. We will also explore techniques that unlock doorways into the inner mind, focusing on our psychological base. We will confront our hidden phobias and irrational short circuits, the different dimensions of self-perceptions for men and women, and whether we are introverts or extroverts. Indeed, many important aspects of mental consciousness are dealt with to help us look at our minds.

You, Among a Diversity of Peoples

To know the self, it is helpful to develop conscious awareness of body and mind, which manifest the feelings of the heart. It is the simultaneous awareness of these two elements that leads to the spiritual within us. Developing awareness of them establishes a greater perspective of the self, a point of view that helps us tune in to the tai chi or yin yang philosophy of the individual self.

When we look at the human race, we see a diversity of peoples so wide-ranging in physical and attitudinal differences that racial, cultural, and geographical groupings instantly come to mind. Yet a visitor from outer space would say we look and think alike except perhaps physically in the variations of our skin color, our physical build, and the way we speak.

We are different from each other, yet we are also alike. We have two arms, two legs, one head, and a body torso. The same internal organs keep us pumping and breathing. We eat, we sleep, and we aspire to have wealth, health, and happiness.

It is only as we examine our mind and body more closely that we become aware of our differences—the color and texture of our skin, our hair, the way we carry ourselves, the length of our limbs, the shape of every part of us, the size of our muscles, and how each part fits in with the rest of the body. More significantly, there are real differences in the way we use our intellect.

Attitudes and aspirations vary so significantly between the peoples of this world that each person on this earth is completely special, unique, and different from anyone else. We should celebrate this uniqueness. Even as we accept that we are part of the human race of planet Earth, thereby embracing the similarities that bond us at a base level, we should simultaneously take joy in delving much deeper into our bodies, our minds, and our hearts.

At a personal level, we can start by examining our mental makeup and our physical body. We can appreciate the subtleties in the way our thoughts flow, and see how the attitudes that govern our actions are formed. Physically, we can appreciate the differences of our body shape, the surface coloring of our skins, and the texture of our pores. To the Chinese, the body is a manifestation of the matter or aggregates that make up the self. We undertake this examination with the awareness that the body is the outer physical manifestation of the self.

Within the human body, the mind, at some subconscious level, controls the self and is the arbiter of who and what we are. Yet the mind is neither physical nor tangible. To reach the mind, we think of the heart, which houses our feelings, emotions, and state of mind. To the Chinese, the mind and heart manifest as energy, or chi, the cosmic breath.

Consciously developing this greater perspective of the self will help us tune in to the tai chi (or yin yang) philosophy that views each of us as a manifestation of the relationship between energy and matter. It is this relationship that defines forms, colors, and textures, and encapsulates all that we can know about ourselves, and about the Universe.

It is extraordinary how human beings, who all have a similar physical makeup, can vary so much in their attitudes and aspirations.

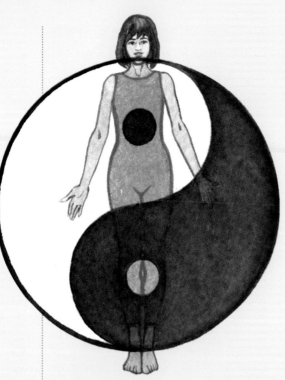

A SENSE OF SELF

To get a sense of self, tune in to who you are. Look at yourself in a full-length mirror. Think of your body in terms of the tai chi, as matter and energy, as yin and yang. Decide which parts of you are yin and which are yang. Look at yourself from different angles and note if you are fat or thin, tall or short, dark or fair. Note the length of your hair and the texture of your skin. Bend your body and stretch it in as many different ways as you can, as you slowly examine the shape and curves of your body. Look at the different shades of color of your body. Dark shades are yin, while lighter shades are yang.

Look at your face, scrutinizing each feature carefully—your eyes, your forehead, your cheeks and cheekbones, your nose, your mouth, your neck, your ears, and your hair. Note the rise and fall of your features, the thinness and thickness of your skin and hair. As you look at yourself, think of the mind within the body. Looking beyond the body in search of the mind requires a certain transcendence

of thought. This enables you to tune in to yourself. It is helpful to connect your thoughts with your feelings. The focusing of your thoughts as you examine your body will give you a sense of the three dimensions of body, mind, and spirit bonding into a single entity.

When you view yourself this way, it becomes easy to think of yourself as symbolizing the tai chi symbol of yin and yang, one part of your body connecting to another part, the outside connecting to the inside, each containing some part of the other and always moving in a flow, representing the whole that is the complete self.

This is the theory of tai chi that reminds us that all of us, and everything in the Universe, comprise two aspects of the same energy flow, one manifesting as yin energy and the other as yang energy, with both constantly evolving and transforming. In other words, there will always be two sides to the self, to the same phenomenon.

Test yourself At the practical level, think through the questions below while examining your body. Become aware of how you feel. Answering questions in this way is a form of analytical meditation.

1 Do you feel uncomfortable examining yourself? Why is this?

2 What are you thinking of as you tune in to your body?

3 Which part of you do you instinctively think of as yang or yin?

4 Do you feel that your body balances well with your mind?

5 Do you notice any negative feelings surfacing as you look at yourself?

6 Can you detect your mind presence at all?

7 Are there special birthmarks, moles, or scars that catch your attention?

8 Do you feel you are too tall, too short, too fat, or too thin?

These questions focus attention on the way that the conscious mind reacts to the body. It is a wonderful start to the journey of self-discovery. The simple act of tuning in to the body dimension of identity engages the mind instantly, making it confront physical, racial, and cultural influences on the physical template. Since physical appearance, race, and culture can be powerful bonding agents among humankind, these aspects of the self have become benchmarks for defining each one of us.

Yet it is quite impossible to stereotype the diversity of human beings according to physique, type, color, and race. Different geographical and weather conditions in addition to so many other things exert an influence over the way people look.

Likewise, different traditions and different historical outlooks can create different mental templates in people. In recent times, global migrations and intermarriages have also added new body and mental templates to the worldwide melting pot, while education and modern-day global communication have created a whole new world of peoples who possess greater depth and breadth of knowledge than ever before. The discovery of self must be viewed in the context of today's world.

It is our perceptions, both of ourselves and of each other, including all the diversity of peoples around us, that define who we are and what we are. We are what we believe.

Exercise

Look at the eight images below and see which one appeals to you. Do not think too much—go for your instinctual reaction.

THE WHEEL

THE DOUBLE FISH

THE BANNER

THE MYSTIC KNOT

THE PARASOL

THE LOTUS

THE CONCH SHELL

THE VASE

How Do You See Yourself?

Allow your prejudices, opinions, and preconceived ideas to flow freely as you soak in these eight beautiful images of auspicious objects. Each image signifies different aspects of personality that could hold some surprises about a hidden you. If you feel that the descriptions do not quite fit your perception of your own personality, try picking another symbol as a second choice.

The Wheel

Introspective | sensitive | reflective
You see yourself as someone who gets to grips more frequently and thoroughly with yourself and your environment than do most others. You feel that this makes you sensitive to people and their needs. You hate superficiality and prefer spending time by yourself than spending time with people who bore you. You like having good, intensive, meaningful friendships. You are also the sort of person who values the inner tranquility of meditation. You are interested in mysticism and comparative religions.

The Double Fish

Independent | unconventional | unfettered
You are a free spirit who dislikes being shackled by convention. You take great pride in being independent and you are determined to be responsible for your own happiness. You are also highly creative and have a certain artistic bent running through your work and hobbies. You are sometimes accused of being excessively individualistic, but you do live life according to the standards that you set yourself. You are sometimes unsure which side of yourself you wish to show to the world. While you like appearing independent, you are also quite aware that genuine freedom comes from acting within a conventional environment.

The Banner

Dynamic | active | extrovert
You are something of a risk taker, always keen to assuage your curiosity even at the cost of putting personal safety at risk. You love life, and you love victory in everything you put your mind to. You enjoy mainly the company of like-minded friends. Making a strong commitment to a cause or to a particular person is never a problem with you, as long as it is something or someone that sounds interesting and varied. You can become easily bored unless strongly challenged, but you are also extremely dependable and you can be relied upon to complete the tasks at hand. You want to be able to make a meaningful difference in everything you take on. Leadership comes easily to you.

The Mystic Knot

Well-balanced | harmonious | loyal

You regard yourself as a well-balanced person and take pride in your ability to stand by your friends. You see yourself as a person whose life is well structured and harmonious. You are dependable and usually deliver more than you promise, so you give those close to you warm feelings of security. You reject everything garish, artificial, and vulgar. You tend to be impatient with impulsiveness, fads, and fashion. When you love, it is forever.

The Parasol

Reliable | dependable | self-assured

You are in full command of your life; you seldom believe in luck or rely on other people. For you, actions always speak louder than words. Problems are always handled in a pragmatic fashion. You are a professional in everything that you take on, and your confidence inspires others to follow your lead. Yours is a realistic view and everything in your daily life is dealt with in a systematic manner. Your support of associates is unwavering. When responsibility is placed on your shoulders you feel you always rise to the occasion.

The Lotus

Beautiful | discreet | popular

You are easygoing yet discreet and take great joy in being liked by just about everybody. You make friends effortlessly, although you also enjoy your privacy and your independence. You appreciate

people for what they are, never imposing your opinions on them. You are peaceful, generous, and loving, and you are seldom aggressive with anyone. You need your own space, but you never lack for companionship and love, and you will seldom be without a soulmate. This is because people are always attracted to your calm demeanor and soothing presence.

The Conch Shell

Romantic | musical | emotional

You have such a romantic view of life that you can be described as being in love with love. You dream, you float, and you sail through life, refusing to see anything or anyone as bad. For you, the heart always rules the head. You have no time for those who are too practical and rational and who scorn romanticism. You are also a great communicator and you have a passion for travel.

The Vase

Generous | trustworthy | logical

You are a very generous person, and you believe in logical thinking. You like to surround yourself with "gems" of wisdom extracted from the classical texts and from great philosophers and thinkers. You also have great admiration for all things cultural and artistic. Your elegant and exclusive personal style is free from the whims of fashion. You place great value on upbringing, appearances, and good behavior in the people with whom you associate.

We Are Mirrors of Each Other

We are reflections of each other. Our perceptions of ourselves and others are colored by our preconceived ideas of physical, racial, and traditional archetypes. We are influenced by our own perceptions and so we all see the same person differently. And everyone will see us differently. To know your true self, you need to know what kind of mirror you are holding up to the world.

To know your true self requires you to know what kind of mirror you are holding up to the world.

It is helpful to determine some basic archetypes—which need not be all-encompassing—and even more helpful to examine our attitudes towards these archetypes. This makes us look squarely at some of our prejudices as well as our insecurities, according to the categorizations of archetypes. This exercise will give us a very good idea about the mirrors in our mind.

We can look at three major archetypes and examine which one we belong to, and then how we feel about where we stand in relation to these archetypes. These three archetypes are:

Physical archetypes
Racial archetypes
Personality archetypes

Physical Archetypes

These can be divided into three categories:

Round | curvy | overweight

A shape often fought against with dieting, associated with excess weight and having undeveloped muscles, fat tummies derisively termed "love handles," pear-shaped bodies, heavy breasts, and big hips and buttocks. The stereotype of the overweight man or woman is that they are clumsy and heavy with short body frames and probably suffering from cellulite! Generally negative connotations are associated with this body archetype, which is less desirable the younger you are, but is more acceptable to more mature people.

Hard | heavy | muscular

These are the muscular types, who tend to look squarish, more manly than feminine. Such people tend to have well-developed shoulders and are of medium height. They are generally considered healthy, sporty, and strong. This body archetype is generally acceptable to both young and old alike.

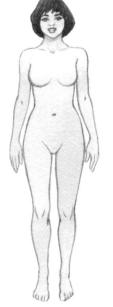

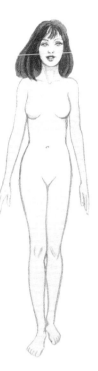

Long | thin | skinny

In women the long, thin look is generally associated with waif-like appearances made popular and desirable by glamorous models and film stars. This body archetype seems to be highly desirable among the youthful crowd for both men and women. Western women who are fortunate enough to have this body type may be the object of female envy.

Test yourself You will find that you do not necessarily fall into any of the three body archetypes described but you will have a perception of yourself which you may or may not like. Test yourself by thinking through these questions.

1 Do you consider yourself to be fat, medium, or thin? Are you happy with your weight? Do you feel you must do something about it?

2 Do you consider yourself short, medium, or tall? Do you wish you were taller or shorter? Do you have a complex about your height?

3 Do you find it hard to buy clothes that will flatter you?

4 Do you feel that your body type makes you unattractive or very attractive?

5 Do you feel that body shape is a direct indication of how sexually desirable a person is? Would you change anything about your body if you were able to?

6 Do you feel that personality is more important than body shape?

Racial Archetypes

These can be divided into four categories:

Caucasians

White Anglo-Saxon type looks. Mainly blonde or light-colored hair, blue eyes, generally light-skinned. Hair on chest in the male. Finely defined and sharp facial features. Double eyelid. Generally tall and of big build. Main representatives of this type are the Northern Hemisphere Europeans. Many now live in the USA, Canada, and Australia.

Aryans

Slightly darker-skinned types with darker hair and brown eyes. Hair on chest in the male. Women said to be exceptionally beautiful. Sharp features. Double eyelids. Tall and considered attractive. Mainly Northern Indians and West Asians.

Black Africans

Dark-skinned, ranging from tan to pitch black. Big and tall, heavy framed. Hair on chest in the male. Tightly curled hair. Mainly dark-colored hair. Sharply defined features. Well-developed breasts and hips in the female. Large and thick mouths. Mainly Africans. Many now live in the USA.

Asians

Mainly Chinese and Japanese. Brown to yellow to white skin tones. Jet-black, straight hair. Generally little body hair. Fine skin with small pores. Single eyelids and small mouths. Fine-boned and small frames. Men tend to be shorter and women tend to be fragile looking.

Test yourself These four racial heritage groupings are generalized categories that are easily recognizable physical prototypes based on geography and race. Even in today's cosmopolitan world there remain those whose view of the world is colored by prejudices and/or insecurities related to their racial type.

Consider if you are comfortable with who you are by thinking through these questions.

1 Do you belong to a minority group? Do you feel that you have ever been discriminated against because of this? If yes, has it made you bitter against any racial group?

2 Are you the product of a mixed marriage? Do you feel ashamed of being who you are?

3 Do you feel you belong to a superior race? If so, in what way would you say you were superior?

4 Do you consider that you belong to an inferior race? If so, in what way would you consider yourself to be inferior?

5 Do you feel that life is unfair?

6 If you could choose to be any race at all, which race would you like to be? Why?

The questions above are designed to make you think seriously about who you are in terms of your racial heritage. Tune inwards to see if you have any deep hangups about being who you are. Meditating on these hangups is very helpful in dissolving them.

In today's world, many countries, including the United States, have become cosmopolitan in their racial composition.

Personality Archetypes

These can be divided into four categories.

Amiable | easygoing

These people are guileless, happy, and tolerant. They exhibit a harmonious balance in relations with others, and are good-natured, sociable, and slow to anger or take offense.

Ambitious | driven

These people are assertive, bold, always busy, and appear to be networking all the time. They have no time for people not useful to them, tend to be impatient, and are very quick to spot opportunity. They are social climbers, often sneering at others. They desire power.

Arrogant | snobbish

These people think of themselves as upper class. They are often smart, rich, or famous. They are self-conscious, like privacy, and are sometimes socially inhibited. They can be insensitive and indifferent, and often are not very likable.

Eager | enthusiastic

These people are fun-loving, adventurous, and energetic. Highly sociable, they can be creative and easygoing. They are playful and are game for most things. They make good social pals.

Test yourself Be honest with yourself and see how many of the attitudes suggested below describe you. Then consider if you like seeing yourself that way or whether you would prefer to belong to another group. For instance, you may think of yourself as easygoing but feel that you should be more ambitious.

Which personality type or types do you think describe you best?

1 Do you like other people who are like you?

2 Are you ambitious? Do you like being ambitious? Do you admire other people who seem to be extremely ambitious?

3 Think of three people you know who fit the arrogant and snobbish category. Examine your feelings about them. Do you secretly wish you could be like them?

4 Do you sometimes get tired of people thinking of you as the "nice type"?

5 Are you a snob? If so, do you think you will always be a snob?

6 Do you think of yourself as someone who has a superiority complex?

Tune in to yourself and assess whether how you see yourself has anything to do with how you see others and how others see you.

Rediscover the Child Within You

Subconsciously, so many of us still live our lives in the past, either weighted by some traumatic event or continually taking strength from some childhood triumph. There is much to be said for consciously delving deep into our memory bank to revisit the child we once were—and to revisit a time when we were free of conditioning and programming.

When you are a baby, your view of the world is filled with light and love and a mother's warm embrace. As you grow older, however, all kinds of conditioning are programmed into your conscious and subconscious mind, and over time the innocence, courage, confidence, and natural loving essence within you can get buried deep until eventually lost, never to surface again.

It is good to meditate regularly, visualizing yourself as a child free of the constraints imposed by adult society.

BE INSPIRED

Jack spent his early years playing computer games. He became something of a hero among his childhood peers and soon developed an almost invincible view of his world as he conquered one new level of the games after another. As a child, his obsession came to rule his days and nights. But, by the time he went to school, Jack's winning aura began to dim as school grades suffered and computer game victories no longer meant very much. Jack did not make it to college, and for years he suffered from a terrible inferiority complex. Then he revisited his childhood days through visualization sessions and convinced himself he still had it in him to be a winner. Jack's personal therapy sessions helped him remember those early moments of triumph and attainment. Today he runs a very successful agency selling computer games!

The conditioning we each receive is as varied as the stars in the sky. Those of us with good karma will meet up with wise teachers who show us how to grow the natural essence of love, compassion, and courage within us so that we learn to develop

Young children move their bodies freely and interact naturally with their friends. As they grow up, they are gradually conditioned to behave in a certain way.

the fundamental nature within us. Then we become balanced, happy people. We do not lose our courage and our faith in ourselves. For many of us, though, the conditioning we receive and are subjected to can be negative and filled with harmful illusions, so that over time we lose our trust in the innate goodness and strength within us. We start to doubt ourselves, and we look for satisfaction in all the wrong places. It is then that we feel the stress and anxiety syndromes that will take their toll on our minds and bodies.

Look within and see if you are suffering from any kind of stress syndrome. Consider the following questions:

> ## The Chinese believe that inside all of us is the child that never grows up.

- Are you overweight?
- Do you depend on artificial stimuli such as alcohol, cigarettes, and drugs to make you feel good?
- Are you suffering from some complex that is holding you back?
- Do you suffer from some irrational fears?
- Do you get tired easily?

These are just some of the symptoms that suggest you might reap benefits from rediscovering the child within you.

No matter what kind of adult we subsequently become, the child within exerts powerful influences on the way we view our world. Present-day phobias, friends and enemies, strength of ambitions, ongoing depression, obsession—many manifestations of behavior and temperament have their root in some long-ago event of childhood.

The Chinese believe that regular meditation involving visualization into a time when you were young is very helpful in recharging the depleted energies of your body.

Empowering with Childhood Chi

Find a picture of yourself when you were young, looking vibrant, radiant, and happy.

> Smiling young faces contain stunning magical powers, especially those that capture all the innocence of your own particular childhood experience.

Note that traditional Chinese meditation techniques differentiate between the energy cycles of males and females. Thus, male energy chi cycles are believed to move in eight-year cycles, while female energy chi cycles are believed to move in seven-year cycles. Incorporate the cycles into the practice of this technique.

Examine a photo of yourself as a young child, looking radiant and cheerful, and try to tune in to that happy time of your life.

See Your Younger Self

If you are a man, look for a picture of yourself when you were eight years old or younger. Look closely at the picture and then lightly close your eyes and try to "see" yourself then. If you can remember the context of the picture, it is even better. Then you will find it easier to "go back in time." If you cannot and the memories are vague, it does not matter. Let your mental consciousness help you along.

Sit comfortably with loose clothing in a room where you will not be disturbed. Get into a silent and calm state of mind by breathing regularly and deeply. You will note that simply by focusing consciously on your breathing you will automatically create a situation of calm in your mind. Breathe slowly and deeply. Do not force the breathing. It should be natural and it should be slow and deep. Breathe in through your nostrils and slowly breathe out through the mouth.

Consciously breathe eight cycles before you start to create a picture of yourself when you were very young, before the age of eight. Tune in to the happiness on your face, the bright trusting eyes, the clear baby skin, the relaxed trust in the world; consciously feel that this beautiful face is yours. Keep your eyes closed and your breathing normal and regular as you concentrate on that time when you were young and innocent, confident and brave.

If you are a woman, repeat the same process, but look for a picture of yourself in which you were seven years old or younger. Consciously breathe seven cycles, and create a picture of yourself at seven years or younger. Tune in to that time of your life when you were young and happy, carefree and innocent. There is an aura of youthful freedom around you. Feel it ...

When you are in that state of innocence, with not a fear in the world, a time when stress has no meaning and pressure is a word yet unlearned,

Picturing yourself as a child and rediscovering the state of innocence can give you the strength to make decisions.

picture yourself floating into a garden paradise where flowers bloom and the air is filled with your favorite fragrance. It is helpful to spray the room with your favorite fragrance to help you create the visualization in your mind. I find that lavender essence works really well for me because lavender is very calming and seems to possess a quality that enables us to access some divine power within us, but you can try any fragrance you like.

Make a Wish

While in a state of innocence, make your wish. Make a BIG wish. Make a VERY BIG wish—not so much for an outcome, but for a personal attribute that will help you cope with your life at the present moment. For example, you might want to wish for courage, the strength to make some decision that

requires you to take a risk, as when you are about to make a major change in your life's circumstance. You might want to wish for strength to withstand some personal tragedy, or to stand up to someone, or face up to some terrible mistake you have made. You might wish for less anger, less stress, less pressure in your life, or wish for the courage to say "no" or to walk away from a bad situation.

When you revisit your childhood you will be reaching deep within you to rediscover the natural strength and essence you were born with, which is your natural birthright, and you will find you are able to recover all that is strong and good and powerful within you.

Remember that you should go back to the time of your first energy chi cycle, before life's conditioning was able to take hold.

Are You a Scholar or a Warrior?

There is a time to be smart and a time to be brave. The scholar possesses a fine mind. He is able to think, to analyze and to strategize. Sometimes, he is so involved in planning that someone sneaks up behind him and kills him. The warrior has the ability to endure physical hardships, and in the life of a warrior there are many opportunities to be brave, to be heroic... and also to be dead.

Right: A Chinese scholar. The scholarly, or yin, part of us will react to a difficult situation by reflecting upon it.

Far right: The warrior, or yang, part of us reacts to a problem with the physical urge to fight back.

Which would you rather be? A scholar or a warrior? Do you pride yourself on your intellect or your physical prowess? Do you believe negotiating is always superior to fighting? Are words always better than bullets?

> Do you believe in the greater power of the intellect, or the strength of your muscles and the courage inside you?

Your immediate reaction to these questions will reveal your subconscious preference and this tells you a basic conviction about yourself. We are—all of us—basically, either scholars or warriors. It is useful to examine your attitude a little deeper, and also in the light of the wisdom of the Tao. It is far better to seek the wisdom within the question, and investigate what this means in our journey of discovery into the self.

The more civilized the society in which we live, the more powerful becomes the written and spoken word. The less civilized our society becomes, the more powerful become the sword and the bullet. The ideal is the warrior whose wisdom arises through scholarship and through his mind, rather than merely through the sheer strength of his physical prowess.

The Chinese believe that the ideal is to apply the wisdom of the tai chi, or the yin and the yang of all phenomena, to our choice. In this situation, we extend the theory of yin and yang to the way we look at our reaction to hostile situations. When forced into a tight spot, how do we react? Like a scholar, reflecting, thinking, analyzing with words? Or like a warrior, with muscle, courage, and weapons, instantly fighting back?

In getting to know ourselves, it is useful to examine the yin and yang of the way we view the world, and the way we react to difficult and hostile situations that unfold within our lives.

THE I CHING

The best way to apply the yin and yang concept is to think through the mental model presented in the traditional source book called the *I Ching*, or the *Book of Changes*, an ancient and revered book that lays down the source of many of the concepts that underlie Chinese thought. The *I Ching* draws on just two basic elements represented by yin and yang lines—broken and unbroken lines respectively—and from there constructs an eight-by-eight matrix that results in 64 hexagrams.

Yin lines signify quiet and inaction, while yang lines signify movement. If we think of the scholar's reaction as the yin line (non-action), and the warrior's reaction as the yang line (action), we will be able to see both sides of any reaction. If we use the wisdom of this analogy, we will realize that within either of the two reactions, yin or yang, will be seeds of the other. Yin can transform instantly into yang and yang can transform instantly into yin. Herein lies the awesome wisdom of the *I Ching*.

If we analyze our reactions to hostile and difficult situations that threaten us, we will find that even as we strategize and think through our reactions, we know that hidden in our thinking will be the urge to lash out and fight back. Here is the scholar reaction being dominant with the warrior reaction lurking within. Similarly if we instantly react like a warrior, hidden in that too will be the scholar urging us to think.

The *I Ching* offers further advice. This is because the *I Ching* can also be used as an oracle. Thus, according to the *I Ching*, in any reaction selected there are 64 possible primary outcomes and these offer further sub-outcomes. The *I Ching* system thus describes outcomes from the initial two reactions. This model of the 64 hexagrams is said to conceptualize all the worldly situations that arise from every response or action. The *I Ching* model has been applied by Chinese scholars and warriors since time immemorial.

Are You a Right-
or Left-Brain Person?

Your brain is the physical manifestation of your mind. It is like a sleeping giant—colossal and awesome in its potential. This potential lies dormant within you, waiting to be used, often to an extent that will surprise you. Your brain functions like a super computer. It has amazing visual, audio, mathematical, analytical, and even psychic abilities.

It is only in recent years that scientific researchers in physics, biochemistry, and psychology have focused on the mysterious depths of the mind's capability, in the process gaining a much greater understanding of the human brain, which can be viewed as the physical mind. These studies reveal that the latent potential of the human brain is far greater than was ever imagined.

The exciting findings of this research address the many intricacies of the human brain, ranging from its various mental functions to the unique characteristics possessed by its left and right sides.

Scientists working with brain scans. The ways that the brain cells react with each other are still not fully known to scientists.

> There are no limits to the brain's inventiveness and abilities.

We can be as creatively imaginative as we allow ourselves to be. We can be as deductive, as analytical, and as instinctive as we wish. The brain functions completely at our command. It is the "hardware" that our mind uses to create the

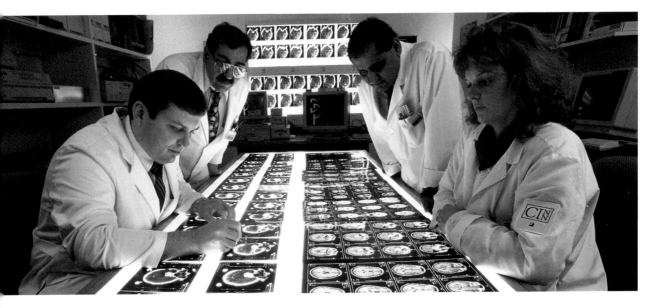

attitudes, feelings, perceptions, expectations, and end results we desire and wish for. The brain is our loyal and obedient servant.

Understand this, and you will begin to free yourself of the restrictions with respect to the way you assess yourself and your capabilities. Learning facts about the brain that have already been discovered will give you the confidence and conviction to move further along your personal voyage of self-discovery into the inner realms of your mind. Then you will begin to appreciate that achieving brilliance and attaining excellence is well within the scope of every individual.

As recently as the days of our grandparents, very little was known about the brain or the way it operates. People were often branded stupid or clever, artistic or numerate, intellectual or obtuse. Educators paid scant attention to the brain and its functions, and few schools taught their students how the brain absorbs, sorts, and regurgitates information. Schoolchildren never really knew which part of the brain they were using, or, more important, how they could use more of the brain.

It is only in recent times that we have come to realize how problems connected with seemingly inadequate mental abilities have less to do with the brain's basic capacity, than with a genuine ignorance of the brain's formidable and awesome potential. Probably the most astounding revelation from brain scientists is the fact that, on average, people use less than one percent of their brains! There is, thus, tremendous untapped potential lying inside every one of us.

We know the brain has strength and resilience. We know it can process a huge amount of know-ledge, emotions, attitudes, and so forth. From this we know it must have tremendous storage capacity for information, and probably a super-efficient filing system. But how does it work? How does it respond to commands and stimuli?

THE CASE OF ALBERT EINSTEIN

Probably the scientific world's most celebrated genius, Albert Einstein was a renowned physicist and Nobel laureate. Einstein proposed the theory of relativity, and his theories changed the way scientists thought about the world and the Universe.

Albert Einstein did NOT formulate his brilliant theory while sitting at his desk working through equations. He developed the theory out of boyhood daydreams. He would take a break from his work and lie outside in the grass, eyes half-closed, feeling the warmth of the sun. He would notice the light from the sun filtering through his eyelashes, then break into a thousand tiny sunbeams, and muse—"I wonder what it would be like to ride in one of those beams of light?" He would allow his mind to drift, taking him on an imaginary journey to the edge of the Universe . . .

Einstein used his daydreams to engage his mind in deep thought. He allowed insights gained during his imaginary journeys to gently slice through his formal scientific training. By allowing the colors and rhythms of his right brain to gently seep into the disciplined reasoning of his left brain, Albert Einstein made a quantum leap into space. Thus was born the theory of relativity.

THE LEFT BRAIN handles numbers, sequences, logic, organization, and other matters requiring rational thought and reasoning, as well as deductive and analytical considerations. Left-brain people are more at home with things mathematical and scientific. Left-brain thinkers focus on lines and formulas, ignoring the subtleties of colors and cadence. Left-brain people tend to be more scientific in their approach, more detached and less emotional. If this description fits the way you think you are, then you are probably a left-brain dominated person.

Left and Right Brains

We have not one, but two brains. We have a left brain and a right brain. The two brains are biologically identical in structure and they work in harmony, side by side. Each brain is made up of millions and millions of cells, which resemble baby octopuses, complete with flailing arms that reach out and connect with other cells.

The two brains have completely different functions, and they each manage different parts of the physical body. The left brain controls the right side of the body and the right brain controls the left side of the body. Injury to the left brain thus causes the right side of the body to become paralyzed and vice versa.

These scientific revelations about the structure and functions of the human brain seem to confirm the application of the tai chi, for it seems that neither scientific nor artistic ability are exclusive to anyone.

Extensive research into left and right brains reveals that each of the two brains controls different intellectual activities. Experiments in this area of research have measured brain waves emanating from minds engaged in different activities that range from the purely creative and imaginary to the exclusively logical and quantitative. These experiments show that each side of the brain takes care of different types of mental activities.

Note that it has been discovered that people who have trained more or less exclusively to use only one side of the brain often find it difficult (and sometimes impossible) to use the other, untrained side of the brain. Thus, those educated to think logically and sequentially, to the total exclusion of creativity, are believed to have a limited ability to think outside of their rigidly set rational boundaries. They become one-dimensional in their thinking!

Similarly, artists who have never been taught or encouraged to use their rational, logical minds may be tremendously skilled painters or designers, but can seem hopelessly inadequate when they are called upon to undertake work requiring sequential thought or analytical input.

More significantly, it has also been discovered that when the less-used of the two brains is somehow activated, through stimulation and encouragement, to work alongside the more often-used side of the brain, the end result, or what is achieved by the marriage of the two brains working together, is often far superior in terms of overall efficiency and effectiveness than that achieved when only one side of the brain is functioning to the exclusion of the other side.

In short, the two brains working simultaneously produce better results, once again demonstrating the wisdom of the tai chi—the left and right sides of the brain can be viewed as the yin and yang sides of the brain.

Scientific revelations about the brain seem to confirm Eastern approaches—neither scientific nor artistic ability are exclusive to anyone. On the contrary, everyone has within himself or herself the potential to develop capabilities in both categories of thought processes. Anyone can be scientific, or artistic, or both—irrespective of which side of the brain dominates. You just need to develop your brain power accordingly.

THE RIGHT BRAIN takes care of different dimensions—it handles dreaming, colors, rhythms, music, and other thought processes requiring creativity, vivid imagination, originality, inventiveness, and artistic flair. Right-brain thinking is said to be less restrained, less bounded by scientific and mathematical parameters. Right-brain thinkers focus on forms and shapes, hues and subtleties, overlooking measurements and dimensions. If this describes you, then you are likely to be dominantly a right-brained person.

Are You a Philosopher or a Manager?

Are you a thinker or a doer, a desk-bound strategist or an operational field person, someone who formulates policies or an action-oriented person? Are you a theoretical conceptualizer or a practical, down-to-earth implementer— the person who analyzes events and makes forecasts, or the person who goes out there to make things happen? Are you a philosopher or a manager?

In the world, there are those who think and there are those who do, those who theorize and those who operate. There are the ideas people and there are those who make things happen. It is not untrue to say that the philosopher feels a certain superiority over the manager, while the manager holds a certain disdain for the philosopher.

Action people maintain that ideas are easy to come by and that it is those who take ideas through to the implementation stage that make all the difference. This group maintains that mediocre ideas that are properly executed and implemented are worth all the best ideas that are never implemented. The thinkers, on the other hand, maintain it is well-thought-out strategy that is the only sound basis for long-term and long-lasting success. Planning, calculation of risks, developing competitive strategy, and working through alternative methods of implementation are all far more important than simple execution. Without the thinkers, this latter group maintain, managing becomes meaningless.

The thinker theorizes, sifting through data, analyzing information, strategizing, drawing conclusions, and making recommendations. Often the role of the thinker can be so removed from reality that the pragmatist finds little time for his or her findings. On the other hand, the hands-on manager who implements, sells, operates, and basically does the job needed to be done can be so near to the task at hand that he or she can often miss the big picture.

While one takes a helicopter view and sees the big picture, the other sees only the perspective from the ground. One looks downward while the other looks upward. As a result, ideas people and action-

A manager does not want to sit and theorize but wants to be out there getting the job done.

oriented people develop very different perspectives of the same goal. Which are you? Do you work at the bigger picture on a strategic level, or do you work in the operational area?

In your work and in your life, do you believe the big picture is more important than the smaller operational picture? Do you believe strategy plays a more crucial role than operations?

Test yourself Reflect carefully on the following statements and see how many of them you agree or disagree with. These questions have been carefully designed to highlight the fine line between strategic thinking and operational thinking. Then look through the rationale outlined in the table below and see how you scored.

1 There are no fixed rules to anything for there are endless permutations in the marketplace. Success or failure depends on the speed of decision-making on the ground.

2 On most occasions, the thinker needs to draw lessons from what has occurred and in the end it is experience that really provides the answers.

3 As in a game of chess, one must continually profit from the quality of experiences gained. Every problem can only be solved within its own context and circumstances.

4 Correct timing is everything, and correct timing cannot be determined when there is only strategic thinking.

5 Like the fermentation of rice wine, quality thinking requires time to mature. Like seeds sown into the ground, thoughts need to be nurtured into maturity.

6 It is sad but true that most people often fail to learn from the past. Mistakes are often repeated again and again.

7 One of the most difficult skills for anyone to master is to be able to adapt strategies and policies to changing situations.

8 Corporate CEOs should never allow their managers to respond intuitively and speedily to signs of danger in the marketplace. Instead, they should await instructions from above.

9 Sometimes the only thing a person can do is wait.

10 It is perfectly fine to lose a battle if one is able to win the war.

The skills of the philosopher lie in thinking and imagining, rather than putting ideas into action.

Answers

	If you agree	If you disagree
1	you're a DOER	you are a THINKER
2	you're a DOER	you are a THINKER
3	you're a DOER	you are a THINKER
4	you're a DOER	you are a THINKER
5	you are a THINKER	you're a DOER
6	you are a THINKER	you're a DOER
7	you are a THINKER	you're a DOER
8	you are a THINKER	you're a DOER
9	you are a THINKER	you're a DOER
10	you are a THINKER	you're a DOER

Are You More Intuitive or Logical?

There are those who believe that our minds operate from two separate levels of consciousness, each of which has its own thought processes for developing conclusions and formulating beliefs. One level of consciousness is the logical mind and the other, the intuitive mind. In your discovery of self, you might want to see which of these is the stranger inside your head.

Conventional wisdom suggests that women tend to be the more intuitive of the two genders and that men depend more on their powers of reasoning and logic. Recent research into the nature of the brain, however, suggests that both genders have the potential to be either intuitive or logical. Nevertheless, in most of us, it is one or the other

From aromatherapy to feng shui to zen mindfulness, the scope for intuitive and experientially generated belief seems to have taken hold of the collective consciousness.

sphere of consciousness that will be dominant. In recent years, with the rise of holistic consciousness and the reemergence of many ancient and esoteric phenomena, it has become increasingly difficult to distinguish between what is real and what is delusion, and between scientifically proven phenomena and the anecdotal presentation of evidence.

Intuition

Some people describe intuition as a psychic gift, others as a "divine conviction" that guides them toward belief systems that may seem alien to others. Others describe the phenomenon as an extraordinary clairvoyance of some sort manifested in the ability to "see" things others cannot see, to

If you are intuitive, you may occasionally see the aura, or levels of auras, as color encircling certain people.

feel energy others cannot feel and to already know things others do not yet know.

In most of us, however, intuition does not have to manifest as any special psychic "gift." We only need to have a deep conviction about phenomena, relying on our inner consciousness to tell us whether something is true or not. If this describes you, then intuition is no stranger to you. Indeed if you are the intuitive type, having to "think things through" probably turns you off. You do not enjoy taking "intelligence tests," and you have little interest in knowing how to categorize data. You will probably be a more right-brained person.

On the other hand, if you find everything that has just been written leaves you cold, then intuition is probably a stranger inside your head. You would be happier if you could be shown visual and empirical evidence to convince you.

Test yourself Ask yourself if you have ever experienced any of these phenomena:

1 A friend calls you to leave a date free. You ask if her daughter is getting married, and she says yes.

2 The phone rings just as you are thinking of someone; it is that person who is phoning you.

3 You know that something is not quite right about a friend's house, and when you voice your misgivings it turns out you are right.

4 You saw a lame dog (or any other signal) as you left the house and instantly felt uneasy. Later, your car got rear-ended and you ended up in the hospital. You do not believe it is a coincidence.

5 You friend tells you she dreamed of white tigers (or other wild animals) and you are instantly convinced the dream means something significant.

6 You strongly believe in a sixth sense.

7 You believe that seeing a rainbow is auspicious.

8 You have sometimes followed up on a hunch with some success.

9 You instinctively like or dislike people.

10 You have sometimes predicted an event just before it happened.

11 You think of someone you have not seen for some time and a letter arrives from that person.

12 You have a premonition of the death of a friend who lives abroad and it turns out to be true.

13 You dream of a friend repeatedly, and when you call her, she tells you she is in deep trouble.

14 You experience a sense of déjà vû when you visit a place.

15 You once met a stranger with whom you felt great empathy and you later became good friends.

16 You have tried self-hypnosis.

17 You have attempted astral travel.

18 You believe in making strong affirmations.

19 You believe strongly in feng shui.

20 Occasionally you can see the aura around certain people.

If you can answer a definite YES to at least half of the statements above, you are probably psychic. If you can answer YES to 75 percent of them, you are probably clairvoyant.

If a friend tells you he or she dreamed of white tigers and you realize the dream is significant, then you may have psychic powers.

What Are You Afraid of?

Nothing is as frightening as fear itself. Yet our fears can be irrational and bear absolutely no relation to the perceived threat itself. Such fears can be caused by the sudden release of stress hormones, which can give rise to a frenzy of panic. Get to know your fears so you can confront them. This is the best way to deal with the phobias in your life.

❝ *When I was 18 years old, I suffered from night panics. I found out that while fear itself was one thing, the fear of fear increases the original fear a thousand times. Once I succeeded in convincing my mind there was nothing to fear, that my dream was merely a manifestation of my vivid imagination and therefore that I could be in control of that imagination, the panic syndromes of my nocturnal hours subsided instantly. Since then I have always coped with my phobias by turning around and confronting them head on.* ❞

It is quite normal to be fearful when walking alone at night, even if you know that statistically you are unlikely to be attacked.

The list of fears and phobias that assail us is long and often irrational, but our fears are not groundless. Usually they are related to some long-forgotten incident or trauma. Anything can cause you to have phobias—for instance, if you fell down and hurt yourself as a child just as you saw a dog passing by, or were bullied by an elder sibling who threw a cockroach, an insect, or even a harmless dead beetle at you when you were a baby; or if someone ever frightened you into obedience by using a pillow, a handkerchief, or a favorite toy as a threat. A programmed moment of fear can create an unconscious trauma that can grow inside the mind as the years pass.

Phobias are not limited to animals and insects. We also suffer from socially transmitted or generated fears such as the fear of flying or the fear of public speaking. These can cause terrible anxiety and stress that might well set off a whole chain of physical and mental events that could cause your mind and your body real long-term damage unless they are resolved.

Test yourself Mentally check the stress level that each of the following activities invokes in you—decide whether you feel completely indifferent to it, whether it causes you some anxiety, or whether it absolutely terrifies you.

Here is a list of social anxieties:

1 Getting on an airplane—fear of flying

2 Attending a cocktail party on your own—fear of rejection

3 Asking someone for a date—fear of rejection

4 Living alone—fear of the unknown

5 Making a speech—fear of the limelight

6 Getting called on in class—fear of the limelight

7 Going to a rock concert—fear of crowds

8 Walking home after seeing a movie at night—fear of the dark

9 Eating a meal alone in a restaurant—fear of being on your own

10 Getting into an elevator on your own—fear of confined spaces

11 Telling someone to do something for you—fear of rejection

12 Asking for a favor—fear of rejection

13 Asking a stranger to give you directions—fear of rejection

14 Being publicly criticized—fear of losing face

15 Being publicly praised—fear of the limelight

16 Telling someone in authority that you disagree with them—fear of rejection

17 Attending an interview—fear of rejection

18 Making small talk—fear of rejection or losing face

19 Going on a subway—fear of losing face or fear of the unknown

20 Taking public transportation—fear of the unknown

21 Introducing yourself—fear of the limelight

Work determinedly at overcoming these social anxieties. Find occasions to confront them in a controlled environment with someone sympathetic helping you. Go slowly. Use strongly worded affirmations to convince your subconscious mind that you simply love doing the very thing you fear. The stronger your sense of panic, the more patient you need to be with yourself.

Here is a list of irrational fears:

1 Fear of insects—butterflies, cockroaches, etc.

2 Fear of frogs, toads, and creepy-crawlies

3 Fear of being tied up

4 Fear of being left alone

5 Fear of ghosts and other frightening creatures

6 Fear of the dark

7 Fear of heights and high places

8 Fear of the sea, of water, or of drowning

9 Fear of being locked up in confined spaces

10 Fear of dogs, cats, or other pets

11 Fear of certain colors

12 Fear of elevators

13 Fear of cars and trains

14 Fear of people in masks

15 Fear of people in uniform

16 Fear of winding roads

17 Fear of fire and burning

18 Fear of getting lost

19 Fear of being abandoned

20 Fear of being rejected

Irrational fears are generally rooted in some childhood trauma. If you suffer from any of these fears, once again try to confront them with the help of an ally. If necessary go and see a therapist.

Many people suffer from a fear of crowds. If you do, try to work at overcoming this fear with the help of a supportive friend.

How Free Are You?

Many people live as if they are confined in a gilded cage, not realizing that the door is open and that they can soar to heights beyond their own imagination. Instead, they build walls around themselves, afraid of the unknown, tormented by fear, troubled by what they believe are their inadequacies. Bondage is a mental thing. Free your mind and your spirit will be free, too.

There are rational and irrational fears. Fears of failure and of stepping out into the unknown are rational fears, which we have to work hard at overcoming. It is natural to be afraid of stepping out of the secure environment that we know to embark on a journey to the unknown. To admit freely to the anxiety of the unknown is fine; you are accepting that what holds you back from doing what you wish to do—from taking a chance, from expanding your consciousness—is you, yourself.

You also know that in reality, you are free to be who you are and what you can be. If, mentally, you are able to understand this at all levels of consciousness, then you will realize that there is nothing that can hold you back except your

own lack of desire. If you lack the nerve and the courage, these are sentiments and beliefs that stop you, but you have to remember that the decision-making process is taking place inside your own head. No one is stopping you from embarking on any course of action you wish to take.

You hold your destiny in
your own hands.

We are all fearful. There is no need to berate ourselves for this. Sometimes the bravest thing is to admit that we are afraid. But we should also know that the greatest courage comes from conquering fear, however rational that fear might be. Heroes and heroines are those who overcome their private fears and then go on to grasp the things they want and do the things they wish to do. It is like jumping out of an airplane. In that split second just before the jump, you will know the terror of jumping, and then you find you are in the air . . . and you are flying.

Before you take your own jump, before anything else, ask yourself if you feel free to be your own person. Ask yourself if you feel trapped in some situation or circumstance. Ask yourself if you

Imagine being as free as a bird. There is nothing stopping anyone from developing into the kind of person they wish to be.

are seeing invisible bonds that imprison you in your present circumstance. For example, are you the only person caring for an aged mother or looking after a disabled child? Are there people depending on you so that you feel trapped and unable to fly out to seek your own happiness? Do you feel caught in a loveless marriage but are afraid to walk out because you are afraid you cannot cope with the idea of being alone?

If any of these situations describe your circumstances, do you feel resentful? Do you blame your circumstances for your unhappiness? Is your anguish caused by the conviction that life is passing you by? Do you feel imprisoned?

We can always do something about our situation, and there should never be a need to feel imprisoned by an invisible cell or prison. These invisible prisons are created by our own minds.

Most of the time it is the mind made numb by years of suppressed anger that does not realize that solutions can be found. When you make the decision to embrace the limitless, you will have started along the pathway to setting yourself mentally free. This can either be through a complete reversal of attitude that enables you to transform your source of anguish and perceived suffering into a source of joy and happiness, or you can start changing your circumstances.

For instance, if you are the sole living relative looking after an old person, you could rejoice that you have this opportunity to do something good and show compassion to another person. Using this technique to change your attitude will give you a measure of contentment, and if you still feel you want to create some private time for yourself, you can start looking around for a way out of your dilemma. Remember that if you make an effort to change your situation or circumstances, it can be done. In the same way, if you truly want to end your loveless or terrible marriage, you should garner the

Many people live their lives as if they were imprisoned. Find the courage to cast aside bonds you no longer want.

courage to do so. Once you really start making some decisions in your life, you will begin to feel a sense of your own freedom.

You will realize that bondage truly is a mental phenomenon. Expanding one's consciousness is a stunningly empowering personal decision, and once the decision has been taken, it creates its own special source of empowering chi.

There is nothing stopping anyone from being the kind of person they wish to be, or living the kind of life they wish to live.

Hidden Dragons, Crouching Tigers

Dragons and tigers are the celestial creatures that reflect the yin and yang of the cosmic individual. Inside us are hidden dragons, our yang side that is courageous and brave, desperate to open our wings and fly into the clear blue skies. But within us also lurks the crouching tiger, poised and protective, ever ready to attack when provoked—the yin side that holds us back.

The human psyche is an ocean of unfulfilled desires and ambitions, and also of hidden fears and anxious misgivings. The mind is very clever at hiding its secrets, burying them deep within its many folds. If you are young, you may be like the courageous dragon, and if you are more mature, it is more likely that your personality will resemble the crouching tiger.

Perhaps you have the powerful yang energy of the dragon and are a natural-born leader.

The Dragon

Youthful exuberance that knows no fear will be prepared to let the dragon have its head, and as a result, all the optimism, exuberance, and ambitions of this magnificent creature will burst forth in a stream of powerful yang energy. Dragon chi is brave and aggressive. Those who manifest it demonstrate the power of natural-born leaders, holding court like ancient emperors, overcoming all obstacles and fighting their way to victory.

When hidden dragons burst forth within you, others will feel the heat of your fierce temper and impatience, but they will also stand in awe of your powerful creative force and your amazing skill and competence. You will be hard to subdue and tough to tame, for once unleashed, the dragon is difficult to hold back. When you are on an energetic high, busily conquering the world and making your mark, you signify both the best and the worst of the celestial dragon. To the world at large, you will show only your public face—so you will come across as brave but also unrelentingly stubborn.

tiger is ever ready to spring in defense of our sedate and honorable lifestyles, guarding us from making fools of ourselves and making sure that we are protected from our own foolishness.

Tiger energy can often be as strong and as powerful as dragon energy, but these big pussy-cats stay very cool, calculating, and aloof. If you manifest the crouching tiger personality, the people around you will have good reason to fear your big smiles and your carefully controlled energy. This is because crouching tigers have a tendency to be very territorial.

Hidden dragons and crouching tigers do not manifest in everyone. They represent the extremes of celestial energy—both the yang and yin—and so they are rare. At their best, the manifestation of their energy creates the stars of the world, although they can also have negative dimensions. These are usually gifted people who possess very strong levels of courage and wisdom. Their energy level is ceaseless, and they project an aura of unrelenting magnetism. Dragons and tigers are very attractive people. Many will find them totally irresistible.

Look at the leaders of the political and business world. It should not be too difficult to identify the dragons and tigers among them. They do not need to have been born in the astrological years of the dragon or tiger. Indeed, you can find hidden dragons lurking in all twelve of the Chinese zodiac signs, just as you can also uncover crouching tigers from among them.

Look out for the powerful bursts of energy and the exuberant optimism that reveal the presence of hidden dragons, and be alert to the unrelenting, wide-eyed stare that hides the wisdom lurking underneath when searching for the crouching tiger.

Both creatures are dangerous. Yin and yang in their extreme manifestations can be deadly, so tread carefully and keep your distance.

The crouching tiger rules the psyche of many people; tiger energy can be as powerful as dragon energy but is more controlled.

Inside your head will be conflicting currents of yin chi that cause you to suffer a sense of ambivalence. Internal struggles created by insecurity and mental upheavals will manifest in emotional uncertainties, which could be quite severe. As a result, you will appear to blow hot and cold. This could be your undoing. You would do well to tame your energy and allow some of the yin chi to slow you down.

The Tiger

The crouching tiger within the human psyche often rules those whose experience of life lends them an air of maturity and wisdom. Like heavenly protectors, these yin celestials rein back the impulsive and headstrong energies within us. The

Are You a Rabbit or a Wolf?

Do you hop around, run, and burrow deep into the earth when confronted with obstacles and danger, feeling safer in the familiar terrain of your own home, or are you a wolf who hunts far and wide, playing the role of the aggressor? When you go deep into your inner mind, will you be brave enough to venture forth, or are you the type who prefers the comfort and safety of the familiar?

The rabbit and the wolf represent two extremes of the living strategy, which seem to reflect the two fundamental attitudes of the human race. When confronted with danger, how do we react? Do we take flight and run away as fast as we can (like the rabbit) or firmly stand our ground and fight to the death (like the wolf)?

The rabbit is usually regarded as a gentle creature, fragile and timid by nature. The wolf is universally seen as a predatory animal, cunning, dangerous, and armed with sharp fangs and a fierce, unrelenting disposition.

If you are happy being what you are, and are a timid person who avoids trouble, then you are close to the rabbit personality.

The analogy of the rabbit and the wolf presents a fundamental hypothesis for us to consider. When threatened, do we run and develop a strategy of survival like the rabbit, or do we make a stand and tough things out?

The natural defense mechanism of the rabbit is simply to take flight. One of the rabbit's outstanding abilities is the speed at which it can run. Rabbits live in big groups, where no predator can reach them. The instinct of the rabbit is always to run back into the shelter and safety of its familiar territory. The wolf, on the other hand, is a predator, a hunter. The wolf is stronger than the rabbit. When threatened, the wolf will almost always stand its ground and fight.

The rabbit uses defensive tactics to survive, while the wolf will always attack. In daily life, are you a wolf or a rabbit?

Test yourself Study the situations below and see whether you would react like the wolf or the rabbit in each case. It is not easy to be a rabbit or a wolf all the time, and although discretion may be the better part of valor, sometimes it seems necessary to stand up to injustice.

1 Someone cuts in line, going ahead of you. Do you tell him off or stay quiet?

a Stay quiet

b Tell him off

2 The waiter in a restaurant ignores you repeatedly. Do you loudly demand attention, or do you continue to wait patiently?

a Wait patiently

b Loudly demand attention

3 In the cinema, the man in front of you talks loudly on his cell phone. You tell him to be quiet and he ignores you. Do you tell him again or put up with his rudeness?

a Put up with his rudeness

b Tell him equally loudly to stop or else!

4 Someone bangs your car from behind and then gets out of the car to demand compensation. It is his fault. What do you do?

a Pay up because he looks threatening

b Get out of the car and tell him to pay you

5 In a nightclub, someone who's had too much to drink makes a pass at your partner. What do you do?

a Ignore him/her and suggest to your partner that you leave

b Demand an apology or else!

6 At the college library, a group of older students talk loudly, disturbing you. You ask them to be quiet but they ignore you. What do you do?

a Move to another part of the library

b Tell them to be quiet or you will take it up with the librarian

7 As you get into your car, two thugs catch hold of you and force you to hand over the car keys. One has a knife. What do you do?

a Give in and hand over the car keys

b Instantly fight back the best you can

8 As you sit down for a meal in an outdoor café, someone grabs your handbag containing all your credit cards. What do you do?

a Scream "Stop, thief" as the thief runs away

b Give chase with the intention of catching the thief

9 You have just received a threatening note from a known troublemaker. You do not know what he will do, but you know it will not be pleasant and that he is serious. What do you do?

a Make immediate arrangements to stay elsewhere so he cannot find you

b Make preparations to fight him and defend yourself

10 A colleague at work has just blatantly stolen your work and taken credit for it. What do you do?

a Accept it since he/she is too powerful to beat

b Take the matter to a higher authority and confront him/her

If you are a predator type who tends to confront problems rather than ignore them, then your life strategy is that of the wolf.

Answers

a If your reaction is to take flight, you're a RABBIT

b If your reaction is to fight or confront, you're a WOLF

Are You Ruled by Your Emotions?

*Do you cry easily? Does sentiment affect you more than rational argument?
Are you motivated by emotional highs and lows more than by intellect?
Emotions are strong inner forces that have the power to galvanize people to
commit irrational acts. Nothing affects people more than emotions—feelings
that cause you to experience either pain or pleasure with great intensity.*

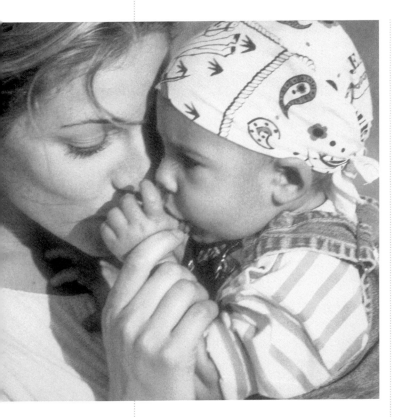

It is useful to differentiate between positive emotions, such as love for a child, and negative emotions, such as anger.

stimulus will vary according to how well we are able to keep our reactions under control. It is negative emotions that give us problems, and usually the more detached we feel toward people and things, the less likely we are to experience negative emotions.

❝ In the early '60s and '70s when women first started joining the executive ranks of the world's corporate institutions, one of the most common accusations leveled against women was their so-called 'weakness,' which in turn was equated to their being 'overly emotional.' I remember those days very vividly and I recall how much I resented being made to apologize for feeling passionate about my job and my opinions. Each time I demonstrated enthusiasm or showed anger, or supported a project strongly, I was told to temper my zeal. In short, I was often told to cool it!

❝ I am so glad I did not cool it. I am convinced that it was the passion I had for my work that propelled me to great success and enabled me to rise to Board level. The whole human race is driven by emotion to some extent, and it is extremely significant for us to know just how much we are ourselves ruled by emotions. It is in knowing that we are then able to judge whether we are being excessively influenced. ❞

Great acts of heroism are spurred on by powerful emotional motivations. Emotions are a strong inner force that can cause adrenaline to flow and move along the pathways of the body, lighting up the whole inner self.

Both positive and negative emotions are equally powerful in their impact on people, but how each of us reacts to a particular emotional

Test yourself Here are 20 questions to assess how much you are affected and influenced by emotions in your decision-making.

1 When someone relates a sad experience, do you feel sympathy welling up inside you?

2 Does listening to a sad aria, like "Un Bel di Vedremo" from *Madama Butterfly*, make you cry?

3 Do you consider yourself a romantic?

4 Does listening to sad songs make you feel quite depressed?

5 Would you approve an extra week's leave for your secretary if her mother had to be admitted to hospital during a particularly busy time?

6 Would you donate money to cover repair bills for your old school?

7 Do you like listening to what went wrong in your friend's marriage?

8 When you are moved almost to tears, do you feel embarrassed?

9 Would you sympathize with your son for bashing up your car?

10 Do you keep all your old college notes even though you have no more use for them?

11 Do you keep pets at home and, if you do, do you play with them?

12 Do you call home when you are overseas no matter how inconvenient it is for you?

13 Do you daydream at work?

14 Would you turn down a promotion for emotional reasons, e.g., because your children needed you to spend more time with them?

15 If your very inefficient manager had five children and was the sole breadwinner, would you consider laying him off?

16 Would you give up a dream assignment if it meant separating from your family?

17 Do you consider the emotional satisfaction at work more important than your salary?

18 Have you ever made a wrong decision because you allowed your emotion to get the better of you, and if so, would you make the same decision again?

19 Do you go by your intuition alone when you are hiring someone?

20 Would you fire an excellent subordinate if they displayed disloyalty?

If you said YES to 12 of these questions you are a well-adjusted human being. If you answered YES to more than 16 questions, you are perhaps over-emotional in the way you view the world. If, however, you answered NO to at least ten questions, it is likely that your head rules your heart in most things. If you answered NO to more than 16, you are supremely detached from most things. You could even be described as dispassionate.

Enjoying playing with pets is one sign of being an emotional person. If a friend has a dog, why not offer to walk it?

You can be excellent at work while still allowing room for emotions; having empathy for colleagues is a positive attribute.

Do You Believe in Coincidence?

When you live in a state of conscious awareness, it is not difficult to find links between every event and person that appears in your world. Viewed this way, life's coincidences offer divination insights. Think about all the things you have done, all the thoughts you have had, and all the people you have seen recently. Then meditate on the common threads that link them all.

Think about the statement "There really are no coincidences in life." Nothing occurs by chance.

> **There seems to be a pattern in the Universe of life, a reason for every occurrence, a purpose in everyone's life, and a role for everyone.**

This suggests that every chance meeting, every phone call, every new opportunity, and every passing event happens for a reason. Viewed from this perspective, even life's disappointments have their reasons in the greater scheme of things. At times, our paths get blocked and our efforts meet with failure, such as when we are passed over for a promotion, when we lose our job, or lose someone we love.

If we believe there is a cosmic reason for every event in our lives—that failure and success are but stops along a longer pathway—then being alert to the reasons should make our lives feel more meaningful. The reasons, however, are never immediately clear, and they may not be what we

expect them to be. If we believe that there is a bigger picture within which we operate our lives, we can also believe that eventually we will see how the pattern unfolds. Alternatively, we can dismiss everything as a coincidence and then deliberately turn our back on the nagging feeling that we may be missing something.

❝ *Many times in my life I have sensed a divine hand in the chance meeting of an old friend, in a book I happened to read, in the way I walk past the telephone just as it rings and it turns out to be a phone call that changes my life. Often I have detected patterns of negativity—when troubles and trials seem to come all at once, as if it were some kind of retribution—but I have also noticed many patterns of great positive significance as well. The key is to live in a state of awareness.*

❝ *When I started to become aware of apparent coincidences happening in my life, I decided simply to accept them. It was this decision to accept them as having some higher purpose that helped me go with the flow. Since then, for me at least, many of the events and meetings in my life have become gloriously and increasingly clear and meaningful.* ❞

If you believe there are no coincidences in life, then stay alert to the pattern of recurring themes that

An important message may come to you through an unexpected meeting. Stay tuned to such events; they may have a significance.

come to you in many different ways. Sometimes it is an item that catches your eye in the local paper, or a television news report you happened to see. Other times it can come as dreams or in a book that somehow comes into your possession.

Most times, however, important messages come to you through unplanned meetings with old friends or associates. It is the unexpected that seems to contain hidden messages from some divine source.

Stay alert. Unless you consciously look for patterns and signs, you will miss them. Be on the look out for the unusual—for instance, a vivid dream that you remember very clearly.

❝ *Once I picked up a very large tortoise shell when my family and I went to Pangkor Island for a seaside holiday. To start with, it was unusual for me to agree to go to the beach, for I am not a beach person.*

❝ *But, it was after that holiday and this seemingly insignificant event that I wrote my first book on feng shui ... and of course if you know about feng shui you will also know how significant the tortoise shell is in feng shui lore—once again it was a sign of things to come.* ❞

So remember to stay tuned in to the special signals sent to you from the great cosmos.

Are You Superstitious?

There are many superstitious beliefs from all the traditions of the world. Many of these beliefs have come down to us through the ages, passed on from mother to daughter, father to son. There is much to be said for giving our ancestors the benefit of the doubt when considering them. That these beliefs have reached us intact must surely say something for their efficacy.

Refusing a final cup of tea or the last piece of cake offered is considered by some cultures to bring bad luck or misfortune.

Would you walk under a ladder? I would not. Why should I tempt bad luck to descend upon me? What does it cost me not to walk under a ladder? Nothing. If I walk under a ladder to prove a point, it is only my ego that is motivating me, and since my ego is an illusion, I would not do it. My attitude toward superstitions has always been one of relaxed respect. Beliefs are real when I believe in them. Someone else may not believe what I believe. To each their own.

Good fortune and misfortune have to do with time and space, but are also linked to symbols and signals from the great beyond. Ritualistic feng shui practices that prescribe correct ways of doing

things—wearing clothes, serving food, drinking tea, eating specific dishes, opening doors in the mornings, sweeping the home, cleaning altars, and so forth—bear a strong resemblance to different superstitious taboos. I have to confess that I believe in these rituals. Mine is an attitude colored by a sense of pragmatism. Where I am unable to observe some of the rituals, I simply move on to something else.

Test yourself   Here are 20 superstitions to help you think about your views. If you incorporate at least half of them into your life, then you are a superstitious person.

1 When you see a ladder propped up against the wall, you make a detour around it because you believe that walking under a ladder is bad luck.

2 When you break a mirror, you pass the broken pieces under your leg three times and wrap them in red paper to be thrown away. Otherwise you believe you will attract seven years of bad luck.

3 You never allow anyone to step over anything important to you because this brings very bad luck.

4 You never eat the last piece of food on the table since this brings you the bad luck of loneliness.

5 You never buy your parents a watch as a birthday present since this is believed to be a bad omen that spells illness or death. If someone does buy any of your family members a watch or a clock, you instantly send a dollar to them as a symbolic gesture of purchase.

6 You never wear black on the first day of the New Year since this creates extreme bad luck in the form of very afflicted yin energy.

7 When visiting a friend, you never decline a final cup of tea or piece of cake offered by your host or hostess since you know that doing so might cause you to have an accident on the way home.

8 You never hang clothes or other personal items outside the home after sunset since this could attract wandering spirits to take shelter in them.

9 You never sweep the floor or clean the house on the first day of the New Year; this means sweeping away all your good luck for the whole year.

10 You never allow your rice urn (or in modern times, your refrigerator) to get completely empty since this would be most inauspicious. You place three coins tied with red thread inside a red packet deep inside your rice urn.

11 You never place empty boxes inside your cupboard since this signifies emptiness and a loss of wealth. You place some jewelry boxes inside the cupboard to signify gold and precious jewels; this is like keeping a wealth vase in the home.

12 You never eat from a rice bowl that is chipped or drink from a glass that is cracked since this would be most unlucky.

13 You never cook food in a broken wok or a broken rice cooker since this suggests bad luck at work or in your career.

14 If you see a snake, tortoise, frog, or bat in your garden, you never kill it since this suggests a good omen. These are symbols of extreme good fortune, said to bring protection from harm as well as to symbolize new wealth coming to the family.

15 You would be most unhappy if someone sent you a gift after dark, as this suggests bad luck, and it is likely you would leave it outside your home.

It is easy to avoid walking underneath ladders. If a belief in a superstition costs you nothing, where's the harm in believing?

16 When you have your period, you never allow your clothes to be washed together with the clothes of the rest of the family since this means bad luck will befall them.

17 You would be reluctant to allow your son to marry a woman born in the year of the tiger since this could bring him premature death.

18 You would also be very unhappy if your son brought home a woman with a square jaw, since this too would suggest that premature death may befall your son.

19 You would never hang pictures or hammer nails into the wall during the nighttime hours—doing this could cause severe illness to befall a member of the household.

20 You would never allow your pregnant daughter or daughter-in-law to use scissors to cut cloth, paint the house, or climb a ladder, since all of these activities would cause some kind of damage to the unborn child.

Are You an Optimist?

Do you believe that the secret to health, wealth, and happiness ultimately depends on your attitude and outlook? If you feel good about your life and all the things around you, would this not reflect an inner optimism that is really empowering? When you take an optimistic view of your life, it becomes a continuing odyssey of fresh insights and exciting discoveries.

Try looking consciously at an old routine in a new way. Let it be a new way of looking at a daily predicament, like working out the best route to get to work or creating a brand new attitude toward an office colleague you hardly noticed before.

Feeling optimistic is all about making yourself feel good. It is knowing that you can reshape your reactions in accordance with each new circumstance. Everything in your world takes on a rosy hue and it makes you feel good about life. When you start looking at your world this way, the person you previously dismissed could well turn out to be a soulmate. So just being prepared to look at anything, or anyone, in a different, optimistic, open-minded way can usually generate some pleasant surprises.

The way we view the world also affects how much we get out of life. Of course life is tough, uncompromising, and full of daily dilemmas. Life can be a grind and a bore. Life can be a colorless nothing. But life can also be a daring adventure with each day bringing stunning new experiences.

VISUAL TESTS

Study this picture (right) carefully. It took me twenty minutes to see the old witch with the hooked nose. It took some others an entire day to see the pretty girl, whom I saw immediately. What do you see below? Do you see arrows and two people talking? Do you see embracing symbols? Do you simply see "you"? If you see the positive side of everything, life is more fun.

If you are enthusiastic and courageous about your life, your attitude will attract exciting experiences for you to savor and enjoy. If you are unenthusiastic and disinterested in everything you do, then even when genuine gold is brought before you, you will automatically think of it as fake.

So be like the moonlight that turns dust into glittering jewels. Be like a magic mirror, reflecting only the best things into your world. Be optimistic.

Test yourself See if you are naturally optimistic. If you agree with six or more statements, you are optimistic. If you disagree with six or more, you are probably pessimistic.

1 You have just received a letter inviting you to attend an interview. You feel a rush of adrenaline and know that this is the big break you were waiting for. There is simply no doubt at all in your mind that you will sail through the interview.

2 The phone rings and your eyes light up. You know this is the call you have been waiting for and that it will confirm what you have known all along.

3 The boss has just told you that you have been transferred to Africa. You feel stunningly happy that he thinks you have what it takes to handle such a tough market and you simply cannot wait to get there and get started.

4 Although you are a service engineer, you have just been asked to fill in for the sales manager who has been taken seriously ill. You feel thrilled that you have been given an opportunity to show what you can do in a managerial position, and you see this as a positive sign for your career.

5 You have just been laid off, which you have been expecting for some time. In some ways you feel relieved because now you will have more time to spend with the children, and perhaps to pursue the idea of working from home.

6 You have just arrived in Milan on a shopping trip and been told that your luggage is still in

An optimist will make the best of whatever news a phone call or letter brings.

Amsterdam, but will arrive on the next day's flight. You feel this is a great excuse to shop.

7 You have just arrived in Singapore on a holiday when you realize you have forgotten to bring your personal organizer with you. As a result, you do not have any contact numbers of people you had been planning to call. You decide to see Singapore on your own instead. The prospect of doing this makes you feel rather adventurous.

8 Your banker has just called to cancel your lunch appointment, which was set for today. You decide that it is not worthwhile trying to figure out the reason why, so you decide that you will simply call him to make another date.

9 You have just discovered that your partner has been two-timing you with your best friend. You feel disappointed in them both, but you can see that finding out was the best thing to have happened, since now you know where you stand.

10 You are driving into the city when you realize that your gas tank is almost empty. Silently you say a prayer that there will be sufficient fuel to take you to the nearest gas station.

Are You a Romantic?

Are you in love with love? Have you often thought of the knight in shining armor who comes into your life and sweeps you off your feet and carries you into the great beyond? Do you yearn to fall desperately, hopelessly in love? It is said that deep inside each and every one of us lurks the romantic, and this feeling, this unspoken aspiration of love, never really dies.

In some of us, the romantic nature is alive and well. It finds glorious expression in the way we view the world and react to the happenings in our life. Among such people are poets, composers, and artists—all the creative people who allow their romantic side free expression. These are the romantics whose passion will not be suppressed and whose belief in love and the power of love is part of their very being. But there are also those who succeed in burying these foolish notions of love, suppressing their romantic urges so deeply that they succeed in burying them totally. Their view of love is colored by practical dimensions that will not allow them to submit to the passion that is awakened by romance alone. For them there are other more sensible ways to manage their feelings, and they differentiate between being emotional and being in love.

So the semantics of the love equation takes over. Being in love is different from loving.

Some people are openly romantic, easily swept up in the tide of love, while others are more reticent and suppress their romantic urges.

> We must understand our own view of love and romance and examine the extent of the vulnerability of our fluttering hearts.

Falling in love is different from being in love. The debate about what is and is not real love fans many flames within us. Yet there is no denying that love, and the passions aroused by love, is one of the most powerful emotions on earth, powerful enough to cause betrayals and terrible wars between nations.

We must know ourselves. We must be clear if the feelings we feel are those that engage our body, our mind, or our heart, and we must learn to tell the difference between them.

Test yourself Consider the questions below to discover whether you are a die-hard romantic.

1 Do you believe in love at first sight?

2 Do you believe that somewhere out there is your perfect soulmate?

3 Do you believe in undying, eternal love?

4 Do you like romantic novels?

5 Do you keep all your love letters?

6 Do you fantasize often about your perfect lover?

7 Do you carry a picture of your beloved?

8 Do you remember the first time you kissed your lover?

9 Do you like to celebrate anniversaries with candlelit dinners?

If you answered YES to at least six of the questions listed above, then you can consider yourself an unabashedly romantic person!

Test yourself further These statements have been designed to stimulate your reactions to the whole question of love, romance, and passion.

1 It is definitely possible to love more than one person at the same time.

2 Love is more meaningful the second time around.

3 Marriage is totally unnecessary these days unless there are children.

4 There is no such thing as love at first sight.

5 It is simply impossible to love someone who does not reciprocate your love.

6 The state of unrequited love arouses deep feelings of rejection.

7 Romance conducted in public will never last.

8 Marrying above or below your social status is a recipe for disaster.

9 The best way to get over heartbreak is to find a new love.

10 Men and women love very differently.

11 The state of love cannot stay static—it is either waxing or waning like the moon.

12 It is the woman who can say no who drives men crazy with lust.

13 There is no more empowered woman than a woman scorned.

14 Playing hard to get makes a woman that much more desirable.

15 No woman or man is worth giving up everything for.

16 The worst betrayal is the betrayal of love.

17 Destiny plays the biggest role in whether a marriage is happy or not.

18 Only men with families can reach the full potential of their destiny.

19 Women are put on Earth only to procreate and serve men.

20 Men are like honeybees, while women are like honey.

21 Love without fidelity, commitment, and honesty is meaningless.

Are You a Concubine, Wife, or Matriarch?

What is your ideal of womanhood? What attitude do you bring to your interactions with the opposite sex—the concubine, the wife, or the matriarch? Which of the three faces of women best describes your view of the eternal man/woman relationship, your emotional outlook, and the way you relate to the epitome of feminine archetypes?

If you have the concubine syndrome, you feel that your main role is to please your man.

The Concubine Syndrome

Is your idea of femininity that of the eternal temptress whose happiness comes from your ability to please and to charm the man in your life? Do you have the concubine syndrome, where your role is mainly to please the man, with less thought for family or children? The concubine can see herself bearing the children of her "husband," but they will always come second in her priorities. If you are a concubine, in your view of the world, the man's role is that of the breadwinner. Thus he provides for you, keeps you in style, clothes you in diamonds, and looks after your welfare. Your role is only to please him in all ways and to dissolve all the stress and pressure of his life.

The concubine syndrome is alive and well in many cultures today. It can be seen in the sexually motivated woman who measures her personal self-worth in the context of her consummate skills in the art of love.

The concubine mentality reflects a powerful aspect of the female view of happiness with a man.

Women who identify with the concubine syndrome tend to be gossipy, crafty, and astute. They are not necessarily submissive; they can be ruthless and scheming. Theirs is the typical secondary wife condition where ultimate survival depends on their ability to stay in favor.

Women who identify with the concubine syndrome are always confident in themselves and enjoy socializing.

In the old days in China when powerful men—ministers, generals, and other strong males in the emperor's court, including the emperor himself—had many wives, the concubine syndrome flourished extensively. Many of the women in the emperor's harem fell into this category where survival at court and the rise to fame and fortune for themselves and their families depended on whether or not they found favor with the emperor—the son of heaven.

Chinese legends and history are filled with stories of the deceit and cunning of the lesser-ranked women of the imperial palace who possessed the concubine syndrome.

Psychologically, the concubine syndrome is still found today. Modern-day women with concubine mentalities appear in many guises, and they are usually aggressive, predatory, self-assured, and confident of their attraction. The concubine route to success and happiness is not necessarily at odds with the rise of greater recognition for working and professional women today. There is simply room enough to accommodate women of different aspirations.

Test yourself See if you have the concubine syndrome lurking somewhere deep in your subconscious. Do you agree or disagree with the following statements?

1 You believe that every man is fair game—even married men.

2 You believe that the best ticket to a good life is to find the "right" man.

3 You like being called "sexy," and you think of yourself as a femme fatale.

4 You prefer the company of men to women.

5 Your idea of luxury is being pampered by a man.

6 You believe that romantic love is for the innocent and the naive.

7 You believe that sex is the best way to keep a man interested in you.

8 You believe that being skilled in the art of love is the most important skill for a woman.

You may not even be aware you have it in you but if you say YES to at least five of these eight questions it is likely your view of the male/female conundrum reflects the concubine mentality. You could well be a predatory female!

A woman who displays the wife syndrome believes that her role is to care for her husband and family. The disintegration of the family unit would devastate her.

The Wife Syndrome

This could almost be called the principal wife syndrome. For you, the main role of the woman is to be a wife and raise a family. Your idea of femininity is to play the role of the consort, the wife. Your idea of happiness is closely tied to the respectability of being a wife who is skilled in being a homemaker, and sexual skills are not as high up on your list of priorities. Respectability is very important to you.

You see your role as being the force that pulls the whole family together. To you, sex is as much a wifely duty as it is pleasure. You are, generally speaking, not a demanding lover and, unlike those with the concubine syndrome, you very rarely initiate the sex act. To you, sex is part of life that comes with being a wife.

When the children arrive, the wife syndrome woman makes a caring mother, although in a somewhat detached way. Deep in the heart of a woman whose self-worth is strongly based on her marital status is the need to be loved and cherished by her man. She strongly believes in the sanctity of marriage. For her, separation and divorce would be a devastating blow.

Women whose view of femininity revolves around being a wife tend not to have the independent spirit. They are creative and epitomize all that signifies fertility and optimism. Procreation is a sacred duty. Their self-worth is strongly interwoven with that of their husband. Like the concubine, they too place the husband as their first priority, but unlike the concubine, they identify strongly with being the husband's publicly acknowledged consort.

Test yourself Women with the wife syndrome are generally married by the time they reach the age of 25, and if they are not, marriage will be paramount in their minds. If they become the second or third wife, they continue to see themselves as the properly recognized "consort." Women with a strong wife syndrome in their consciousness rarely participate in illicit love affairs. Do you have the wife syndrome? See if you disagree or agree with the following statements:

1 You believe life is incomplete if you do not have a husband.

2 You believe that women's main role in life is to create the family unit.

3 You think of marriage as a sacred trust.

4 You like the company of men and women in equal measure.

5 Your idea of luxury is having your family intact and at home together.

6 Love, duty, and fidelity are virtues you respect.

7 The family unit and children are the best way to hold a man's heart.

8 Your husband is the most important person in your life.

If you said YES to at least five of the eight questions, you definitely view yourself as a wife sort of person, and finding a husband is extremely important to your sense of self-worth.

The Matriarch Syndrome

You are the traditional earth mother, the compassionate and powerful matriarch. You are also the epitome of the independent woman—strong, firm, and able to support everyone in your life. You take pride and joy in running your family, and you enjoy mothering your husband, whom you probably treat like your eldest son. You control the family finances and all aspects of your husband's and children's welfare. Whether or not you are married, you are the kind of woman who can build a meaningful life for yourself. You might be a formidable corporate CEO, the matriarch of a big family, or the powerful patron of a charitable committee—whatever you are, people look up to you for your self-assuredness and confidence.

You will be naturally drawn to weak men. It is likely that you will have given up sex with your husband after about 10 to 15 years of marriage and you might even find him a concubine or a second wife. If your husband were unfaithful you would probably turn a blind eye. However, you would lay down conditions and would also have the clout to make sure your husband was discreet in his affairs, never bringing shame on the family. You choose the type of relationship you desire, rather than conforming to anyone else's concept of what makes a happy marriage.

Though matriarchs may appear to be intimidating, they are also extremely kindhearted and compassionate. Love, affection, and family count for something in their view of life, but they are rarely overtly sentimental.

Test yourself Are you the matriarchal type? If you say YES to at least 5 of these questions, you definitely view yourself as a potential matriarch. If you answered YES to less than 5 questions, you do not have a matriarchal personality.

1 You believe all women should be educated, as they have the potential to become leaders and have great success in their fields.

2 You are not a feminist, but you do believe that women are superior to men in many ways—if not physically, then definitely mentally and spiritually.

3 You think of marriage as a sacred institution but not a necessity. Any unmarried woman can be perfectly happy.

4 You believe that the best way to a man's heart is through his stomach.

5 Your idea of luxury is seeing every member of your family well cared for and eventually having responsible jobs and being part of the family.

6 Compassion, nurturing, and caring, as well as a sense of responsibility, are virtues you hold dear.

7 You believe that women should get involved in social and charitable work.

8 Your children and grandchildren, as well as your employees, are important people in your life who deserve your care and attention.

The Chinese believe that matriarchal women have the fire energy of strong yang in them, and they are said to be stronger than ten men.

Find the Goddess Within You

"I am the mother who feeds you, the sister who supports you, the daughter who charms you, and the nymph who enchants you…" Here are four goddesses from the Asian pantheon of goddess deities—Chinese, Hindu, and Tibetan. See which strikes a chord of personal affinity at the mental consciousness level. Do you see the goddess as mother, sister, daughter, or nymph?

Goddesses signify the flow of energy within us.

Asian goddesses are powerful, compassionate deities that personify all that is best in the female archetype. It is believed that hidden deep inside all of us—men and women alike—are the qualities and attributes of these goddesses. They lie dormant until awakened by the powerful stimulus of seeing their image in glorious color.

They exemplify the substance that embodies our inner consciousness, giving form and identity to the highest good and to the purest aspirations within the human psyche.

Goddesses represent material reality, and they stand at one end of the metaphysical spectrum. Gods, on the other hand, represent spiritual reality. Thus, it is to the goddesses that we turn for the bounty that enhances our lives in the material existence of samsara, the cycle of birth and rebirth, the realm of our existence.

Tara

Tara is the Tibetan goddess mother liberator, the compassionate mother goddess who protects, heals, and guides you. There are many inspiring stories of Green Tara, the swift liberator who emanates in 21 physical appearances to remove all fears.

Visualize the goddess Tara appearing in the space in front of you. From her heart, rainbow-colored light goes out in all directions. She is seated in the cross-legged position on a golden lotus. Her left leg is drawn up into her body and her right leg is slightly extended. This symbolizes how swiftly she will fly to the side of those who

The Tibetan goddess, Tara, is endowed with the power to heal all sorrow, grant all wishes, and dissolve all obstacles that block the rise of true wisdom.

invoke her help and her blessings. She appears compassionate and stunningly lovely. Her body appears as emerald-green light, youthful, and exquisitely beautiful.

> **Mother Tara offers a hand for all who need guidance during difficult times of their lives.**

The goddess's right hand on her right knee is in the gesture of giving blessings; her left hand at her heart is in the gesture of refuge.

Tara's face combines a hundred autumn moons at full moon. Blazing with light rays, her visage shines as brightly as a thousand stars. Tara is endlessly triumphant and, having reached every perfection, she has light rays emanating from her body and her crown. She smiles with serene rejoicing even as she subjugates all of your fears and all of the demons of delusion that threaten to engulf you with bleak despair.

Tibetan Buddhists believe that with the help of Mother Tara, wise realizations come to mind, like rainfall bringing true enlightenment and the development of the spontaneous kind heart.

Saraswati

Saraswati is the Indian goddess of knowledge, wisdom, and the arts. She embodies the wisdom of the all-powerful mother goddess Devi. She is described as the flowing river of consciousness that energizes creation. She is the dawn goddess whose golden rays dispel the darkness of ignorance. Her appearance instantly transforms chaos into order and confusion into clarity. To realize her presence, it is necessary to transcend the worldly pleasures of samsaric senses and rejoice in the serenity of the spirit.

Saraswati is usually depicted playing a musical instrument—the lute—and she is flanked by two peacocks that signify the arts. She is usually dressed in white and is said to be an emanation of the mother goddess Devi, who emerged from Brahma's mouth riding a swan.

Through the grace of the goddess Saraswati, you can acquire the power to sense, to think, to comprehend, and to communicate. Chaos is transformed into order, and the wisdom that arises from this allows you then to see all the promise and all the potential contained in every individual circumstance. And so it is also said that Saraswati is a personification of speech and sound and every form of communication.

This illustration shows Saraswati, the Hindu goddess of learning and the arts, seated on a white lotus flower. By contemplating her image, it is said that knowledge arises that helps people to find possibilities where before they could see only problems.

Even the gods salute her and the demons of the four directions sing songs to her glory. Sacred elephants raise their trunks in salute as they consecrate the space around her with life-sustaining water. With Lakshmi comes the wish-fulfilling cow with enough milk to feed the world for all eternity. From the ground arises the money tree that bears every kind of flower and every kind of gemstone. In her hands Lakshmi holds the basket of elements overflowing with grain and gold. She reveals all the locations of all the gems, minerals, and secret hidden treasures to the lords of the land and she shares all the secrets of the earth's fertility with the spirits of the Cosmos.

Along with Lakshmi comes the handsome prince of pleasure who shoots arrows that drip with desire into the hearts of all maidens. He rouses their senses, excites their minds, and inspires their hearts. With him come also the dakinis of love and longing, who bring with them bees plump with honey, flowers filled with pollen, and birds that sing songs of romance.

> ## Lakshmi brings all the manifestations of wealth, abundance, and power.

Lakshmi brings the white-skinned elephants and the seven-headed flying horse. She brings a crown, a throne, a parasol, a flywhisk, a cushion, a fan, a bow, and a conch—all the eight symbols of celestial authority and kingship. In short, Lakshmi brings all the manifestations of wealth, abundance, and power. But Lakshmi seeks those who would not be corrupted by wealth or made arrogant with power, those who do not succumb to the allure of pleasures and riches and prosperity. She looks

Lakshmi, the Hindu goddess of wealth and abundance, will bestow these gifts only on those who will use them wisely.

Lakshmi

Lakshmi is the Hindu goddess of wealth and abundance. She personifies the beautiful and the bountiful aspects of nature. Seated on a 108-petaled, dew-drenched lotus and dressed in pink silks, she nurtures life, gives sustenance, bestows power, and offers worldly and temporal pleasures. Hindu legend describes Lakshmi as having risen from an ocean of frothing waves. Bedecked in gold, she is the embodiment of affluence, abundance, and auspiciousness. As she rises, life-giving nectar flows from her body in every direction. The earth palpitates in ecstasy. Joy fills the air.

for someone strong, wise, and virtuous who understands the deceptive and temporary nature of samsara and strives instead to uphold the order of the Cosmos.

If wealth is what your heart most desires, meditate on the image of Lakshmi to know the balance of life and the order of the Cosmos.

Kuan Yin

Kuan Yin is the Chinese goddess of mercy, the Buddhist divine madonna to whom devotees turn in times of sadness, grief, and sorrow.

> Kuan Yin is the goddess who shows mercy to all who call on her for help.

Many legends abound telling of the various manifestations of this beloved goddess, who is said to have appeared many eons ago as the beloved Chinese princess Miao Shan whose virtuous purity and beautiful visage have inspired millions of Chinese to turn to her for help and blessings.

Dressed in beautiful white robes, and always drawn with a serene expression on her face, Kuan Yin carries a small bottle of nectar in one hand and a flywhisk in the other. She is depicted sitting on a lotus or standing on a dragon, or on a tortoise crossing turbulent waters.

Kuan Yin is the Compassionate Buddha Avalokiteshvara himself, who has assumed different forms throughout the centuries. Some say she may even have taken reincarnation as Queen Maya, who gave birth to the Lord Buddha Shakyamuni and passed away seven days later. Kuan Yin is seen as the goddess who shows mercy on all who call on her for help. She is perceived as the light for the

blind, the shade for those who suffer from the heat, the stream of water for the thirsty, and the bestower of fearlessness for those who abide in fear. She is the remedy for the sick, and and is a mother for all suffering beings.

Kuan Yin portrays hope for the hopeless in her "thirty-three manifestations and fourteen bestowals of fearlessness." These many different beautiful images of the goddess provide a wealth of visual and spiritual inspiration for those who choose to practice her meditations.

Kuan Yin, the Chinese goddess of mercy, offers solace in times of grief and great sorrow.

The Eastern and Western Mind

In terms of value systems, spiritual perspectives, and a view of the great Cosmos, is there a difference between the Eastern mind and the Western mind? Test yourself with this sampling of statements and see what you think. Consider if you agree with any of these statements and whether your spiritual perspective reflects more of an Eastern or Western mind.

1 Thought processes seem to have evolved from different starting points in the East and West. Do you agree?

2 The West views life as a constant battle between good and evil, between materialism and spirituality. Western thinking generally holds that most of what is undesirable in life originates from the excesses of overindulging the senses—excess indulgence in the pleasures of the flesh and excess indulgence in stimulants like drugs and alcohol. These indulgences are seen as blocks to the purity of soul. Do you agree with this theory?

3 The West associates evil with diabolical satanic forces, which seem to have their roots in the pursuit of material wealth, power, and the pleasurable appeasement of the senses. Do you agree with this?

4 In the Eastern mind-set, there are no such things as absolutes. There is no absolute evil and no absolute good. There is no belief in an almighty creator god or in the devil. All negative behavior is believed to originate from ignorance. All that is desirable comes from wisdom realizations and the enlightened mind; these are within people's control. How do you feel about this?

5 Western belief systems insist on a rejection of the polygamous state, while polygamy is accepted in many Eastern traditions. Where do you stand on this matter?

6 Western value systems focus on the rights of the individual, while Eastern value systems focus on the obligations of the individual and the rights of society in general. Where does your own value system fit in?

7 In the Eastern view of gender differences, women generally have fewer basic rights than men, although they are respected, while in the West, both genders enjoy equal rights. Which view of women is more in accordance with your own?

8 Whatever injustices and discrimination women suffer in the West, these arise from personal prejudices. In the East, they arise from accepted social traditions, and in some instances are even legislated for. Do you agree?

9 There are no Western equivalents to the Eastern concept of the duality of yin and yang in the Universe, the concept that there is a negative and a positive dimension to all things. Do you agree with this philosophy?

10 The West views the galaxy in terms of the sun revolving around the earth—it is sun oriented. The East views the Universe in terms of the moon revolving around the earth—it is moon oriented. Which view most agrees with your own?

11 While Eastern medicine has some interesting concepts, we should look to the West for treatment for illness. Do you agree?

According to Eastern ways of thinking, the Universe is seen in terms of the moon revolving around the earth. This moon-oriented way of thinking is reflected in the lunar calendars of many Eastern religions.

How Do You View Marriage?

Within every male is the ideal female goddess prototype, and within every female is the ideal male god prototype. How do you relate to the Western and Eastern view of male/female ideals as personified in the god/goddess legends? Examine your inner male and female instincts by seeing which of the god/goddess pairings described here you relate more readily to.

Right: The Greek goddess Hera with Zeus; she endures his infidelities in return for sharing his prestige and power.

Opposite, top left: Juno and Jupiter. Juno is said to ensure the happiness and well-being of a woman in marriage. Many consider June to be the favorable month for marriage from a woman's standpoint.

Hera and Zeus

The Greek goddess queen Hera is described as being equally strong and equally influential as her male counterpart. She endures the infidelity of the powerful patriarchal figure Zeus because she is instinctively drawn to his vigorous masculine energy, but she stays stubbornly monogamous herself even as she turns a blind eye to his indiscretions. She sees this as a small price to pay in exchange for the prestige and

power of being his official consort. In today's times, Hera would manifest as the powerful corporate wife who expects to share her husband's authority and status. The man who identifies with Zeus would reflect broadly similar sentiments, in his mind placing his wife and his other women in different categories. The wife in this scenario occupies a dominant and unshakable position.

Juno and Jupiter

The powerful Roman goddess of tradition, also the wife of Jupiter, Juno personifies the established norms and behaviors of her times. In love relationships, she prefers the open declaration of honorable intentions, as much to assuage her need for security as for her desire to protect her public image. Juno is honored as the patron of marriage,

THE MOTHER GODDESS

Asian legend explains that in the beginning of time, there was only the Mother Goddess, the bringer of life, the nourisher, the lover, the comforter. Her image graced stone caves of antiquity, and her statues stood alone in ancient temples.

In Japan, the Mother Goddess was Amaterasu, the sun goddess; in Greece she was Demeter, the corn goddess; in Egypt she was Isis, the river goddess. The Vikings knew her as Frejya, the Eskimos called her Sedna, the Romans knew her as Artemis. The Tibetans worship her as Tara, and the Indians know her as Shakti. Then came the powerful warrior gods who forced the mother goddesses into submission.

So the inner female essence is that of the Mother Goddess—instinctively nurturing—while the inner male fundamental nature is that of the all-conquering warrior who seduces the Mother Goddess into submission. Are these the basic attitudes in our love relationships?

the human body. Shiva is the meditator, the indifferent husband won over by the wifely qualities of his consort.

Lakshmi and Vishnu

In this coupling of the great goddess of wealth with the guardian of the Cosmos, it is Lakshmi who chooses Vishnu by placing a fragrant garland of victory around his neck, thereby making him her consort.

Vishnu is the stern keeper of cosmic laws—he restores moral order—while Lakshmi is seen as the goddess of mercy who understands the frailties of man. She is also the goddess of prosperity and good fortune, and as such, she provides Vishnu with the capability to be the protector and preserver of the world.

Lakshmi serves Vishnu well in his battle against chaos and corruption, and he pleases her hugely by being completely diligent in carrying out his duties as guardian of the world. She ministers to his every need, mothering him and tending to him as a devoted wife should.

Parvati is totally devoted to her husband, Shiva, and they enjoy wonderful marital bliss.

Lakshmi attends to Vishnu's every need and is a devoted wife.

and she was worshiped for her championing and protection of women. Her counterpart, the powerful god Jupiter, is not unlike Zeus in that he typifies the masculine attributes associated with the vital and energetic lover.

Parvati and Shiva

From the start it is Parvati who gives chase. Each day she visits the cave of Shiva to sweep, decorate, and offer him fruits, hoping to win his love. Shiva ignores her advances, and it is only after she goes into retreat that Shiva accepts her as his wife. Parvati melts the stern heart of Shiva with her total devotion and continuing affection. As a result, they enjoy great marital bliss and this brings order and stability to the Cosmos.

Parvati is regarded as the divine homemaker, the goddess of the household, of marriage, of motherhood, and of family. She wears 16 love charms, decorations that celebrate the divinity of

How Do You Cope with Stress?

Stress comes from anxiety, fear, guilt, and pressure; it is basically an inability to cope accompanied by a deteriorating sense of self-worth. Stress erodes confidence and causes illness and self-destructive behavior. Stress indicates a state of anxiety, frustration, and fear, which can sometimes lead to an unexplainable sense of terror. How do you cope with it?

Stress at work is increasingly common, but there are many ways to change your responses to it and start to tackle the root of the problem.

Stress is the opposite of calm. Stress is the opposite of relaxation. Stress is a measure of how unfit we are at the mental level. The inability to cope with stress directly affects our sense of well-being and our happiness. Physical results of stress show up in a thousand different ways. It causes headaches, earaches, toothaches, chest pains, palpitations, skin rashes, and butterflies in the stomach. Stress makes us hold our breath or breathe unevenly, gives us indigestion and diarrhea, or causes constipation. Stress leads to an inability to speak coherently and remember basic facts, and a fatigue that is not in proportion to our workload.

Sometimes stress causes us to lose our appetite and makes it hard for us to concentrate. We are easily distracted and often overreact to people and events. The worst effect of stress is behavioral. Stress makes us negative in our attitudes and in our emotional reactions to others. It causes us to lose our patience, to become angry and short-tempered. Stress is one of the most self-destructive phenomena of the modern living environment, and unless we learn to cope effectively with stress and its effects, nothing we do will ever be much fun or give us any real satisfaction.

Test yourself Your journey into self-discovery must take account of the stress level under which you operate. Look within to see what causes you to feel stressed. Consider the following stress-inducing situations, and see if anything is causing you anxiety.

1 Are you feeling inadequate at work?

2 Are you feeling inadequate in your love life?

3 Do you compare yourself unfavorably with your peers?

4 Are you dissatisfied with your marriage?

5 Are you having a problem at work?

6 Are you having problems in a relationship?

7 Is someone you love chronically ill?

8 Are you having cash-flow problems?

9 Are you in danger of losing your job?

10 Have you just been fired?

11 Are you feeling dissatisfied with life for no reason at all?

12 Are you feeling bored?

13 Are you finding it hard to cope with your work?

14 Do you feel stuck in a stress cycle?

15 Are you hiding a terrible secret?

16 Are you suffering from a secret addiction?

17 Is there something in your life that is causing you resentment?

18 Are you desperately afraid of something?

19 Have you made a promise you cannot fulfill?

In attempting to dissect the causes of stress in your life, you will also come to recognize your level of stress tolerance. Different people have different levels of tolerance. Invariably the cause of all stress can be reduced to three sources:

1 People around you who cause you to become emotionally stressed.

2 External events that cause you to become physically stressed.

3 Lifestyle-related issues that cause you to be psychologically stressed.

If you examine these three main causes of stress, you will see that they all have to do with the way your mind reacts. It is the mind that is the root of all stress. You cannot change people's behavior toward you, you cannot change the events that happen, and you cannot change the physical circumstances in which you find yourself. But you can change your responses and your reactions to them. The key to dealing successfully with stress starts with pinpointing the root of stress. Everything that causes us to feel stressed comes from the mind. Guilt, pressure, ego, vanity, ambition, frustration, and fear—they all originate in the mind. There are many different ways to transform the mind and cope with stress.

It is important to generate a sense of mental calmness; find time to indulge in relaxing activities, such as walking in the woods, to help you to slow down and give you time to think.

Five Sure Ways to Cope with Stress

First, we generate a sense of mental calmness. We slow down our reaction to people, events, and circumstances that cause us stress. For example, each time something stimulates anxiety and makes us reach for the phone, we immediately put the phone back in the cradle, count to ten, and give ourselves a day to respond.

Second, we learn to reverse the negatives in our life. For example, we can reverse our view of everyone who causes us stress in our lives. Think of all the difficult people currently causing you grief as wish-fulfilling jewels brought into your life for you to practice patience and tolerance. Think of every setback as a blessing in disguise. This is the process of transformation that operates simultaneously at the mental, intellectual, and even spiritual consciousness levels. Do not expect instant success—it takes time.

Third, try some physical relaxation methods. Start with deep breathing exercises. Learn some basic exercises. Take up simple yoga or chi kung, or learn a few stretching exercises that can relieve you of physical aches and pains. You will be surprised how effective a simple exercise regimen can be in reducing your stress levels. Once a week have a body massage concentrating on the shoulders, the neck, and the back. Once a month have a reflexology massage, and occasionally treat yourself to the full works—aromatherapy, Bach remedies, mineral therapy, homeopathy, a complete detoxification, and a full pampering regime. When you look after your body, it looks after your mind!

Fourth, create powerful and positive affirmations. Think up short, powerful statements that continually enhance your confidence, build you up, and convince you of positive outcomes. Then write them out, stick them in places where you can see them, and most important, repeat them like mantras in your head over and over again until you believe your own rhetoric. Be very selective in your choice of words. Craft your sentences carefully. Use the present tense. Use only positive words. Make them believable.

Fifth, try mental and creative visualization exercises. Picture yourself happy and relaxed, lying on a beach, or going for a walk. Images have the power to convey moods and nuances. Pictures will add powerful energy to all your words. Say to yourself, "Every day in every way, I am getting better and better at everything I do."

There are some wonderful deep breathing exercises that can help you to relax. In chi kung, you breathe in through the nose with your arms raised, then bend down and breathe out at the same time.

TEN SURE WAYS TO RELAX

1   *Grip your hands very tightly so that your fingers dig deep into your palms and then let go. Feel the release of tension.*

2   *Tighten your forehead, close your eyes, and contort your face into an ugly frown. Keep frowning until you can't go any further and then release. Feel the tension lift instantly.*

3   *Stretch your arms out horizontally so they are parallel with the ground. Stretch them far out until you cannot stretch anymore. Then relax and feel your body relax.*

4   *Place your palms flat against a wall and then push. Keep pushing until you cannot push anymore, and then release. Feel your arms relax.*

5   *Open your mouth as wide as you can and make it into a big O. Then close it. Feel your facial muscles relax.*

6   *Rub your hands together until they warm up, then place them flat against your face. Close your eyes and feel the relief.*

7   *Lie on your back and put your feet up. Feel the blood rushing to your head.*

8   *Lie completely flat with your back to the floor and systematically flex and release every part of you. Start at the feet and move up through the legs, to the face, and even your scalp. Feel tension drain out of you completely.*

9   *While lying on your back, breathe in through your nostrils slowly and deeply. Feel your abdomen expanding like a balloon. Then slowly breathe out through your mouth and feel your abdomen flattening like a balloon, releasing air. Visualize fresh, energizing chi flowing in; and stale, stagnant chi flowing out.*

10 *While lying on your back, close your eyes and begin to daydream. Think pleasant thoughts, and then visualize a positive outcome to something you are working on at the moment. Smile happily to yourself.*

1 Start by gripping your hands very tightly. Make sure the fingers dig deep into the palms. Feel the release of tension as you open your hands out.

2 Close your eyes and contort your face into a frown. Feel the tension lift as you relax.

6 Rub your hands to warm them, then place them on your face and close your eyes. Feel your anxiety begin to melt away.

Blueprint of a Woman's Life Cycle

What is your self-image? What attributes and perceptions make up your view of yourself as a woman at each stage of your development? What are the dimensions of being a woman that excite you the most today? Do you view yourself evolving within the fixed template of the traditional roles, or do you see yourself creating your own template?

The Child

We start out as the child whose life is shrouded in innocence and childish delights. The great responsibilities of later life have not yet entered into our young and as yet unformed consciousness. This is the stage when curiosity and adventure dominate life—we constantly seek out stimuli. We are searching, learning, experiencing. What we eventually become, how we feel, and how we assert ourselves is determined by our role models and our circumstances in life.

The Young Maiden

We become the young maiden when we first discover many things about ourselves. The post-puberty stage is when body changes bring exciting new vistas. Freedom from childhood restrictions and the sudden entry into adult life lead to thrilling new feelings. This is the time of life when love and romance bring new, strange feelings into our world. This is also the stage of life when the opposite sex, men, take on new significance. It is an exciting new period of life indeed.

How you see yourself as a woman will depend very much on which phase of life you are in.

The Mother

Next come marriage and motherhood, when we accept the responsibility of caring for our children. This can be a most fulfilling period when a woman can wholeheartedly embrace her role in the evolution of the life cycle itself—but it can also be a traumatic period of great stress.

This is also the longest-lasting period of a woman's life. The mother role of a woman can span twenty to thirty years, and it also coincides with that time of her life when other issues will come to dominate her thoughts. At this period of a woman's life, she is most likely to make important changes.

The Matriarch

Finally we arrive at the stage when we transform into the wise woman, the grandmother, the influential aunt, and the powerful matriarch. It is the postmenopausal period when we are given a new lease on life. We are freshly empowered. Our responsibilities as a mother are, theoretically at least, all but over. We have come to terms with marriage and life. At this stage of life we can call the shots. We can be anything we want to be—whether or not we know it.

Woman's Life Cycle— a Blueprint

Although it is possible to map out a stage-by-stage blueprint of a woman's life cycle, each woman develops at her own pace so that at every stage the psychological manifestations do not always fit a fixed pattern. In the context of modern living we now also have to take account of the increasing numbers of women who have careers and generally turn their backs on the traditional blueprint of a woman's life cycle.

Today's woman can choose not only whether she wants to be a mother and start a family, but also the size and structure of her family. Whatever your view of yourself at any moment in time, however, it is useful to look at the inevitable flow of a woman's life. Irrespective of the choices she makes, eventually a woman will enter into the phase of the matriarch. What her life becomes at this last stage is the sum total of the choices she has made in the earlier stages of her life.

Test yourself See how you respond to the following statements, which highlight some of the very serious issues confronting women today. Should you be facing any of the dilemmas listed, perhaps you can get a measure of comfort in knowing that you are not alone in having to confront these matters.

1 If you were desperately unhappy in your marriage, would you get a divorce?

2 If you were single and getting on in age, would you adopt a child?

3 Would you be upset if your 25-year-old daughter told you she was gay?

4 If you discovered that you had feelings for another woman, would you suppress them?

5 Would you urge your 17-year-old daughter to get an abortion if she became pregnant and had no wish to get married to the baby's dad?

6 Would you resent your daughter-in-law deciding she did not want children?

7 If you discovered your husband was cheating on you, would you confront him?

8 Would you ask for a divorce if your husband had a child with another woman?

9 Would you tell your husband if the child you were carrying was not his?

10 What would you do if your husband told you he was gay?

11 How would you feel if your parents divorced, or if your mother told you your father made her unhappy, or had an affair?

The Men of Our Times

The men of our times can be viewed in terms of five principal masculine archetypes—the autocratic emperor, the family man, the courageous warrior, the learned scholar, and the ardent lover. These archetypes also reflect the men of past eras, and they're prominent in legends and myths, literature and poetry, and in the fairy tales handed down through the generations in the East and the West.

Examine the attributes of the masculine archetypes presented here. If you are a man, see how closely they fit your view of yourself. If you are a woman, see which of these categories of men best reflect the attributes of the man in your life.

The emperor archetype is confident and self-assured and sees himself as the provider for his family.

The Emperor

This is the leader, the visionary, the king, the autocrat. He epitomizes the primeval yang energy of the trigram Chien in the *I Ching* system of eight trigrams. He is the patriarchal archetype who views himself as the temporal head of all he surveys. Such men are confident, self-assured, and usually clear about their life directions, their aspirations, and their view of the Universe. Men in this category tend to be traditional in their outlook and comfortable in the role of provider and patriarch, and they also possess an instinctive respect for women.

In disposition, the emperor is calm and measured. Here is a man who is practical, traditional, and old-fashioned, and who brings order out of chaos; he is the ultimate reliable person. He is also a man of few words, but do not think he is a pushover. He is a leader who expects obedience from his family and loyalty from his loved ones. Betray him, cheat him, and he will not forgive you.

The Family Man

Here is the man of many women's dreams. This is the all-around guy whose attitudes toward life and love, work and play, male and female, correspond most closely to the cultural and behavioral mores of his time. If you take up with such a man, be prepared to be bored or charmed by his predictability. The family man is unlikely to let anyone down. He neither fools around nor thinks of doing so. He is not difficult to love or to please. He maintains a healthy respect for family and will not mind his wife going out to work or being a homemaker. If your man belongs to this category, hang on to him. In this day and age, such men are rare!

The Warrior

Courageous, brave, and exciting, here is the swashbuckling hero of every maiden's dream. He epitomizes the winds of change, of transformation. The warrior takes risks and is a free spirit. If you

Scholar types tend to live in a world of their own, and seldom have eyes for women other than their own partner. Scholars tend to be secure individuals. They are deep thinkers with an inner world that is alive with color, activity, and knowledge. It is hard to read what the scholar is thinking, but this is not because he is secretive. He is simply a thinker rather than a communicator.

If you are mentally his match, the scholar is never boring. If you are not the clever type, you had better pass on this man—you could end up being exceedingly miserable.

The Lover

Here is the ardent lover who features repeatedly in literature and all the works of dramatic fiction. With him, any woman will surely feel the joy and anguish of romantic love, although you might find his passion a bit overwhelming.

The lover can be jealous, but he is also quick to turn off those who do not match his ardor. He is sensitive, sensual, passionate, and very vital in the way he woos a woman. In fact, the lover cannot live without a lover, be this a woman or another man. He can be possessive.

The lover has an impractical view of the world, and he neither likes nor thinks about work. If you find that this description fits the man in your life and you insist on being carried away by his grand and amorous protestations of love then enjoy . . . if not, come down to earth immediately and look elsewhere for love.

Left: The warrior archetype is courageous and exciting, but he will not be a deep thinker. If you are searching for a kindred spirit, you would be wise to look for someone else.

Below: If you are looking for romance and passion, the lover archetype could be for you. Yet he may have an impractical view of the world, with his head always up in the clouds.

like adventure, then follow him to the ends of the earth—but do not expect fidelity or commitment.

He is the sort who will avoid the intimacy of personal love. He loves his independence too much. If you love such a man, then match him in his quest for new worlds to conquer and new risks to take. But beware—the warrior is a dangerous man to give your heart to because there is a certain lack of stability in his psyche.

The Scholar

This is also the sage, the counselor, and the eternal advisor. The scholar will either hold you mesmerized by his wonderful intellect or drive you mad with his insistence on teaching you everything, from how to read the paper to bringing up kids or mowing the lawn. The scholar is fastidious and is usually a perfectionist.

The Courtesan Condition

There are women who adopt a strategy of life that can only be described as the courtesan condition. Their behavior is reminiscent of the geisha women of Japan—long-suffering, apparently docile, and seemingly compliant to the needs, wants, and demands of others. Some see this as the ultimate manifestation of weakness. Others view it as a secret strength.

Geishas in Japan are trained to please men, but they are independent women, often with powerful intellects.

The courtesan condition is a behavioral response to the outside world that depends entirely on always seeming to want to please others. Some see this as a weakness, others see it as as the ultimate

strategy of life, for in apparently never wanting to prevail they have already done so.

There is an implied yielding yin force in the behavioral response of the courtesan. The ultimate yin energy is represented in the trigram Kun which also signifies the yielding woman who always wins by always giving in.

The courtesan will always appear to be self-effacing, will always seem eager to please, will always be undemanding, and always grateful for the tiniest gestures of appreciation or approval. She seldom loses her cool and will be very soothing in her reactions to every kind of behavior. The popular image of the courtesan is one of abject humility. She seems to give credit to others, generously heaping praise on those around her, and always acknowledging other people's superiority (especially in the case of men).

To the uninitiated, such behavior appears to imply some sort of basic emotional weakness. Many people—especially those who live in the West—seem to think that it is weakness, insecurity, and a sense of over-dependence that motivate submissive behavior. They conclude that such behavior manifests a strong desire for approval, a craving for appreciation, and an almost compelling need for acceptance. They see apparently submissive women as long-suffering creatures desperately in need of rescuing. Nothing, of course, could be further from the truth.

The courtesan condition showcases one of the greatest secrets of Eastern women. In their interaction with men, Eastern women almost always hide their true inclinations, so that it is from strength that their submissiveness comes. The women of the East who have been trained as courtesans have often gained full control over their senses and over the way they respond and react to any kind of behavior.

> **Playing the role of the compliant female requires a great deal of strength and self-control.**

Thus, they are able to deflect unwanted attention and propositions and still seem to be submissive and wanting to please. Far from being the clinging type and dependent on others for their strength, many courtesans are inwardly ambitious and possessed of powerful intellects. With perfect training, they have learned never to show their claws, and never to reveal their true feelings. Instead they will always appear to be full of sympathy and humility.

There is a great deal to be said for this geisha-style approach to the art of interacting with the men in our lives. It is not an easy strategy. It is born of great strength, for in appearing to fulfill the imagined expectations, they are able to submerge their own self-cherishing thoughts, their own ego, and their own vanity, all of which calls for a great sense of purpose. However, it is well worth considering this style of human interaction, especially in professional situations.

Test yourself See if you are able to use the courtesan strategy in your love life.

1 When someone criticizes you, can you smilingly accept the criticism?

2 When someone insults you, are you able not to respond?

3 When someone says your dress is unsuitable, do you change immediately?

4 Do you believe that men are basically weak and easily manipulated?

5 Can you let someone else be the center of attraction?

6 Can you pretend to be stupid and not appear to feel bad about it?

7 Can you lose a game and not mind?

8 Do you mind serving others?

9 Can you appear attentive even though you are feeling bored?

10 Are you good at hiding your feelings?

If you answered YES to at least six of the above questions, you exhibit great potential.

There can be great strength in appearing submissive and eager to please. Many Eastern women have learned not to reveal their true feelings and they have full control over the way they interact with others.

Are You a Samurai or an Emotional Coward?

In Japan, the samurai is the brave warrior who prevails in a hostile and dangerous world. The samurai syndrome reflects the masculine instinct for self-preservation. The samurai is competitive and highly motivated, and always on guard. The emotional coward, by contrast, is the fence-sitter, the uninvolved and indifferent observer who does not like to take a stand.

The Samurai

The samurai syndrome is alive and well in the corridors of the corporate world. Like it or not, the corporate work environment is now exceedingly competitive, and it is hostile. It is an environment that encourages the pursuit of self-interest. Only the strongest and fittest will survive.

The corporate environment brings out the best and the worst of the human condition. Those in play in such environments do not look only to survive, but they expect to thrive, to gain power, and to rule. Power is the name of the game—power to control people as well as events.

Enter the samurai, who thrives on strategic power play and skillful manipulation. The samurai is cold and calculating, devoid of emotion, suspicious of even his best friend. The samurai can be a man or a woman who has honed his or her manipulative skills to a fine art. All their relationships are motivated purely by self-interest.

Test yourself If you work in a corporate environment that is filled with intrigues and plenty of corporate politicking, consider how you would react in the circumstances described below.

1 You have just started dating one of your colleagues when you hear through the grapevine that both of you are in line for a sought-after new assignment. Do you instantly start planning how you can get the better of him/her?

2 You find yourself in a situation in which if you betrayed your boss, you would be promoted and offered his job. Would you betray him without a second thought?

3 Do you dislike being in situations where you are not in control?

4 Do you consider competitiveness as being healthy for the company?

5 Do you prefer being in the background to being in the limelight?

6 Do you believe that being emotional is an obstacle to upward mobility?

7 Do you regard an angry reaction as a loss of control?

8 Do you always assess what's good for you before anything else?

9 Would you grovel if you had to?

10 Would it be true to say that you don't care what others think of you?

If you answered YES to at least six of the above questions you are certainly a political animal. You can consider yourself an active practitioner of the samurai syndrome.

The Emotional Coward

The detached observer of the world who balks at making any kind of commitment suffers from the anxiety of a loveless and meaningless existence. While such people appear to be reasonably self-sufficient and independent, they are likely to be very lonely and unhappy individuals. This is because theirs is a conscious strategy of detachment. They will find it hard to allow anyone to get too close, because of a probably deep-seated fear of depending on anyone for their well-being. Emotional cowards live their lives free of emotional highs and lows. They depend on no one and no one is allowed to depend or rely on them. They do not take advantage of anyone and no one will be able to take advantage of them. They live in splendid isolation, afraid to love, terrified to trust, and fearful of commitment of any kind.

If you find yourself veering into such a state of conscious isolation, make an effort to break free, for isolation creates its own downward spiral, and negative avoidance of involvement leads to a serious contraction of spirit that will leave you drained and unhappy. Learn to love. Keep a pet. Make friends with children. Create openings for the yin chi inside you to flow upwards, diluting the hardness of distrust deep inside you.

Test yourself Consider your responses to the following questions:

1 Are you afraid of depending on anyone?

2 Do you want to hide from others?

3 Are you shy but no one knows it?

4 Do you secretly harbor a superiority complex?

5 Do you feel uncomfortable when anyone gets too close to you?

6 Have you often been afraid to kiss someone?

7 Have you often felt rejected?

8 Do you prefer watching television at home to being out partying?

9 Are you afraid to get hurt or appear vulnerable?

10 Are you afraid to ask people out?

If you answered YES to six or more of the above questions you certainly seem to be afraid of making yourself vulnerable to anyone. Think through your hangups—it will help you to break loose of the invisible but powerful walls you seem to have constructed around yourself.

A Japanese man in traditional samurai clothes. In most corporate offices today, you need to have some of the spirit of the samurai to survive.

Your Happiness Base

Not many people can really define happiness, except to say that it is a state of mind. Happiness is the absence of unhappiness, the absence of pain, and the absence of sorrow. More than that, happiness is a deep-felt joy that rises from somewhere very profound inside you. It rumbles forth, surfacing upwards into your consciousness, causing you to break into smiles.

Examine yourself and see what really stimulates happiness—a touch, a smell, a picture, a sound, or a taste? The bear hug from your dad, the warm embrace of a friend, the cuddle of love from a sweetheart? These are all powerful touch stimuli that bring a warm glow to the heart.

Aromas also have the power to make you happy—the smell of fried onions, a favorite perfume, a lover's scent, the smell of your father's tobacco—smells that bring back a memory of affection that reaches deep into the heart.

Then there are pictures of loved ones, photographs of smiles and joyous occasions, of treasured moments, of triumphant times, of inspiring scenery, of sunrises and the morning dew. The sense of sight is perhaps the greatest source of feelings of happiness.

Our happiness base can also be built around positive sounds and music that we have absorbed into our subconscious—the voices of loved ones, a favorite opera, music that brings back a time of happiness, rhythms and beats, the sound of water flowing, a morning birdsong.

Finally, there is the happiness associated with the touch sensations, with physical pleasure—the happiness of tastes, foods, drinks, and textures that

Our happiness base can be built around positive sounds such as the gentle lapping of water against the shore. The mind remembers many settings associated with calm sounds that establish a wonderful background to feelings of joyousness.

CREATING THE HAPPINESS BASE

- *Delete all negative motivations, convictions, and beliefs from your consciousness. Write them down and then burn them. Compile them and then box them away. List all the negative fears you have ever felt and then tear them up and scatter them to the four directions.*

- *Destroy ugly pictures of unhappy moments in your life. Keep only positive photographs.*

- *Do not listen to sad music whose lyrics make you think of broken dreams and unrequited love—but do differentiate between inspiring music, which does have touches of melancholy, and outright sad music, which can give you an overdose of yin feelings.*

- *Keep a safe distance from people who bring out negative emotions in you; who make you feel bad about yourself; people who make you feel inadequate, irritated, and anything else that shakes your self-confidence. Until you feel able to stay detached from their power, it is better to remove them, at least temporarily, from your space.*

- *Seek out those who build up your self-esteem, who encourage and inspire you, whose energy lifts your spirits.*

make our taste buds glow with satisfaction. Some people are able to feel their happiness base with no effort in the world. The smallest excuse sends them into gales of laughter. Such people operate from what we call a happy base. They seem to find it much harder to get angry or feel sad than naturally unhappy people.

The person in charge of this base is you yourself. If you create sensors within the brain and say to yourself that you really prefer happiness to unhappiness as a regular state of mind, you will find it increasingly easy to create this happiness base and to build on it.

The highs and lows of life are part of the natural process of the evolving and changing Cosmos. Within happiness lie seeds of depression and inside the core of depression are seeds of great happiness, too. For those whose lives seem filled with tragic events that make them feel constantly unhappy, think of the seeds of happiness that lie at the core of their unhappiness. These seeds provide the hope that must convince them things will change for the better.

For those whose lives shine with happiness, stay grounded to the reality that it is the sharing of happiness that creates the flow, and it is this flow that will ensure that the seeds of unhappiness never take root to overwhelm your sense of well-being.

Build up your happiness base by spending time with friends who make you laugh, lift your self-esteem, and encourage you to feel great about yourself.

Are You an Introvert or an Extrovert?

The mind is a vast sea of complex thinking that reflects a tuning inwards as well as a tuning outwards. The mind is both object-oriented and subject-oriented, extroverted and introverted. These manifest as a range of interactions rather than simply as two categorical types. Both introverted and extroverted people can come across in either a positive or a negative way.

Your basic attitude—whether you are inward or outward looking—will reflect the way in which you interact with the world. How this influences the way you organize your life and lifestyle will depend upon whether your temperament is yin, dominated by the darker negative forces, or yang, dominated by the lighter positive influences.

Extroverts can appear talkative and socially responsive, but on the other hand, they can also seem aggressive, edgy, and restless.

If you wish to know yourself and want to examine better pathways to realizing your destiny, it is useful to reflect on where you stand in the spectrum of polarities that define the parameters of your thinking. It is from these that the manifestation of introvert or extrovert attitudes is projected and take on greater clarity.

The complex process of thinking and the formulation of attitudes resemble the endless knot that has no beginning and no end. In the process of thinking, any number of inputs can influence our attitudes. These different inputs take the form of thoughts, instincts, feelings, and sensations. What is then manifested as the output of our mind is our attitudes. Visualize all of your mental pathways and ask yourself what kind of an extrovert or introvert you are.

Extrovert

To begin with, consider which side more accurately reflects your attitude. Are you basically an object-oriented person? Do you tend to be more in tune with the world outside you? When you arise each morning, is your first thought about your external circumstances or about the state of your mind? Are you very aware of your living space, your external environment, the events that happen from day to day, the people in your life? Do you like interacting with people, socializing, partying, and responding to external stimuli? Are you happiest when you are in the company of other people?

If you are all these things, then you are probably the lively, socially oriented person who is more at home communicating and interacting with people rather than being alone. Your hobbies and sports tend to be social and team-oriented, and your destiny is best played out in the external arena of people and events.

Introvert

The opposite end of the spectrum is if you are more of a subject-oriented person. You are given more to self-reflection and meditation than to interacting with people. You are happiest when left alone with your thoughts. This manifests as reserve, aloofness, a disinterest in the world around you, and even a tuning out of the world. You dislike social gatherings, cannot make small talk, and are puzzled by meaningless interactions.

Both extroverts and introverts can be happy individuals or they can be moody, rigid, or restless in their outlook. Happiness or unhappiness is not the monopoly of either type. Their motivations and outlooks may be different, as are their instincts and sensations, and these reflect in the way they design their life, but both are capable of creating stability or instability in their lives.

> Your basic attitude—whether you are inward or outward looking—will reflect how you interact with the world.

Knowing their outlooks, however, gives strength to their motivations and a certain assurance to

The key to maintaining a happy mental attitude is good balance. A balanced introvert comes across as a relaxed, calm person.

their behavior. The key is the maintenance of balance so that what manifests is stability of attitude. Thus, balanced extroverts are pleasantly outgoing and responsive, a joy to be with, while unbalanced extroverts come across as touchy, restless, self-centered, and aggressive. This latter type manifests their attitudes as a mass rather than as a flow, imposing their will and their circumstance on you rather than allowing the interaction to flow.

It is the same with introverted people. Those who are balanced in their outlook will come across as controlled, calm, and peaceful, and these types can often inspire others with their demeanor. Unbalanced introverts can come across as moody, pessimistic, and unsociable.

Part Two

DISCOVERING
SECRETS OF
YOUR BODY

Our physical appearance, and the circumstances into which we are born, is the manifestation of what the Chinese term our heaven luck. This is similar to the Buddhist (and Hindu) concept of karma. How we perceive and define ourselves physically, whether positively or otherwise, reflects our benchmarks of physical desirability and acceptability. How we view our appearance affects our thinking and has an impact on the nature of our aspirations.

We will learn to read our own faces and look closely at our dominant facial expressions. Smiling and gloomy faces project inner perceptions, while signs and marks on the body, face, hands, and feet—lines, birthmarks, moles, and indentations— help us find out more about a person's character and destiny. These marks on the physical body reveal temperament, sensitivity, and emotional makeup, which are all part of the complex human personality.

How Do You Breathe?

Our breath is magical. It gives us life, and determines the state of our bodies and our minds. Blown onto freezing fingers, our breath warms us. Blown onto hot soups, our breath cools what we take into our bodies. Breath nourishes our internal chi. It is even more vital for our well-being than food. The way we breathe determines how healthy and balanced we are.

Breath is the link between mind and body. Every breath we inhale feeds our body and nourishes our mind. With every exhalation, we expel unwanted molecules and negative energy. As you begin to understand your body in this section, think about how your breath affects your state of mind as well as your physical well-being.

Once we know how we breathe, and once we know how to progressively improve the way we breathe, we can harness an incredible and powerful life force and ensure a healthy chi flow within the body. This, in turn, will affect the way we feel, giving us full authority over the state of our minds, our hearts, and even our bodies.

Correct breathing gives us greater control over our hearts and minds. It enables us to increase our sense of well-being, and will also enhance our chances of realizing our fullest potential.

Most of us do not know how to breathe correctly. This is especially true for those of us who get insufficient exercise.

This chi kung pose shows the in-breath, with raised arms. It illustrates how to breathe correctly, expanding the lungs to their full capacity.

As a result, the amount of new air (and chi) that is taken into the body is usually grossly inadequate.

> ## Correct breathing is the secret remedy to a great many ills.

Worse, because the out-breath matches the in-breath, what is expelled is equally inadequate. As a result, insufficient fresh air is breathed in, and insufficient bad air is expelled.

Bad Breathing

Check how many of these symptoms of bad breathing describe your state of body and mind. Be honest with yourself. If even one or two of these situations describes you, there is good reason to consider learning how to breathe correctly.

1   Irregular breathing patterns—usually short, shallow, and relatively fast
2   Stooped shoulders and a constricted throat and chest
3   Suffering regularly from dizzy spells and being prone to headaches
4   High blood pressure and easily short of breath
5   Extra sensitive to heat and cold
6   Tiring out easily—lacking in energy and vitality

7   Usually easily upset and quick tempered

8   Easily stressed out and pressured

9   Usually tense, finding it hard to relax

10   Completely lacking in stamina

Good Breathing

Good breathing is all about posture. When you open your shoulders, your chest cavity opens. This in turn expands your lung capacity, thereby increasing the amount of air you take in. Air fills up your entire lungs—all three cavities as shown—when you breathe in deeply and slowly, and it flushes out greater quantities of stale air as you slowly breathe out. There is no need to stick out your chest or pull in your tummy. Just breathe slowly and deeply in and out without contorting any of your physical muscles. As long as you hold a good posture without stooping your shoulders, you will soon get the feel of the technique.

You can either breathe in and out through your nostrils, or you can breathe in through the nostrils and out through the mouth. Just visualize your breath filling all the three parts of your lungs as shown in the picture below, left.

It is unnecessary to breathe too deeply when you start. The lung capacity must open slowly. Likewise, it is advisable not to attempt to hold your breath—just create a regular and steady pattern of deep, slow breaths and focus on making this kind of good posture breathing a habit.

Feel your whole body suffused with wonderful fresh air, and experience all the stagnant energy flowing out of you.

If you wish, you can go deeper and engage your tummy in your new breathing exercises. Visualize the chi entering your tummy, filling it, and then visualize your tummy contracting as you breathe out. Do this lying down or standing up. If you like, you can place your palms on your tummy to feel it expanding and contracting.

Visualize the chi going all the way down to the ends of your limbs—your toes and your hands. This is a powerfully energizing technique that will fill you with renewed energy and stamina.

> You will discover that with good breathing, your sense of well-being is considerably improved.

Systematically create a feeling that fresh new chi is washing through your body and mind. It will not take you long to get the hang of it. Your capacity to achieve, and your motivation to get out there and do the things you want to do, will also be considerably enhanced.

When you breathe in, visualize your breath expanding all three parts of your lungs.

When you breathe out, ensure that you exhale fully to push the stale air out of your lungs.

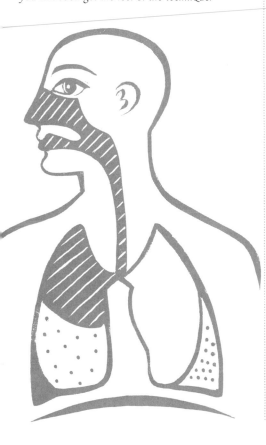

Left: This diagram shows the parts of the body that are involved in breathing, including the sections of the lungs.

Body Prototypes

It is not clever to try to emulate every role model that takes our fancy at any moment in time—it is better to adapt and create our own version of what's cool. We live in a diverse world filled with different body prototypes, and comparison is a futile exercise. It is best to try to accept your body and work at making it the best it can be. Learn to be comfortable in your own skin.

A young woman with mixed African and Caucasian parentage.

A woman with typical Caucasian features: fair hair and skin, with blue eyes.

Right: You may be Caucasian but not fit the stereotype. Perhaps you have dark hair or darker skin than many other white people.

If you are not as slim, as long limbed, or as curvaceous as you would like to be, becoming stressed about it will not make it happen. Instead, try to find creative beauty in the way you are.

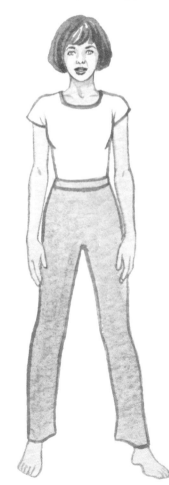

We all belong to social groups defined by race, culture, geography, and religion. Some of us belong to dominant groups, while others are part of minorities. For example, body shapes and looks can be categorized to reflect three different groupings—white Caucasian, black African, and colored Asian.

Caucasians have features that are sharp and well defined. Their limbs tend to be medium to long, and their body frame is light. Hair color is mainly blonde but can be brown or red, and the hair tends to be naturally wavy.

If you are Caucasian, do you fit this stereotype? Or are you a Caucasian with dark straight hair or darker skin? Do you have mixed parentage? Ask yourself how well you fit into the body prototype of your racial heritage. How do you feel about the body prototype you have inherited?

EXAMINE YOURSELF

Examine your body to see how closely you typify the norm of your own cultural and racial benchmark based on the three defining attributes that describe a human body—shape, color, and weight. Look at the body prototype shapes overleaf. See where yours fits in on this prototype benchmark. Most of us fall somewhere in between two prototypes.

Black Africans usually have a bigger, heavier build and a swarthier look. Hair is black to brown and tends to be tight and curly. If you are black, how true to type are you? Have you ever wished you had different features? Do you like being dark skinned—are you proud of your heritage?

Asians are lighter in build and have shorter limbs. Facial features tend to be Mongolian, with fine, almond-shaped eyes with single eyelids. Noses tend to be finer and flatter. Hair is usually black, generally thicker, and almost always straight. If you are Asian, which type of Asian are you? Are you Indian, Chinese, or Arab Muslim? Asia is a vast continent with many different types of "looks."

Do you find it easy to define yourself according to your racial prototype? Are you comfortable with doing this? Are you light skinned for an Indian, or are you very dark skinned for a Chinese person?

Obviously there are many other groupings within which further generalizations can be made, but by drawing your attention to three major "types" when you try to read your body later, you will be able to bear basic racial stereotypes in mind and make allowances for your own group.

There is a profusion of styles, shapes, and looks when it comes to defining body types, and attempting to classify the human body can only be partially successful. It is more important for us to examine how we fit in as individuals within the diversity of the human race.

Asians from China, Japan, and other Far Eastern countries tend to have Mongolian features, with fine, almond-shaped eyes.

Black Africans usually have black hair and more clearly defined facial features than Asians and Caucasians.

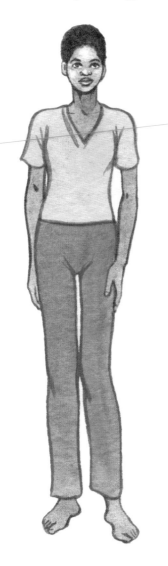

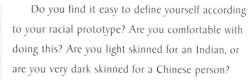

Far left: Black Africans display huge variations in their appearance, with skin color varying from near black to pale brown.

Left: Asians also vary widely in skin color and facial features, but they generally tend to be lighter in build than Africans and Caucasians.

Three Body Prototypes

Large | round

These people tend to have soft bodies and smooth skins. Usually associated with the matriarchal archetype, they tend to have arms and legs that are shorter than the body torso. Fat is stored around the abdomen and the hips. This body type can have a problem with weight, and may enjoy cooking for their family and entertaining friends with dinner parties. As men they tend to be jolly. Heavy, round people are usually warm, generous, and down-to-earth, and often even-tempered, good-humored, and ever ready to shower those around them with affection. They are usually popular.

If you belong to this body type, chances are you are resigned to being curvy, and being of a practical nature, you have probably accepted your body shape and focused on other aspects of your persona for improvement and development. You will probably benefit from more physical activity.

Far right: The hard and muscular person generally has an upright posture and is of medium build.

A person who fits the large and rounded body prototype tends to be heavy with short limbs.

Hard | muscular

Such people exude an aura of confidence and power. These are the warrior types who tend to live their lives in a very physical way. They are usually of medium build or tall, with firm body parts and good posture. They are active, love sports, and move with a certain grace. Strong, muscular people tend to be somewhat self-assertive and impatient. They have a zeal for life and are natural leaders. They tend to be visionaries, and are ambitious and inclined to be rather grandiose. They could lack sensitivity to other people's feelings, but physically they are beautiful people. Women of this type can be frighteningly ambitious and efficient. The men are domineering and ruthless.

If you belong to this body type, chances are you are ambitious and are aware of your own physical beauty. You might benefit from being a little more perceptive of those around you and developing more sensitivity.

Lean | thin

These people usually have a boyish look with a flat chest and a reed-like appearance: thin, long, and lightly muscled. If tall, such people tend to stoop, and when short they tend to look fragile. There is a certain vulnerability attached to this body prototype. Limbs tend to be thin, the face has little flesh, and the skin usually looks stretched. People who are thin and lean generally tend to be private, quiet, and socially inhibited. When you engage them in conversation, they are intense and dogmatic. They are self-conscious individuals who prefer being left alone to being in the public eye.

If you belong to this body type, you are probably not very interested in your body, or in making an impression. Emotionally you could be slow to nurture relationships, but once you find your soulmate, you are a one-lover person. You could benefit from being more sociable.

The lean and thin person usually has a rectangular appearance, a boyish body-shape, and long limbs.

When you next find yourself with a group of people, see if you can identify the three body prototypes among them.

The Body According to the Five Elements

The Chinese distinguish between five types of physical build, and these are categorized according to five elements, five planets, five shapes, and five coloring types for the complexion. According to what element and planet defines your build and coloring, the Chinese have also developed correlations of behavioral tendencies, success potential, and energy levels.

ELEMENT	SHAPE	COLOR	PLANET
FIRE	Triangular	Red/purple	Mars
WOOD	Rectangular	Green/brown	Jupiter
METAL	Round	White/metallic	Venus
WATER	Wavy	Black/blue	Mercury
EARTH	Square	Yellow	Saturn

To start with, think of body types in terms of five-element and five-planet types. From the above chart, a human figure can be conceptualized using shape definitions. This enables us to broadly categorize according to element and planet. Note the planet that is associated with each element type as shown in the chart, and from there think through the definitions that arise.

Thus, Mars (fire) is a planet of aggressive energy, so fire body types have a great deal of stored-up energy. Jupiter is the epitome of growth energy, while Venus is balanced energy. Mercury energy is fluid and elusive, and Saturnine energy is solid and grounded. These associations are to be

read according to how much the body frame and shape is "true to type."

The five elements have other distinguishing characteristics, and these offer further levels of categorization. Different kinds of frame, build, shape, coloring, and so forth can be discerned from an examination of our bodies. These are found in different combinations in every human being.

Examine yourself and see which element best defines your body frame, coloring, and temperament. Most people manifest a range and assortment of elements that govern their life.

The key to analyzing elements is to know which element is governing what part of a person's life. From the summary of characteristics given in the table at the top of the opposite page, it is possible to think through the elements and planets that have a primary or secondary influence in your life, and from there to use the cyclical theories of the elements to enhance some of the characteristics that are beneficial to you.

The table summarizes the various different manifestations of element type based on body frame and coloring. For instance, if you are slim and muscular, you are a fire energy person ruled by the planet Mars; if your coloring is ivory or white, then your body frame will be simply too strong for

This man has a rectangular face with brown eyes—he is ruled by Jupiter and is a wood element.

BODY FRAME:	Slim | muscular	Tall | angular	Balanced frame	Large | round	Solid | sturdy
Your ELEMENT is	FIRE	WOOD	METAL	WATER	EARTH
Your PLANET is	MARS	JUPITER	VENUS	MERCURY	SATURN
COMPLEXION:	Red | maroon	Olive	Ivory | white	Dark | tanned	Ocher | earth
Your ELEMENT is	FIRE	WOOD	METAL	WATER	EARTH
TEMPERAMENT	Energetic	Calm	Vivacious	Flexible	Grounded
ASPIRATION	Fame	Wisdom	Status	Wealth	Confidence
PASSION	Adventure	Sciences	Career	Money	Environment
CHARACTER	Active	Steady	Enthusiastic	Easygoing	Reliable

your complexion. This is because fire burns metal, so it would be better to use earth-based tones in your clothes or makeup to take fullest advantage of the fire energy suggested by your body frame. Accumulating earth energy will help you to build confidence in yourself and stay grounded in the way you conduct your life. Building more solidity into your frame will benefit you, also.

Generally each person will have a predominant element, which will be suggested in the "whole look." Usually this is defined by the body frame, although there will be instances when another attribute, for example color and complexion, could suggest an overwhelming dominance of another element. Once you are able to identify the different elements that dominate your "look," you will be able to work toward subduing them, or expanding the element you would like to dominate your physical appearance. Finally, remember that it is the combination of all the different elements that ultimately defines any particular person.

The four defining attributes that manifest according to the elements are your temperament, your aspirations, your passions, and your character. Examine each of these within you and see which of the attributes best describes you, then add them to your basket of elements. From this you will start to build a composite of what and who you are. The following sections discuss the dominant body and personality types based on the five elements.

The olive complexion of this woman indicates that she has a calm and steady approach to life.

The theory of the cycles of elements:					
ELEMENT:	Fire	Wood	Metal	Water	Earth
Enhances	EARTH	FIRE	WATER	WOOD	METAL
Is enhanced by	WOOD	WATER	EARTH	METAL	FIRE
Exhausts	WOOD	WATER	EARTH	METAL	FIRE
Destroys	METAL	EARTH	WOOD	FIRE	WATER

The Wood Element Body Type

Two kinds of wood element body frame are distinguishable among the diverse people who make up the human race. The first type is tall and muscular resembling a tree with branches. These types tend to be serious, calm, and rather intellectual and scholarly. The second wood type tends to be finer boned and shorter. This type tends to be more superficial, naive, and romantic.

Wood Body's Personality Type

Wood body types tend to belong to people whose voices are low but clear and who speak with pronounced inflections. Their speech is usually slow but fluent. They do not make charismatic speakers and have a tendency to be monotonous and boring. An injection of fire energy will lend them much energy and make them more energetic speakers. Their movements are calm and studied.

Wood people will always have a tendency to look younger than their age. They are lucky in that they tend to stay within healthy weight levels. Although they are not known for their strength, they do tend to enjoy the luck of longevity. Their mental capacity will not deteriorate with age either.

If anything, health disorders in old age tend to result more from excessive worry caused by anxiety, nervous tension, and insomnia rather than anything physical.

In terms of personality, wood type people tend to be calmer and less agitated than, say, fire types. However, their anxiety and worry, though well hidden or camouflaged, still exists and can cause health problems. They are neither energetic nor athletic types, and will often appear rather spaced-out, lost in their own thoughts. They love the company of intellectuals with whom they feel a special kinship. They do not like gossip, nor are they the kind who can make small talk successfully.

Wood body types tend to reveal a preference for the slow and relaxed lifestyle of the country to that of the fast frenetic pace of the city. They enjoy taking meditative and contemplative walks. They have aspirations to attain great heights of achievement but seldom give voice to their secret dreams. Wood body types have a tendency to a certain reserve and aloofness.

In the realms of romance and family, wood body types will exhibit loyalty and fidelity and a certain romanticism, which manifests in poetic sentiments rather than the extravagant gesture. They avoid being in the limelight, preferring to be the kingmaker than the king.

Elemental Combinations for Wood People

Water

The presence of water attributes and symbols will seriously enhance the sense of well-being and increase the effectiveness of wood type people.

Water enhances wood, providing it with material things that make daily living more pleasant. Water also attracts economic success, helping wood type people to be more successful in their careers.

Water coming into a wood type means they will be darker in their coloring and they will put on weight and appear fatter. According to the theory of five elements, therefore, people with wood type bodies will benefit from putting on some weight and becoming more tanned or adopting a darker coloring for their complexions.

The strengthening of the water element in a wood type's body frame and coloring promises material achievements and an enhanced income.

Metal

The presence of metal on the other hand has a destructive impact on the luck of people with wood body shapes because metal inhibits the chi of wood and will bring failure and loss. A wood/metal combination suggests that complexions become smooth and pale—even white.

Fire

The presence of fire attributes on wood body types is not beneficial and tends to be exhausting for the person concerned. Wearing red could make wood people wilt unless they were born in winter, in which case the warmth of fire will help to bring the energy that causes wood types to blossom.

Earth

The presence of earth attributes is beneficial to wood type people since wood can be nurtured in earth. This also suggests a darker coloring and a more solid muscular build, which brings greater self-assurance and confidence. Wearing earth-colored clothes and keeping hair long, tied up in a bun, or hanging loose, will enhance the luck essence.

The typical wood body type is characterized by long limbs and a long, rectangular-looking body frame, with a long, slender neck and elongated head. The shoulders are broad.

The Fire Element Body Type

Fire-shaped people tend to be tall, thin, strong, muscular, and full of energy. They tend to project a vision of litheness and agility. Their skins are usually taut and smooth. They exhibit a healthy and lively spirit that seems to attract wealth and success. They tend to be dynamic individuals who are naturally courageous and rather fiery. Fire people are full of chi—sometimes too much!

Fire Body's Personality Type

Fire people look youthfully energetic most of the time, and are vivacious and active. They tend to speak fast, in low, hoarse voices, and have boundless energy. The element of fire has life only when it is active. When it is still, the fire is out, so fire people must keep themselves active to be happy. The extreme manifestation of this is a restless spirit and a thirst for adventure. Fire

people's bodies have a high metabolic rate and they are able to maintain their slender silhouette. Their personalities are directly related to their store of energy. Much of what they are and do is directly determined by how energetic they are. Hyper fire people will manifest a restlessness that requires their energy to be channeled productively, otherwise they will simply direct their energies into negative, non-beneficial pursuits.

Fire people are attracted to people, noise, and anything that symbolizes adventure and activity. Their horizons are limitless, and their dreams can be very lofty. Fire people tend to be superficial and lack the intellectual depth of wood people. They are sometimes impatient, intolerant, and critical, although they do not bear a grudge and are quick to forgive and forget. Fire people love parties and socializing, but theirs is a quicksilver approach to life and friendships.

Their enormous need for action, change, and movement makes them action-oriented people who participate—they do not sit by the sidelines. They are also free spirits who love taking risks, gambling, and moving on. Fire people are less reliable and trustworthy than most, unless theirs is a life tempered by the influence of wood characteristics, which make them slow down and take a slightly more intellectual and caring attitude to life.

Elemental Combinations for Fire People

Wood

The effect of the wood element in the lives of fire type people is always positive. An olive complexion will benefit them, as will a heavier bone structure and a slightly squarish-shaped face. By wearing green, fire types will have their energy calmed down. They will benefit enormously from wood-element attributes, which will make them slow down and take a slightly more thoughtful and caring attitude to life.

Water

Water can have a negative effect on fire people. For example, fire people with plump hands and feet are considered less likely to succeed. It is important for fire types not to become very overweight or to wear too much black or blue in their clothes. This will have the effect of dousing and sapping their energy.

Metal

When fire types take on metal attributes, such as developing a pale complexion or a thinner physical build, the effect will be a severe curtailment of the fire person's energy. The passion for attainment and the courage to take risks and move resolutely forward will be lost. The effect of metal is not necessarily negative, but it will temper the pure fire energy quite significantly.

Earth

When fire types combine with earth attributes, the effect can prove exhausting for fire. Thus, when fire-type people change their coloring to earth tones and begin wearing earth colors, they will start to walk slower and their ambitious nature will be curbed. Their energy levels drop to such an extent that it seems that their joy of living has become seriously curtailed.

Fire-type people look rather triangular, with small heads and long bodies that tend to be bigger at the hips. Women tend to have small breasts and large bottoms.

The Earth Element Body Type

Earth types have square, strong bodies and they tend to be short rather than tall. They look sturdy and strong, fit, and totally reliable. They have thick limbs and short muscular necks. Their hair appears thick, with a tendency to be curly, and their foreheads are square and smooth. Their eyes are large, they radiate energy, and they are full of hidden agendas and untapped secrets.

Earth Body's Personality Type

The earth is deep and holds many untapped secrets. This is the impression that emanates from earth types. The earth person's personality is quiet but suggestive of strength and authority. Both men and women have loud, imperious voices. Their speech will be authoritative but monotonous, deep but not melodious. Earth types are very studied in their attitudes and very labored in the way they work. They tend to be grounded in reality rather than being dreamers. They are very practical and down-to-earth. As a result, they tend to be hard-working people who believe in the merit of industry rather than the chance of the windfall. Earth people succeed mainly through perseverance, and they demonstrate patience and resilience in their attitude. They prefer to be sure before proceeding, as they are not risk-takers. Although they do not lack for courage, they prefer the known to the unknown. They will never ever act hastily. Earth people make excellent bankers. They work toward attaining economic and financial security, and they plod through their careers with the earthbound certainty that one day they will take the CEO's seat. Since they are very conservative by nature, they make reliable but unexciting friends, husbands, wives, and employees.

The Chinese differentiate between two kinds of earth people—the type that exhibits some fire energy in their domineering and aggressive behavior, and the type that are more pure earth types, being people of fewer words but who are deep and mysterious in their outward behavior. The first type tends to be dogmatic and inflexible in their thoughts and actions, while the second type tends to be mysterious and deep rooted. Both types will frustrate those who are impatient and are risk-takers. It is likely that earth types will have

Earth people have square faces with thick, solid skin. Their features are usually big and protruding; the nose may seem large for the face, and the jawline is solid and square.

become reasonably successful by the time they reach their early forties.

The most outstanding charac-teristic of earth types is that they are amazingly resilient and never give up. They will do almost anything to preserve the security of their family. They are not greedy for enormous wealth, and what they strive toward is complete security for themselves and for their loved ones. They dislike the risk-taking of gambling and are not prepared to take unnecessary risks with their hard-earned savings.

Earth types love the environment and nature. They are avid gardeners, and they are likely to enjoy keeping pets. They love any kind of activity that brings them close to the earth. Because they tend to be heavy looking, they usually look older than their chronological age, and they will have a tendency to seem to age quicker than other types.

Elemental Combinations for Earth Types

Fire

The effect of the fire element in the lives of earth type people is always positive and beneficial. This means that a reddish complexion or red hair coloring will always benefit them, as will a lighter bone structure and a slightly more pointed face. By wearing red, earth types will have their energy jazzed up. Their placid nature is imbued with a boost of energy, and their thinking will be raised to surface level, becoming less deep rooted. They should also incorporate red around their home. If they do, they will benefit enormously from the input of fire energy.

Metal

On the other hand, note that the influence of metal simply exhausts the earth types. It is not advisable for earth types to wear too much white or choose light-colored foundation for makeup.

Water

The effect of water on earth is to create a darker complexion and a tendency to gain weight. Water will also temper the earth person's passion for security and reduce their levels of confidence and self-assurance.

Wood

The effect of wood can be very negative on the earth element body type, since wood destroys the energy of earth. Thus, the earth type's self-confidence is likely to take a severe beating when they take on an olive complexion or when they become thinner or weaker.

The Metal Element Body Type

Metal body types are average height with a well-proportioned body. They have good bones, and their flesh and skin radiate health. Muscles are smooth, and the proportions between body parts exhibit an amazing symmetry. Although the metal element is described as round, this refers more to the non-angular appearance than to actual roundness of form.

Metal Body's Personality Type

Metal people are graceful and refined, with soft, intimate voices. The metal person's personality is most amiable and is suggestive of smiles and friendliness. Metal types are very calm in their demeanor and rhythmic and disciplined in the way they work. They are seldom in a hurry, and they are always well disciplined in their attitude. They have enormous self-control. As a result, they seldom gain weight beyond what they wish, and they always make sure that they appear well groomed.

Metal people succeed mainly through their sense of self-discipline. They are patient people and have diplomatic skills in handling people. They are very good at seeming to be flexible and easygoing, radiating a serenity that is most reassuring. They also hide a will of iron. They are knowledgeable and do not lack for courage. They tend to be elegant, classy, and chic in the way they dress, being neither casual nor formal but always looking good.

Metal people are intensely private people. They seldom get caught in illicit adventures and generally do not get swept away by their emotions or passions. They tend to marry within their own social status. In their careers, they tend to rise to become very senior managers although, surprisingly, metal types are not madly ambitious.

There are two types of metal people. The first type is the iron metal type who tends to be more commercial and business-minded. The second metal type is the more refined manifestation, and this type can be described as a real gem-quality type of metal person.

These second types tend to find themselves gravitating to the performing arts—they are often opera singers, ballet stars, and musicians. Those who make it become greatly adored and loved.

Elemental Combinations for Metal Types

Earth

When metal people display signs of earth attributes, such as in the color of their skin or hair or in the way their frame becomes more muscular, the effect is most beneficial since they become more industrious and certainly more in tune with the practical aspects of survival.

Water

When metal people are affected by the water element, it shows up as a tendency toward gaining weight and a more money-conscious attitude. Although water does exhaust metal, in general the effect is neither good nor bad, as it depends on what the person feels is important in his or her life.

Fire

When metal is combined with fire, either by changing hair color to reddish tones or by wearing red or gaining weight in the hips, the effect is definitely non-beneficial. This is because fire burns and destroys metal, and the effect of this is to destabilize the lifestyle and attitude of the extremely disciplined metal person. This is thus not something that can be encouraged.

Wood

When metal combines with wood, this shows up in the height of the person and the coloring. The effect is to introduce a more introspective and serious mental state to the metal person. The impact of this state can sometimes be difficult for the person to come to terms with, thereby creating a mixed-up state of mind.

People with metal element body types have an overall tendency to be fastidious in their grooming—so they will always look smart. This is because their intrinsic self-discipline is reflected in the way they carry themselves.

The physical appearance of metal people displays extraordinary symmetry and balance. They have a beautifully rounded forehead and skull. The limbs are well proportioned and rounded, the arms shapely and smooth.

The Water Element Body Type

This is the smooth-talking, sharp-looking charmer who loves money and enjoys being at the center of social gatherings. The water type is mercurial, very friendly, and usually extremely popular. They fall in easily with other people's plans and are superb at networking. Water-type personalities are blessed with the ability to make friends easily and with panache.

Water Body's Personality Type

Water people move gracefully, appearing fluid and very loose. They tend to be agile despite their roundness, but they are seldom athletic. As they get on in years, water types have a tendency to put on weight. Many water types have a sweet tooth, and diets do not work easily for them.

Water people usually come across as rather serene since there is a perpetual smile on their faces. They tend also to be sentimental and are easily moved. It appears that, like the element they personify physically, they tend to cry easily, but they also radiate warmth and friendliness. There will always be people around the water person, so they can be classified as sociable types. Water people are attractive sexually and make friends with little difficulty. They lead busy social lives, and since they are also easygoing and flexible, they never come across as dogmatic or stubborn.

As lovers, they tend to be romantic, and they are extremely attentive. In fact, they make very pleasant companions indeed.

Water types are also rather skillful at making money. They gravitate naturally toward influential people. They are strongly motivated by the good things in life, so money is an important means to their ends. They are also socially conscious and do like keeping up appearances. They are usually successful at what they put their minds to, and they are also good at finding spouses that are higher up the social scale than they are.

There are two kinds of water people. The first is the industrious type who is excellent in parlaying their skills at networking and their natural charm into profitable deal-making. The second type is the financial genius who tends to have the ability to rise to prominence in the financial field.

Elemental Combinations for Water Types

Metal

Water type people benefit most when there is the presence of metal attributes. The presence of metal enhances the water type's success and ability at making money. Physically, the influence of metal manifests as pale skin; finer skin texture; and less round, better-proportioned limbs.

Earth

When a water type shows earth attributes, such as coarse hands and darker skin, the effect is not promising in terms of luck potential. The earth element inhibits the natural vitality of the water person.

Wood

Combined with wood attributes, such as olive skin coloring and heavier bones, the water body type will take on characteristics that will prove frustrating and exhausting. It is better for the water person not to develop wood tendencies.

Fire

The effect of fire attributes and characteristics on water types is also not promising since this is a classic clash of elements. Water types are discouraged from wearing too much red. Although water controls fire, fire tends to diminish the flexible and easygoing attitude of the water person.

Generally, people with water element type bodies exhibit a fluidity of movement that is both graceful and rather charming. They flow rather than walk, and they usually look very good in clothes that allow this trait to manifest. So flowing dresses look better on them than structured clothes. Formal attire and corporate stiffness in work outfits tends to make them uncomfortable; they need flexibility and softness in the way they dress.

Water-type people tend to have curvaceous bodies yet do not appear fat. The face looks fleshy and the mouth wide and full. Hands and legs are generally shorter than those of the other body types.

Dragon and Phoenix Archetypes

The dragon and phoenix are the celestial archetypes that manifest all that is paramount in the universal Chinese philosophy of yin and yang. Traditionally, yang (the dragon) is viewed as the powerful, dominating force, while yin (the phoenix) is passively receptive. The two are direct opposites, but they do not compete. They are cleverly balanced within human beings.

Right: Yang energy is personified by the dragon, which is the archetype of aggressive, masculine energy.

Far right: The phoenix personifies yin energy, symbolizing the passive, yielding, introverted, feminine archetype.

How much within us reflects the dragon, and how much reflects the phoenix? Irrespective of our gender, we contain variations of both archetypes within us. They manifest on every plane of our consciousness—in the way we project ourselves; the way we dress; in our preferences for colors; in our affinity for light, shade, noise, and silence; in our like and dislike of nocturnal or daytime activities; and in the attitudes we bring to the way we work, play, and interact with people.

The Dragon

The dragon archetype symbolizes the ultimate yang energy. It is masculine, domineering, extroverted, and aggressive. The dragon symbolizes sunshine and the essence of light and sound. He is cheerful and optimistic. He moves inexorably forward, taking the lead and always demonstrating courage.

Dragon archetypes tend to be workaholics and compulsive talkers. They are action-oriented people who keep moving and changing. They are dogmatic, resilient, and pioneering. Dragon types are described as handsome, with well-shaped and well-proportioned bodies. They have medium-sized heads with shapely foreheads, shining eyes, and straight noses. Their voice resonates deeply. The powerful effect dragon types have on other people sets them apart. The dragon is the leader.

DRAGON ARCHETYPE	check here	PHOENIX ARCHETYPE	check here
Prefers the sunshine		Prefers nighttime activities	
Prefers summer		Prefers winter	
Prefers white or bright colors		Prefers black or dark colors	
Likes to take the lead		Prefers to follow	
Prefers to plunge right in		Likes to think things through	
Likes being action-oriented		Considers planning to be vital	
Likes being center of attention		Prefers to be unobtrusive	
Generally a positive person		Generally a negative person	
Likes warmth and heat		Prefers the cold	
Generally cheerful		Usually morose and gloomy	
Usually optimistic		Generally pessimistic	
Hard and tough		Soft and yielding	
Likes flamboyant clothes		Likes tailored outfits	
Usually domineering		Usually submissive	
Identifies with the sun		Identifies with the moon	
Loves the mountains		Prefers the sea	
Likes to fly		Likes being grounded	
Loves pop music		Loves classical music	
Very materialistic		Tends to be spiritual	
Never satisfied		Easily satisfied	
Tends to be tall		Tends to be short	
Big-sized and heavy		Small-sized and dainty	

The Phoenix

The phoenix, on the other hand, personifies the ultimate yin energy. She symbolizes the feminine archetype—yielding, receptive, passive, quiet, silent, introspective, introverted, and submissive. In this analogy, the phoenix is the matriarchal woman, life-nurturing and calm, soft and serious, more of a follower than a leader, resilient and dark; strong, but in a less obvious manner than the dragon. In essence she also represents the negative; the dark side; and the cold, unmoving force.

Phoenix archetypes also signify the mysterious brooding aspects of personality. She is never impulsive, always careful, seldom stubborn, and always prepared to give in. The phoenix type is regal and extremely elegant. She radiates a smoothness and purity that sets her apart as well. This is especially evident in those extremely rare women who manifest the pure phoenix archetype.

The assessment listed above should help you gain greater insights into where you are in the yin and yang spectrum, and whether you identify more with the fearless and dominating dragon archetype or the yielding and submissive phoenix archetype.

Dragon and phoenix types seldom manifest as perfectly pure types. The list of dragon and phoenix attributes above reflects extreme ends of the spectrum. No one is completely yin or completely yang. There will always be a little dragon and a little phoenix in all of us. Dragon-phoenix balance is needed to create a whole individual.

Fair Skinned and Dark Skinned, and All the Colors in Between

Skin and hair color are among the most visually obvious ways of differentiating people. There are white people and black people. There are red skins and olive skins. There is black hair and blonde hair. If we look closely enough at all the peoples of the world, we start to discern that the human race is made up of a huge variety of skin and hair colors. This is what makes for a colorful world!

The huge variety of skin and hair colors exhibited by the human race makes for a colorful world.

great lengths to keep my face out of the sun simply because I had equated my tanned skin to being ugly. Today I have successfully shrugged off that psychological affliction and no longer have a phobia about getting tanned. That was because sometime in my early twenties I met the most delightful guy at college who found my 'tanned skin' irresistible! **"**

Confronting the prototypes of skin color is a vital part of the discovery of self. It forces us to tune in to how comfortable we are inside our skins. Are we happy with our skin color, or does some incident in the past buried deep in our psyche still color our view of the world?

" *I remember when I was 12 my grandmother told me how ugly I was because I was so dark. My Chinese olive skin tans really badly, and in my young days, being something of a tomboy, my skin was always suntanned. For years thereafter, I did everything I could to make myself fair, and I went to*

Test yourself   How comfortable are you in your skin? Answer YES or NO to the questions below: Would you say that your skin color:

1 Has no impact on your social life?
2 Is a social stigma?
3 Makes you more acceptable to your peers?
4 Is a social disadvantage?
5 Causes you to stand out in your group?
6 Is a bone of contention between you and your sweetheart?
7 Makes you feel like you belong?
8 Emphasizes how different you are?
9 Makes you feel happy and thankful?
10 Gives you an inferiority complex?
11 Makes you feel attractive?
12 Is the cause of all your problems?
13 Gives you a feeling of superiority?
14 Puts you at a disadvantage?

If you answered YES to five or more of the even-numbered questions, you obviously don't feel comfortable in your skin. If you answered YES to five or more of the odd-numbered questions, you are probably quite comfortable in your skin.

Hair Color Reflects Personality

Our natural hair color is usually a consequence of our physical coloring and body type. It is easy to change our hair color, and generally we tend to select a color that we feel reflects our personality.

For example, blondes and light-haired people are often thought to be cheerful, lively, and extroverted. Red-haired people are normally associated with fiery and strong-willed personalities. Dark-haired individuals are generally regarded as serious, conservative, and mysterious. Our preferences for different shades and colors can alter as we mature and our personalities change. Hair color, however, reflects the superficial side of our personality—so there is no need to look for insights or hidden meanings here.

YOUR COLOR PREFERENCES

The colors you like generally reveal your intrinsic nature. Pick out the most dominant color in your wardrobe and match it against the characteristics here. See how much of a match they are to your own view of yourself.

Dominantly Red:

Indicates vibrant yang fire energy. You are ambitious, love attention, and will tend to be impulsive. Your direction is the south. You attract people easily into your space by the sheer force of your personality.

Dominantly Yellow:

Indicates an earthbound personality. You are very practical, tend to be motherly, and can be as solid as a mountain. Bright sunshine yellow reflects the sunny side of your nature, while deeper yellows reflect a more earthy personality.

Dominantly Green:

Indicates a steady, cautious personality. You have an optimistic view of the world and of people. You like a quiet life where you are free to do your own thing and grow at your own pace.

Dominantly Blue:

Indicates an extremely creative and sensitive personality. You have imagination, intelligence, and artistic flair. There is a quiet resilience in you, and you attain all that you want without anyone realizing it. There is a certain relentless zeal about you.

Dominantly White:

Indicates a self-assured, confident personality who takes charge easily. You can cope with pressure and are the consummate professional.

Dominantly Black:

You are strong-willed and very resilient. You are highly disciplined, but what you lack is confidence, although you do a great job of hiding your fears.

Dominantly Purple:

You are very much an intuitive person, with deep emotions and feelings. There is a tendency toward arrogance, but also toward things metaphysical. You are equally comfortable in company or by yourself.

The Yin and Yang
of Facial Expressions

If you want to charm, impress, or merely get on the right side of someone, make sure that you are conscious of your facial expressions when you are with them. The way we carry our face expresses our inner mind and heart, and if we wish to understand the essence of our inner nature, it is worth making an effort to study and analyze our dominant facial expression.

According to the classical texts, our dominant facial expressions indicate the strength of yin or yang chi within us. We are seldom fully aware of how we carry our expressions—whether we show a yin or a yang face to the world. Since displaying yang chi to the world attracts so much good fortune, this is something worth examining.

When the chi is positive, it is said to be yang. Yang energy moves from great yang to bright yang

Each time you scowl or frown, think about what kind of yin energy you are showing to the world.

to lesser yang. These three levels reveal the intensity and extent of positive essence in the hidden nature of an individual. Yang expressions manifest as smiling faces, but there are different types of yang smiles. The truly joyous expression reflects bright yang, which is well balanced. Lesser yang shows a reduced level of joy where some yin seems to be creeping in. Great yang indicates an excess of joy indicating a touch of smugness.

Yin faces reflect negative, depressed, gloomy, bored, or unhappy emotions, so they manifest as sad and unsmiling expressions. Sometimes they can also manifest as a scowl with furrowed brows, and sometimes they may appear as angry. A great yin expression is said to reflect the state of grief, while lesser yin indicates mild feelings of sadness or anger. Reducing yin symbolizes the input of some yang. Angry faces are described as yin turning yang.

A yin face reflects unhappy emotions, varying from mild feelings of sadness to expressions of huge grief.

Your Temperament

If you wish to know how yin or yang your attitude is, look at your dominant expression. Yet in order to define your dominant or base temperament, you will need to look at the shape of your face.

There are five basic face shapes that offer clues to aspects of your personality and indicate careers in which are you most likely to find success. They are based on the element that rules your face.

WOOD ELEMENT FACES are long, oval, or oblong shaped. Such people are usually optimistic and have a natural elegance. They thrive in environments where they can express themselves. They work well by themselves but are also good team players. When matched with yang expressions, wood element faces indicate people whose optimism turns into enthusiasm, thereby propelling them into careers that allow them to take center stage. They do well in the communicative industries. When wood element faces carry yin expressions, they tend to be more serious and conservative, and their success will come from being the brains behind public figures.

FIRE ELEMENT FACES are triangular or heart shaped. People with fire element faces tend to have powerful but hidden ambitions. Those with bright yang expressions always look good, and they have the ability to charm and persuade others to their way of thinking. Fire element faces with yin expressions also do well, especially those with the lesser yin faces, who usually come across as equally mysterious and irresistible.

EARTH ELEMENT FACES have square face shapes that look full and stable and they emit an aura of stability and strength. Earth types have steady temperaments. Being private and usually successful within their sphere of work, they tend to

project a detached disinterest in the rest of the world. Yet earth types pick up more than they will let on. They seldom lose their cool and always show the best side of themselves.

METAL ELEMENT FACES have round face shapes. If they are dominated by yin expressions, they project a perpetually depressed look. Smiles transform metal element faces into very attractive people whose expressions attract good luck. Temperamentally, metal-faced people tend to be inflexible and others have to accommodate them. They do not socialize easily and are single-minded about their work, especially about wealth creation.

WATER ELEMENT FACES are curvy faces with high cheekbones and rounded, slightly protruding foreheads. Such faces indicate an extrovert who is slow to anger but quick with the repartee. They are usually witty and find success in the entertainment and communication industries. Smiles do not work as well for water faces as for the other elements.

Nothing warms the heart more than receiving a genuine smile. When you smile, consider the kind of yang energy your smile is emitting.

The Yin and Yang Secrets of Body Shape

Ancient Chinese knowledge always describes the life force of the human person in terms of the yin and yang—the cosmic forces of female and male. The body thus contains both male and female parts, and it is when these parts are in balance that we are said to have a good body, with the cosmic energies so well balanced that we feel good and look good.

The Chinese believe that good health and a pleasant and attractive body shape can both be attainable if only we make the effort to know which parts within us are yang and which parts are yin, which parts of us are male and which are female. Thus, the bones in the body, which are hard, symbolize the masculine yang, while skin and flesh—the soft parts—signify the feminine yin. A good body has a good balance of bones and flesh. When this is out of proportion, as when there is too much flesh or too little flesh, the body loses harmony. An underweight or overweight body is said to have too much yang or too much yin.

Generally speaking, metal types tend to be the most balanced of all the element types. Wood and fire types tend to have an overabundance of masculine energies, while water and earth types usually have more feminine energy within them.

This means that it is the water and earth types that have the greatest tendency to put on weight. Water types tend to have too much liquid in them, while earth types tend to have too much muscle.

Body shape or weight maintenance reflects the male and female energies within the human body. There are people whose weight gain or loss is well distributed throughout the body, while others tend to gain weight in particular parts of their bodies.

In terms of the latter, there are two types of weight gain that are worth examining:

- Those who gain weight in the upper parts of the body while the lower parts stay constant—this describes the person in whom the male yang energy dominates. To balance this weight gain, it is beneficial to get more sleep and rest, thereby strengthening the yin energy.
- Those who gain weight in the lower parts of their torso, i.e., in the hips and thighs—is the predominantly feminine, yin type person. To balance out the excessive weight gain in the hips and thighs, it is advisable to engage in yang-type pastimes, which means exercise and activity.

The masculine yang energy generally refers to the skeleton of the body, which operates during the daytime hours when the sun is at its zenith. It is said that it is the yang part of the body that works to create the success of the individual. The feminine yin energy refers to the softer, more receptive, and darker sides of the person. These energies will dominate during the nighttime hours when darkness rules. Thus, yin-dominated personalities will tend toward the restful and the calming. Together, the yin and yang aspects of the life force keep the body in good shape.

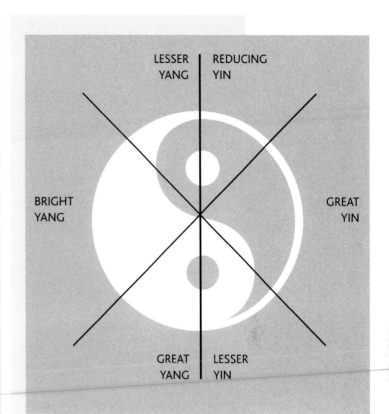

LESSER YANG

REDUCING YIN

BRIGHT YANG

GREAT YIN

GREAT YANG

LESSER YIN

According to the Chinese, everything in the Universe can be explained in terms of the evolution of the tai chi symbol, which reflects the interaction of yin and yang energy. This is as true for the environment as it is for the human individual. From the tai chi chart here, you will see that yin and yang is expressed in terms of what is known as the six energies. This fine-tunes both positive and negative energy into three levels of intensity.

This dynamic ebb and flow of the yin and yang energies influences the interactions of the five elements of existence—wood, fire, water, metal, and earth—which in turn give birth to the "ten thousand things"; i.e., the Universe. These profound concepts are the basis of Taoist philosophy, which is the basis of the sciences of China.

The Three Regions of the Body

The proportions of the body offer useful clues to personality and temperament. Three types of body proportions form the basis for body reading. The key is whether your head, torso, or lower body dominates. You can examine your body proportions with body-reading techniques and see what type of person you are and where your propensity for success lies.

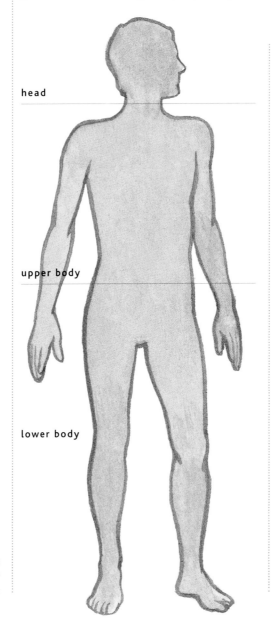

head

upper body

lower body

An illustration showing the division of the body into three regions.

THE HEAD is the upper portion of the body, and the Chinese believe that it is the head that reveals the most about a person's personality and their potential for success. To be well proportioned, the head should ideally make up one-seventh of the height of the person.

THE TORSO is the middle part of the body, and this includes the neck, the shoulders, the arms, and the upper body down to the waist. This part of the body offers an indication of the strength and health of the body as a whole. To be well proportioned, this part of the body should be two-sevenths of the height of the whole body.

THE HIPS AND LEGS make up the lower part of the body, and the Chinese believe that this part reveals the physical and intellectual courage of the person. This part of the body should ideally make up four-sevenths of the height of the body.

When the body is well proportioned, there is said to be a good balance between the three regions. Such a person is described as being healthy in mind, body, and spirit and will generally do well in life. To determine the variations in intellectual or physical dominance or skills, it is possible to categorize three types of body proportions.

Type A

The first type (type A) is where the HEAD dominates, so in terms of proportion, the head will be bigger than the perfect one-seventh. People with "big heads" are described rather generously by the Chinese, who view such people as being intellectuals who are imbued with the potential for great wisdom. They are seldom materialistic in the sense of aspiring to become wealthy. Instead, their aspirations lie more in the literary or scholastic fields. Many, however, attain leadership levels in different fields because their propensity to succeed is high indeed. The best professions for them are the teaching, research, or academic professions.

Type B

The second type of person (type B) is where the TORSO dominates. These types are generally very conscious of their body shape. They love eating, and they are also very physical people. They tend to be the most materialistic of the three types of body shapes, but they are also the most practical and action-oriented. Being physical people, they get into action relatively quickly, and they usually find success in areas that require initiative and fieldwork. So they are good in sales and in the communicative trades, as well as in sports management. Many also find huge success in business and in commerce. The type B person is extremely practical and reliable.

Type C

The third type (type C) is where the LOWER BODY dominates. These types usually have a longer lower body and a smaller head. They are the most adventurous and courageous of the three types. They take risks, they look for challenges, and they usually love traveling. They tend to look tall and rather stiff in their demeanor, so they usually gravitate toward the military or law enforcement professions. They can also be found in the financial industry as dealers and brokers. They have the aptitude for taking big risks and the ability to stay relatively cool in a crisis.

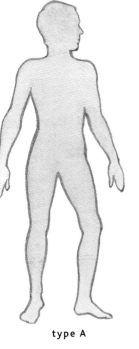

type A   **type B**   **type C**

In type A, the head dominates; in type B, the torso. In type C, the lower body is dominant.

The Palaces of the Face

When your forehead, your cheekbones, your nose, and your chin protrude, you are considered to exhibit features that indicate a good life. These are the "mountains" of your face, the yang indications of prosperity and a good life. Mountains should stand out and look prominent. Your eyes, nose, ears, and mouth are the organs that bring balance and stability; they should be clear.

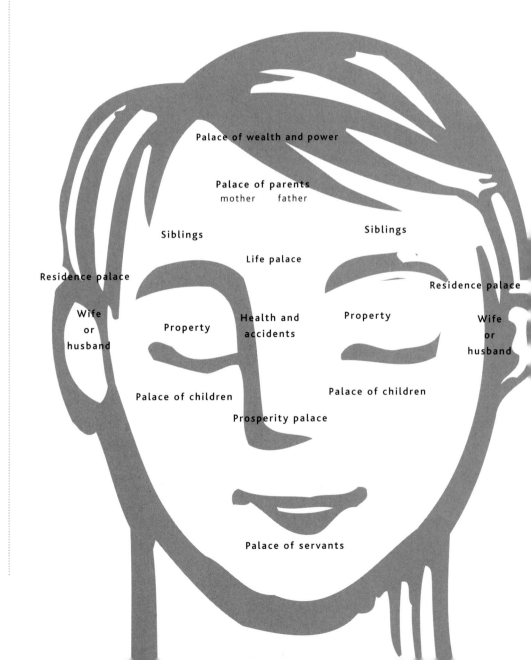

Detailed readings of the face are best analyzed in accordance with the different palaces of the face. These govern different kinds of luck and are shown on this sketch of the face.

The Palace of the Parents

The palace of the parents indicates the kind of parent luck you have. When this part of the face is smooth and high, it means you have parents who care for you. When this part of the forehead is sunken, it is said to be one indication that either of your parents could have a premature death.

Your Children Luck

The number of children you have, their gender, and how filial they will be are indicated by the appearance of the face just under the eyes. Generally, if you have a slight "fold" here it means good descendants luck. If this part of the face looks pinched, it is unlucky. Dark circles under the eyes are not a good sign. Ensure you get enough sleep and if they persist, use a camouflage stick to improve their appearance. This will greatly improve your children luck. Black spots in this part of the face are a bad sign and could mean early death.

Sibling Luck

How well you get along with your siblings is indicated in the area above the eyebrows. When this part of your face has an indentation of any kind, it means your siblings will depend on you and sometimes even cause you grief. If the flesh is firm and smooth, however, your brothers and sisters will be of enormous help to you. Protruding eyebrows are an advantage; they indicate fame and glory. When eyebrows are arched, smooth, and shiny, they are indicators of great good fortune.

Property and Residence Palaces

When the property and residence palaces appear full and well endowed, you will live in a large cottage or mansion. However, when this part of the face is thin-skinned and pale in color, you have little or no asset luck. You may very well live in a small home that you rent rather than own.

The Life Palace

The most important palaces are those located along the center line of the face, and especially the life palace. This area between the eyes should look clear, bright, and firm of flesh. It should have an open space between the eyebrows, as this is another indication of a good and balanced life. This part of the face should never have spots or a mole, and it should not have hair. This part of the face is also the entry into the spiritual third eye, and the clearer this part of the face, the better is the indication in terms of luck. Moles, discoloring, or indents here suggest major obstacles and mishaps. Looking further down, along the bridge of the nose, if there are any markings here, they indicate accidents during middle age.

The Ears

The location of the ears is also significant in face analysis. Ears that are high and reach the eyebrows indicate success at an early age. Lower down, success comes later in life. When the ears are placed really low—when the top of the ear is level with the eyes—only modest success can be expected. Perfect ears usually have long lobes, and these indicate a long life. When the hollow in the ear is large, it indicates wisdom and intellectual prowess. Ears are said to be auspicious when the coloring is lighter than that of the face.

The Mouth

The mouth is an indicator of personality. When it is well shaped and well defined in a woman, it indicates good fortune. When there is a "pearl" on the mouth—when the center of the upper lip protrudes like a pearl—it is the surest sign that she will marry into wealth or that her husband will treat her like a princess. Thin lips indicate a more reserved or introverted personality. A fuller bottom lip than top indicates ambition.

The Face According to
the Five Elements

The Chinese distinguish types of faces according to the five elements and combinations of the five elements. The element of the face is defined according to its shape, and this gives vital clues to the person's temperament. The elements also define the essence of a person's chi vitality and offer clues to the kind of expertise that can best be developed to bring success.

The table opposite gives the specific face shapes that define the element. However, since most people possess combination faces, it is impossible to find perfectly triangular, round, or square faces. The best way to determine what element your face belongs to is to see which part of your face has the greatest width and to note the curves and width of the rest of your face.

Based on the five elements, there are three types of combination faces that can be defined specifically for purposes of face reading. The three combinations are as follows.

This is a classic heart-shaped face, with full cheekbones and a small, pointed chin.

The Heart-Shaped Face

The heart-shaped face is a combination of the wood and water elements. It is widest at the forehead, with very full cheek bones, a rounded or curved jaw, and a small, pointed chin. This type of face belongs to the eternal charmer who has a natural attractiveness. The heart-shaped face is said to be auspicious because the elements are harmonious and indicate constant growth. The wood and water face also suggests a very equitable temperament and calm disposition. People with heart-shaped faces tend to be romantics and usually stay faithful to those to whom they give their heart. They are also creative and have a literary talent. They will find success in doing anything related to the creative arts. They are ambitious people, but never overtly so. Such people only need to guard against their tendency to float. It is vital for them to stay grounded and also to keep an eye out for the risks they take in their lives.

The Diamond-Shaped Face

The diamond-shaped face is a combination of wood and fire. Here the face is very wide at the place of the cheek-bones and then the face tapers towards the jawline and the forehead. The central portions of the face—the nose and cheeks—tend to

ELEMENT	SHAPE	DESCRIPTION OF SHAPE	BASIC TEMPERAMENT
FIRE 火	TRIANGULAR	Widest at the forehead and tapering slightly toward the jawline, so it looks like a triangle. Face is longer than it is wide.	Active, strong-minded, extroverted, and magnetic. Loves fame and attention. Success in high-flying careers. Can be bad-tempered. High energy.
WOOD 木	PEAR-SHAPED	Widest at the jawline and narrowest at the forehead.	Idealistic, intellectual, dreamy personality. Honest and has integrity. Righteous and high-minded. Psychic. Ambitious; reaching upwards.
METAL 金	ROUND (like a curved square)	Prominent cheekbones with a round, curved face. Width and length of face are the same.	Usually rich and fortunate. Creative and charming and possesses an elegant grace. Also glamorous and classy.
WATER 水	CURVED	Widest at the cheeks, with curved chin and forehead.	Flexible, clear-headed, popular, charming personality. Excellent with finances.
EARTH 土	SQUARE	Same width all over, and the face is as wide as it is long. Both forehead and jawline look square.	Reliable, determined, and full of power and strength. Stubborn and dogmatic personality. Also patient and thoughtful.

be rather prominent. This is also an auspicious face that combines the best of the two elements—a courageous disposition with a calm and steadied manner. The high energy of fire combines well with the intellectual capability of the wood element. Diamond-shaped faces usually belong to people who are enterprising and have initiative. They can be competitive and have the vitality to see through projects to successful completion. They should be wary of taking too much on, as they could end up working themselves to death.

The Oval-Shaped Face

The perfectly oval-shaped face combines metal and water elements. In appearance, this is often the most beautiful shape for a woman's face, as it is both curvaceous and slightly elongated. The forehead and the chin are both curved. This, too, is an auspicious face shape, and it suggests a life of ease and luxury. This analysis is based on the productive relationship between metal and water, and since water signifies wealth, such a face shape suggests the potential for a great deal of wealth.

People with oval-shaped faces tend to be dreamy in the way that they approach life. The danger that lies before people in this category is that their life can become too easy, so it is necessary to guard against being too indolent. In other words, do not allow too much water to drown you!

Above: The oval shape.
Below: The square face.

The Nine Wealth
Features of the Face

The Chinese believe in lucky and unlucky faces, and a great deal is made of the mountains and rivers of the face, which indicate wealth and fortune. Generally, the central axis of the face is deemed to be a crucial indicator of a person's lot in life, and when this appears to balance both sides of the face, the powerful trinity of luck is said to be properly aligned for prosperity.

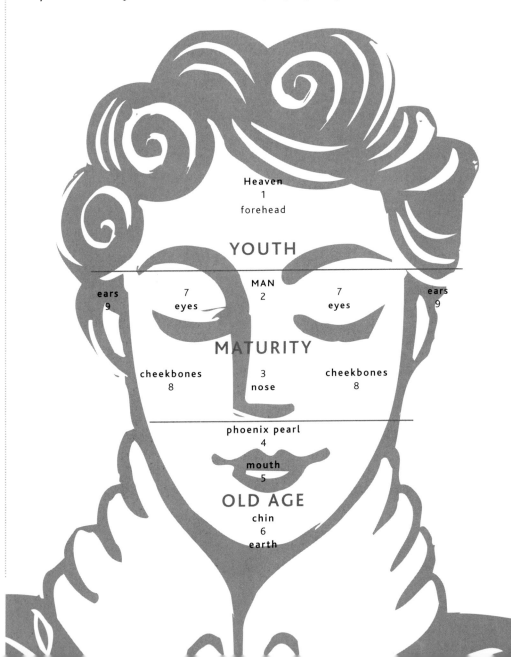

Heaven
1
forehead

YOUTH

MAN
2

ears
9

7
eyes

7
eyes

ears
9

MATURITY

cheekbones
8

3
nose

cheekbones
8

phoenix pearl
4

mouth
5

OLD AGE
chin
6
earth

The nine wealth features of the face. The central axis of the face indicates much about your lot in life, and ideally, balances the face.

The First Wealth Spot

The first wealth spot, the forehead (which also represents the luck from heaven and is the foremost mountain of the face) is round, high, curved, and protruding. Such a forehead indicates power, wealth, and great authority.

A perfect forehead is rare, but as long as this protrudes and looks prominent and wide, good fortune is indicated. A good forehead augments all the other luck features, since this also signifies the place of the heavenly celestial dragon. This is a yang spot in the face and means a great deal in terms of one's luck potential.

Look after your forehead and keep it clear of blemishes, spots, and unsightly pimples. Use artificial aids to ensure a smooth forehead. Moles on the forehead are acceptable unless they are placed in the dead center, in which case they should really be removed. Black moles here are deemed to be most inauspicious.

The Second Wealth Spot

The trinity of luck is expressed in terms of tien, ti, and ren—heaven, earth, and humankind, with humans in the center, located at the middle space above the nose and between the eyes. This is the man spot also referred to as the "life palace." Here the space should be clear, bright, and luminous if it is to represent a life of good fortune.

There should be no hair, colorings, spots, or moles in this area since these collectively or by themselves signify obstacles to one's luck. When this space is clear and luminous, it symbolizes a life of affluence and influence.

The Third Wealth Spot

The third wealth spot of the face is the nose. This is deemed a yin spot, and it signifies one of the rivers of the face. In the Chinese classic texts on face reading, the nose signifies the river Jie, which brings

wealth. The rounder and fleshier the nose looks, the better is the wealth luck indicated. Nostrils should not be too small nor too large.

The nose must look balanced and smooth. Spots—white or black—are seen as obstacles, and moles at the tip of the nose are regarded as a major sign of misfortune. The Chinese always regard a big nose with some indulgence, no matter how out of place it looks in the overall face. This is because the nose is the repository of money fortune, and it indicates wealth from many different sources.

The Fourth Wealth Spot

Directly below the nose is the tip of the lips, and if you are deemed to possess the mighty gift of gab—tremendous prosperity luck from speaking— you will see here what is termed the phoenix pearl. It looks rounded and is protruding, and usually those who have it will probably have had it from childhood. Like the cleft chin or the dimple, the pearl is deemed also to be a beauty spot. It brings good fortune in both men and women. The pearl is considered the fourth wealth feature on the face.

The Fifth Wealth Spot

Directly below the pearl is the mouth, which is considered the second river on the face. It is known as the river Huai. The mouth is deemed auspicious when it is soft and succulent. Irrespective of its size, the mouth must never appear dry, since this indicates loss of luck. As long as the mouth is always moist, it indicates money luck. The mouth is the fifth wealth spot on the face. Moles around the mouth, as long as they are not black, are deemed to enhance the good luck of the mouth and indicate that the person will never lack for food.

The Sixth Wealth Spot

The sixth wealth spot is the second mountain on the face—the chin. This is also the place of earth in

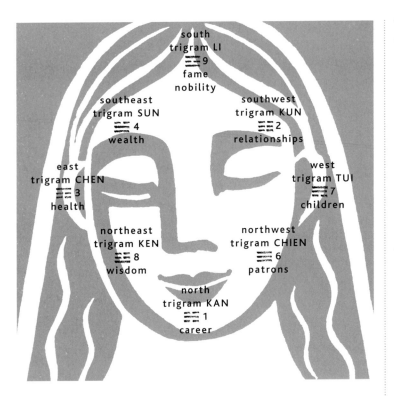

south
trigram LI
9
fame
nobility

southeast
trigram SUN
4
wealth

southwest
trigram KUN
2
relationships

east
trigram CHEN
3
health

west
trigram TUI
7
children

northeast
trigram KEN
8
wisdom

northwest
trigram CHIEN
6
patrons

north
trigram KAN
1
career

The nine Chinese trigrams make up the *I Ching* and, when superimposed on the face, indicate good luck and fortune.

the trinity of tien ti ren and is sometimes viewed as the jawline. To be auspicious, the chin should be protruding and prominent. A receding jawline is one sign of misfortune in old age, or it can even be a sign of premature death. A prominent chin indicates a strong base mountain, and this is also suggestive of longevity.

The Seventh Wealth Spot

The seventh wealth spot on the face is the eyes. The eyes are said to indicate great good fortune when they shine and are slightly moist. It does not matter what shape, size, or coloring the eyes are—what is most significant is their vitality, When eyes are bright and are well protected by arched eyebrows, life is healthy and prosperous. Eyebrows should never be overly plucked or shaved. When a face lacks eyebrows, the person simply cannot climb up the ladder of success. When one eye is smaller than the other, it is a good idea to use artificial aids such as eyeliners to correct the imbalance.

The Eighth Wealth Spot

The eighth wealth spot on the face is the cheekbones. In terms of age luck (see opposite), one enters into the center section of the face, which indicates the mature years, at the age of 21. When the cheekbones stand out prominently and appear bright and shiny, it is one of the surest signs that serious wealth luck is about to manifest.

Cheekbones should always have flesh and never look bony, since this would indicate excessive yang. For cheekbones to appear balanced, they must look good enough to pinch!

The Ninth Wealth Spot

The final indicator is the ears. When your ears are well formed and proportionate, they indicate great good fortune and wisdom. They are said to represent the flow of the Yellow River.

Remember that face reading is based also on manifestations of yin and yang, and clues can also be gleaned by superimposing Chinese trigrams— shapes that make up the hexagrams of the *I Ching* (see page 27)—on the face. These trigrams, which are made by combining yin and yang lines, are another way of looking at the kind of luck intrinsic to the different parts of the face.

Of the nine wealth features, only one is placed in the youth section of the face, and two in the old age section. This suggests that our destiny manifests mostly during the time of life between youth and old age—this is named the age of maturity.

Thus, while face reading gives you a good idea of luck potential, it is essential to note that the bridge between heaven and earth is humankind. It is humankind luck that has the most impact on our destiny as it unfolds. The face over time can undergo change. Mountains can flatten and rivers can run dry. It is vital to stay ever watchful, as much over our physical bodies as over the luck that we are constantly creating for ourselves.

THE AGE LUCK OF YOUR FACE

Check the part of the face that shows where you are at this year. If your age is on the right side, the pleasurable interests dominate. If you are on the left side, it is career matters that occupy your attention. If your age is on the center part of the face, you are standing at a crossroads. The center years indicate significant changes taking place.

Chinese face reading assumes that a person's life moves from point to point. The childhood years are governed by the markings on the ears. As a child, your control over your destiny has yet to manifest itself. The teenage years and the early twenties are indicated by the forehead; at this time heaven luck dictates much of your life's circumstances. Generally, the smoother and larger this part of the face the easier these years will be.

Marks, indentations, black spots, creases, and moles here indicate obstacles, accidents, poor health, and problems related to relationships with parents. Generally when the forehead is flawed, there are difficulties in communicating with parents. When this part of the face is small and bony, indications are that parents lack the resources to give you much of an education. You tend to be a loner. On the other hand, when the forehead is broad, round, and smooth, it is an excellent indication of a happy time.

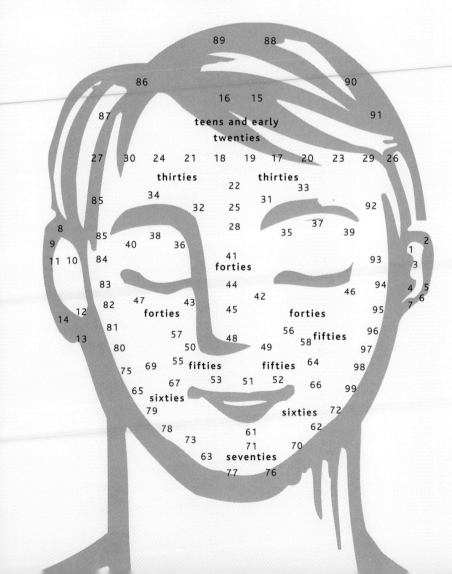

Use this diagram to check the age luck of your face. Any discolorations, spots, or indentations indicate problems at that age, whereas smooth skin is an indication that you will have a trouble-free time.

The Secret Meaning of Moles

The surface area of the skin should ideally be smooth and unblemished. However, special rules attest to the meanings of moles. Depending on where they are found, their size, color, and indentations, moles are either positive or negative indications of luck. Thus hidden moles are better than visible ones, and moles on the front of the body are to be preferred to moles at the back. Here's why . . .

The most auspicious pearl mole on the face is to be found between the two eyebrows but a little off center. Such a mole indicates high achievement and plenty of recognition.

Moles on the back of the body from the neck down are said to symbolize burdens you carry all through your life. The worst kinds of moles are those found on the upper back and on the back of the shoulders. Below the torso, moles do not signify burdens, but they do indicate obstacles to success. Moles on the back of the neck or head, however, are said to be protective, as they signify secret warning signals that alert you to danger.

Generally, moles range from light pink to jet black and may appear simply as spots on the body or as raised protrusions. The Chinese make a distinction between light and dark moles. Light-colored moles are said to represent pearls, while dark-colored moles are said to signify the droppings of the gods. This suggests that lighter-colored moles are to be preferred to black moles. One is said to be yang while the other is yin.

Moles found on the ears, eyebrows, and nose are also considered to indicate good fortune. In fact, a mole anywhere on the ear is said to be most auspicious. A mole at the tip of the nose is inauspicious and is especially unfortunate for men.

Moles on the feet suggest a great deal of travel and adventure, while moles on any part of the hands indicate an industrious person. Moles found on any part of the limbs indicate that financially and economically this person will have good life. Moles on the hands and feet are usually quite dark, and in many instances they appear as single black spots that one cannot miss even though they may not be protruding.

Moles found anywhere on the stomach on the front of the body indicate a very good life with plenty to eat. Economically and intellectually, this is a big person indeed.

Above: All moles below the eye are auspicious, and are said to imbue the person with innate sex appeal.

Above: Moles on the lower part of the face are also lucky. A mole just at the end of the mouth indicates a person who will never go short of food.

Above: A pearl mole on the forehead, just off center, signifies high achievement in business or politics, but also indicates that family life may be disappointing or nonexistent.

BIRTHMARKS IN PRIVATE PLACES

Much like moles, birthmarks that are hidden usually have auspicious meanings, while those that are exposed take on connotations of blemishes that signify obstacles. When you have a dark stain-like discoloration on any part of your face, it warns of some misfortune in the year indicated by where the spot is. Camouflage these blemishes if you can.

There might be some notable exceptions to the rule. Thus, when you have a birthmark that is usually hidden and that looks like or resembles any of the celestial creatures, for example dragons, tortoises, phoenixes, or any kind of birds, horses, or elephants, the meaning is said to be auspicious. Other equally lucky signs on your body include the mark of the lotus, the trident, the fish, coins, and the vase. These marks are said to be even luckier when they appear on the front of your body around the stomach area or hidden between the legs near the genitals. Moles on the genitals are most auspicious.

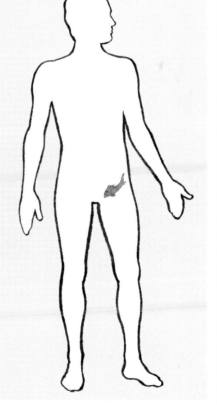

The Five Elements of the Human Body and Organs

The Chinese use the five elements theory to understand the inner and outer physical functioning of the body. Thus, in traditional Chinese medicine, each of the five major organs of the body—the heart, the spleen, the lungs, the liver, and the kidneys—represents one of the five elements. Illnesses are diagnosed according to imbalances in those elements.

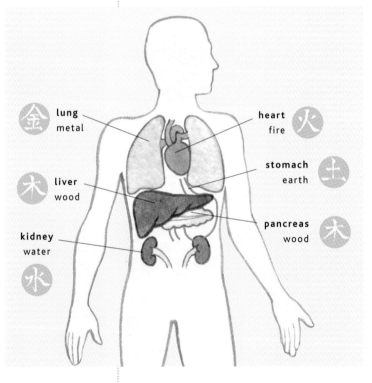

金 lung metal

火 heart fire

土 stomach earth

木 liver wood

木 pancreas wood

水 kidney water

An illustration showing the five elements of the body as represented by the organs of the human body.

yourself succumbing excessively to any of the emotions that represent any one of the elements, then you can suspect that something may be wrong with that particular organ within the body. When worry, depression, excessive thinking, fear, or sadness start to dominate your waking hours, you can suspect some kind of malfunction of the flow of chi into these internal organs.

It is a good idea to try to overcome these problems, otherwise they simply get "stuck" inside your system, thereby causing the flow of chi to also get stuck. The vital meridians inside you get clogged much as a drain gets blocked when there is excessive dirt stuck inside.

According to traditional Chinese medicine, one of the most common causes of blockages in the system is stress. This villain of modern living causes chi to get stuck and stagnate within the body, preventing the organs from functioning properly, especially the liver. An afflicted liver means an affliction of the wood element within the human body. An afflicted liver also starts to affect all the other organs.

This is because the five elements are all interrelated. Anger is the emotion most often associated with the liver, so when you find yourself feeling irritable, losing your cool, and barking at everyone,

The illustration above shows the five elements as represented by the organs of the body. The heart is of the fire element; the liver and pancreas are of the wood element; the lungs are of the metal element; the kidneys are of the water element; the womb and stomach are of the earth element.

Each of the five elements signifies a ruling planet and an overriding emotion. When you find you have good reason to suspect that your liver might be malfunctioning. Meanwhile, there are a great many clues, such as a yearning for sour food, excessive weight gain, headaches, indigestion, yeast infections, and eye problems.

❝ *When I became alert to the many signals of liver malfunctioning inside my body, I drank a great deal of water, because water produces wood and is good for it. I also ate a lot of black foods (like Chinese black mushrooms) since black symbolizes water. In a month, I had become less stressed, and calm, and my weight problem stabilized. I was back on track again.* ❞

Chinese medicine approaches the treatment of ailments from a totally different angle than Western medicine does. If you look at the table below, you will see that by examining how you feel and checking the time of the year you can see which part of your internal or external system could be unbalanced. The next time you feel something amiss in your body, it is not a bad idea to consult

If illness strikes, a doctor qualified in traditional Chinese medicine can prescribe the correct plants to rebalance the five elements of the body.

a doctor qualified in traditional Chinese medicine. The doctor will recommend remedies and cures that use the five-element theory in order to restore balance and harmony. Using the productive cycle of the elements, it is possible to rebalance your five elements, and you will feel better again.

ELEMENT	FIRE	WOOD	METAL	WATER	EARTH
ORGAN	Heart	Liver/pancreas	Lungs	Kidneys	Stomach
EMOTION	Joy	Anger	Depression	Fear	Worry
TASTE	Bitter	Sour	Spicy	Salty	Sweet
SEASON	Summer	Spring	Fall	Winter	Winter
BODY PART	Blood	Limbs/tendons	Skin/hair/bone	Waist	Muscle
FACE PART	Eyes	Tongue	Nose	Ear	Mouth
WEATHER	Heat	Wind	Dry	Cold	Damp

Shoulder and Arm Luck

Your shoulders and arms reveal the strength within you. The Chinese believe that merely looking at a man's shoulders will reveal if he will be a success or failure in life, and that by simply looking at the curves of a woman's shoulder, one can tell if she will bring luck to her husband's family. The arms are judged by examining the bones that make them up.

The Shoulders

In the male of the species, thin, narrow shoulders always suggest a lack of physical and mental strength. Softness of the muscles suggests a serious lack of determination, and such men are not destined for greatness. Similarly, shoulders that are hunched up and too high reveal an inner restlessness that suggests an instability of purpose. Such men lack the focus and determination required to succeed.

It is said that the luckiest shoulders for women are rounded, curving out from the neck in a smooth line. Shoulders should always look straight and balanced.

Male Shoulders

The luckiest type of shoulders for men are said to be broad and muscular, for these are shoulders that indicate great power. Such men are said to have the luck to succeed. They are usually self-confident, sensitive, and sensible. Broad-shouldered men are also big-hearted and generous, and they are said to make the best lovers.

Female Shoulders

For women, the luckiest shoulders are said to be rounded, curving out from the neck in a smooth line. Shoulders of this shape suggest an apparent submissiveness of attitude, which is said to attract good fortune to women. If the shoulders are also fleshy, it is a further indication of the woman's beauty and intelligence.

Balance

Shoulders should always look straight and balanced without sloping either to the left or right so that one side is higher than the other. When the right shoulder is higher than the left, a tendency to conceit and arrogance leading to a serious reduction of success luck is indicated. When the left shoulder is higher, however, it also indicates a serious weakening of luck, but this time it is because the person is overly generous and weak.

The Arms

The arms of a person are made up of dragon and tiger bones. Dragon bones are the bones from the fingers to the elbow, while tiger bones are the bones from the elbow to the shoulder. A quick way of gauging the success potential of a person is to see if the dragon bones are longer and stronger than the tiger bones. When they are, it suggests that most of the ambitions of the person can be realized. When tiger bones dominate, the person will meet with a series of frustrations.

Long Arms

When the arms are extraordinarily long—when they reach the knees—this is a fantastic indication of great success, although this is rare. Generally, long arms suggest an influential and powerful person. Those with short arms tend to have a harder time attaining their ambitions. The shorter the arms, the larger the obstacles to success.

Muscular or Skinny Arms

Those whose arms are balanced to their body size also tend to enjoy success, especially if the arms are round, muscular, and solid. They will have success at work and enjoy happy relationships.

However, arms that look flat and skinny usually indicate a life of difficulty. Such people are seldom satisfied with their life, and although they may appear happy, their thin arms give away their unhappy state of mind.

ARMPIT HAIR

Bushy hair in the armpits is believed to be a sign of success, especially when the hair is healthy and thick. Dry, unhealthy hair in the armpits, however, suggests worrisome problems that are usually related to lack of financial success.

YOUR HAIR BRINGS YOUR MARRIAGE LUCK

Hair should always look smooth and be long and free flowing. It should appear rich and shiny if it is to attract the full power of yin luck. This is the luck of marriage and family. A man with hair that is fair and shiny with good health, not too wavy and not too oily, is said to have plenty of business luck. A woman with beautiful, free-flowing, healthy hair is believed to be able to contract a happy and auspicious marriage.

When there is too much hair, the Chinese believe that the person has excessive yin energy that should be balanced by introducing more yang energy, for example by wearing white. When there is thin hair, however, luck is said to be missing, although balding hair is believed to be better with age.

Characteristics based on hair type suggest the following broad generalizations:

- *Fine-haired people are intelligent, creative, and romantic, and are risk-takers.*
- *Very curly-haired people are fickle, and frizzy hair tends to make you ill-tempered.*
- *Straight or wavy-haired people are kind, caring, and humble.*
- *Coarse-haired people tend to be impulsive and unlucky.*

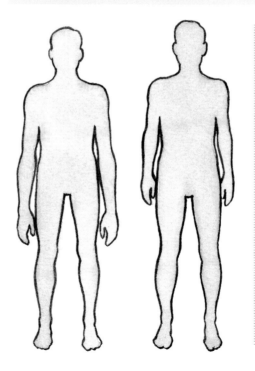

Long arms (left) indicate great success, while those with shorter arms (right) will find it harder to reach their goals.

Your Chest and Breasts
Reveal the Real You!

The chest in men and the breasts in women reveal their ability to cope with their roles in the context of their lives. They are indications of the physical health and the mental attitudes of the real person lurking within the body. In men, the chest is a symbol of the determination of the patriarch, while in women, the breasts are a symbol of motherhood.

A broad, protruding chest indicates a strong man who will persevere until he is successful in achieving his goals in life.

Broad, Thick Chest

A man who has a broad and protruding chest is strong, energetic, and achievement-oriented. When hair is sparse on the chest, he is the sort who will persevere and ultimately succeed, whether in the military or sports field. When the hair is silky and soft, the potential for success is magnified. In a woman, a large, broad chest suggests a positive, optimistic attitude. She is likely to be a successful career woman. Her success in her role as wife and mother, however, is indicated by her breasts.

Flat, Narrow Chest

Men with flat and narrow chests tend to be introverted. They are generally mild-mannered and reserved, and commonly find success in the arts. They have tremendous mental capabilities and are often successful in research and creative pursuits, but they do not tend toward leadership.

Rounded, Full Chest

Men with full, rounded chests tend to be impulsive and adventurous. They are not aggressive, but they like taking risks and doing things their way. These men are independent-minded and usually find success in business. They display initiative and are friendly and sociable.

Breasts

In women, the breasts reveal the kind of mother attitude they possess, and in men, they symbolize fertility. Thus, according to the Chinese, if you want to gauge the fertility of a man, you should look at his nipples. If they are large, they indicate lots of children; and when there is a bit of hair on them, the man's ability to father children is assured. Too much hair on the nipples indicates that the man's fertility is in question. In women, the breasts are an indication of success in the role of wife or mother.

Flat, Circular Breasts

Flat, circular breasts are said to reveal a woman who is reserved and withdrawn, but also practical and efficient as a homemaker and mother. She will raise her children meticulously and with great care, but she expects the father to be a proper provider.

Round, Full Breasts

Round, full breasts like inverted bowls indicate a woman who will be faithful and a good mother to her children, but she is motivated by what is expected of her rather than by any great passionate love for them. She tends to be selfish to some extent, and her wants and needs will have equal priority with the needs of her spouse and children.

Round and Bouncy Breasts

Round, bouncy breasts indicate an exceptionally fertile woman. This is a woman who loves life and is independent-minded. Her children are not her whole world. She will have other needs and desires. If she has big nipples, it is also an indication that she could desert her family. These breasts also indicate a woman who could be unfaithful.

Upward Pushing Breasts

Upward-pushing breasts indicate a woman who is pleasant, optimistic, and cheerful. She is also

arrogant and has a tendency to be moody; at times she may be incredibly loving, but at other times she can be difficult and bad-tempered.

Full and Spreading Breasts

Full and spreading breasts indicate a motherly type who tends to gain weight easily and transform quickly into an earth mother. She is ambitious for her husband and for her children. She is faithful and will create a warm, loving home. Her children will be brought up with a lot of love and attention.

Hanging, Oval Breasts

Hanging, oval breasts indicate a woman who has reached a stage when her breasts have begun to sag. This indicates weariness and a physical weakness. This woman is likely to manifest a melancholy nature and may have a tendency toward depression. This woman is unlikely to make a great mother unless someone can infuse some real yang energy into her and find a way of making her feel happy.

A full-breasted woman takes her duties as a mother and wife seriously but does not put her husband's needs above her own.

What Do Your Back and Stomach Reveal?

The human backbone keeps the body upright and standing. When this part of the body is sturdy and strong, it suggests a good reservoir of cosmic chi and hidden strength. These reserves are as intangible as they are powerful. The back carries the weight of living responsibilities, and it also fuels the body, ensuring not only good health but also a full and meaningful life.

The Back

Extending all the way from the shoulders to the waist, the back supports the spinal column located vertically down its center. The back is where the reservoir of one's cosmic energy is stored. A strong back indicates wisdom and a depth of purpose in life. It also stands for the firmness of yang energy within the self. When the back is straight and firm, it denotes a healthy, well-adjusted balance of yin and yang energy within the body. Success is attained through a healthy composite of mind and body. When the back is crooked, hunched, or weakened, all kinds of troubles and obstacles manifest in the person's life. Many people suffer from back problems so, not surprisingly, it is common to suffer a certain number of setbacks in life.

Broad Backs

People with broad backs have a reservoir of strength, vigor, and ambition. Broad-backed people are like the tortoise—they have a natural, inbuilt protection against politicking and power struggles, so they usually win in any power games played against them. In a man, the broad back suggests an ability to protect the family. In a woman, a broad back indicates that she has an independent nature.

Rounded Backs

People with backs rounded like a dome possess an acute skill in business. They have a shrewd commercial sense and are also skillful with money. Such people attract success and wealth luck easily. They are good at deal-making and negotiating. They love the good life, and their homes are likely to be luxurious and comfortable.

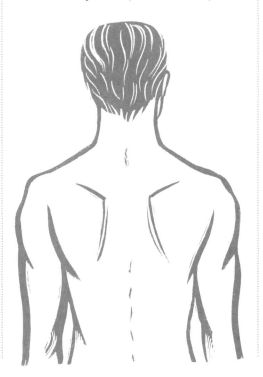

A straight, firm back represents a good balance of yin and yang energy and strength of purpose. A weakened back shows that obstacles in life are likely.

Triangular Backs

People with triangular backs where the top is broad and the waist is narrow are usually very sensual and creative. They are not very ambitious, being easily satisfied. Men with this kind of back tend to travel a great deal.

Thin, Narrow Backs

People with thin, narrow backs will generally suffer back problems. Such people tend to be arty types who are not very realistic about life. They are dreamers rather than doers. However, their introspective natures give them a tendency toward inner development and spirituality.

The Stomach

The abdomen is one of the most highly prized indications of prosperity and status. The ideal stomach is one that is round and protruding and, in a woman, looks like she is in the early stages of pregnancy. This kind of tummy is a symbol of longevity and wealth. In fact, the laughing Buddha who has a fat tummy is seen as a symbol of happiness and good fortune precisely because of his fat stomach. Many Chinese believe that stroking the tummy of an image of the laughing Buddha strategically placed inside the home is one sure way of attracting good fortune. So invest in this happiness Buddha and make it a morning ritual before you leave for the office each day to stroke his fat tummy.

A popular way of knowing exactly how large one should be in order to attract wealth luck is to use feng shui dimensions to measure your waistline. The easiest way to do this is to use a feng shui dimensions tape and measure the waistline of every person you know. You will be surprised at how accurate the indications of prosperity are. Otherwise, try checking your waistline against the chart at the top of this page.

MEASUREMENT	MEANINGS
23.5–24 inches	Blessed with many good children
24–24.5 inches	Additional income from unexpected sources
24.5–25 inches	A very successful son
25–25.5 inches	Excellent all-round good fortune
25.5–26 inches	Very good examinations luck
26–26.5 inches	Good gambling and speculative luck
26.5–27 inches	Improved income
27–27.5 inches	Property, power, and honor for the family
32–32.5 inches	Lots of money flowing in
32.5–33 inches	Good luck in examinations
33–33.5 inches	Plenty of precious jewels in your life
33.5–34 inches	Abundant prosperity and good fortune
34–34.5 inches	Money luck
34.5–35 inches	A safe filled with jewels
35–35.5 inches	Six types of good fortune
35.5–36 inches	Abundant good fortune

A curvaceous belly-dancer with a soft stomach. The Chinese believe that a rounded stomach is a symbol of wealth.

Discovering Your
Male and Female Essence

The Chinese have long held that within us all are both primary and secondary traits of sexuality. Both the male and the female essence is present in the human life force. This is expressed in the symbol of the tai chi—the yin and yang—which eloquently describes the dualism of chi that makes up the whole. Both male and female exist in all of us.

A feminine-looking woman and a woman with masculine elements. Although feminine traits will dominate, most women deviate in some small way from the norm of soft, delicate features and a small frame.

Chinese wisdom accepts that the nature of our sexuality is indicated in our body shape, or more accurately, in the extent that it varies from the traditional view of the male and female body.

This implies that, generally speaking, male and female sexuality is expressed outwardly in male and female physical attributes. Thus, men with feminine physical features will have a greater tendency to be bisexual or gay, while women who exhibit masculine physical attributes will have a greater tendency to be bisexual or lesbian.

Feminine Facial Features

The Chinese describe feminine facial features as being soft, delicate, and fine. Complexions are smooth, and pores tend to be small. Females are also generally fairer skinned than their male counterparts, irrespective of race. Shoulders are round, and arms tend to be shorter and weaker than those of men. Women are usually small-boned, and the female frame always appears smaller and daintier. The ribcage and upper portion of the body is narrow, while hips are round and full. The abdomen is the same—round and full. A woman's body shape is generally more curvaceous. There are many lyrical descriptions of the ideal female body in the Chinese classical texts, and these can apply equally to women of all races, but the ideal is, of course, a rare occurrence.

Most women will have some traces of masculine energy, which manifests in some small way in the shape of the body and in the features of the face. Usually, however, any deviation from the norm is insignificant and the presence of any masculine essence often adds to the uniqueness of the individual, makes her whole and adds to her overall charisma rather than making her appear masculine. In women, the feminine traits will always be the dominant characteristics.

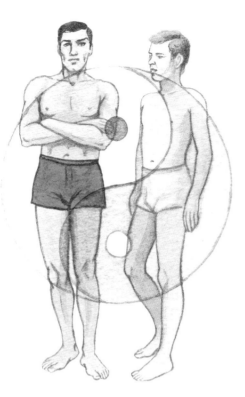

Masculine Facial Features

Masculine facial features tend to be square and thick, and eyebrows are usually coarser and harder than in their female counterparts. Shoulders are broad, limbs are muscular and relatively longer. A man's frame is generally larger and stronger. The torso is wide with a narrower lower body. Men are supposed to be flat-chested and more muscular than women. The Chinese classical texts have many poetic descriptions of the male hero who epitomizes the ideal male body. It is not unusual for men also to possess yin or feminine traits in their body shape or facial features.

Confused Sexuality

When masculine traits in the female body are significant—for example when there is an overall masculine look to the frame—it is possible that sexuality can become confused. Likewise, when feminine characteristics are evident in the male body—for example, in men who manifest finer facial features—they too can feel the stirrings of confusion in their sexuality. This confusion is usually a source of great unhappiness during the early formative years, and due to peer group and family pressure, it is often hidden and even denied.

It has been suggested that having both gender characteristics is more the norm than being completely male (yang) or completely female (yin). It is how these attributes balance within us that makes us comfortable with our sexuality—or not.

Test yourself   Check the balance of yin and yang in your physical shape, and see if your comfort level makes you whole as an individual.

1 Your facial features are:	
a fine	b coarse

2 Your shoulders are	
a narrow	b broad

3 Your breasts are	
a full	b flat and small

4 Your hips are	
a full	b slim

5 Your limbs are relatively	
a short	b long

6 You have more	
a fat	b muscles

7 Your body looks	
a delicate	b strong

8 Your face tends to be	
a curved	b square

9 Your buttocks are	
a rounded	b muscular and slim

10 Your feet are relatively	
a large	b small

11 Your hands are	
a delicate	b strong

A score of seven to nine As for women and six to eight Bs for men is usual.

Between these numbers, you exhibit a healthy balance of yin and yang in your body.

A completely masculine man and a man with feminine elements. Few men fit the masculine ideal perfectly; many possess some feminine traits—for example, wide hips or fine facial features.

Are You a Tiger
or a Dragon in Bed?

The Taoist way of harmonizing yin and yang between lovers reveals the way sexual energy is released during the act of lovemaking. Whether the act of love enhances or depletes you of energy depends on whether you are a tiger or a dragon in bed: a tiger is the dominant female and a dragon is the dominant male. How do you see yourself?

A Chinese watercolor painting of tigers, which represent dominant females in the act of love.

Opposite: A Chinese watercolor of a dragon, which symbolizes the dominant male.

The act of love is described as a fusion of the fire trigram Li, with the water trigram Kan in the Dragon Tiger classic of sexual alchemy. These two energies signify the waxing and waning of yin and yang energies during the act of love.

Whether you represent fire or water energy depends on whether you see yourself as a dragon or a tiger in bed. Knowing this will tell you if your approach to sex enhances you with new energy or depletes you of your chi each time you indulge in the act of copulation. In other words, find out if

you are a dragon or a tiger in bed! The tiger signifies the essence of the male, regenerative energy hidden in the female. This is represented by the water trigram Kan, which is made up of a single yang line sandwiched between two yin lines. Women who take on a dominating role in the act of love—either taking the initiative most of the time or assuming the leadership role from foreplay through to the final release of energy—are said to take on the spirit of the tiger. Such women can be differentiated from the submissive, yielding types, and from those who look upon sex as an act of love between two people of equal energy.

The dragon, meanwhile, is representative of the regenerative energy hidden in the male, and this is signified by the fire trigram Li, which consists of a single yin line sandwiched between two yang lines. Men who take on the dominating role in the act of love are said to embody the essence of the dragon. This type of man is to be differentiated from those who surrender the initiative to their partner.

> The tiger and dragon essence materializes when fire and water are united.

The Dragon Tiger classic defines the way sexual energy is released and conserved between partners in love. The Taoists believed that the energy released during the act of copulation offers a powerful source of longevity chi. This procreative energy, however, is released only when the sex act takes place between partners where love is not the primary passion but longevity is. Can you imagine yourself making love this way?

LEGEND OF THE 16 LOVE CHARMS

Legend has it that Rati, the plain-looking daughter of Mara, turned in despair to Lakshmi, the goddess of beauty. Lakshmi gave her 16 love charms and said, "Anyone who decorates her body with these love charms will enchant the man of her dreams and attract the forces of prosperity into her household." Rati became the beloved wife of Kama, the lord of desire. Women wear these love charms (shown in the picture above) at their wedding, to ensure conjugal bliss. The 16 love charms are:

1   a red dot on the forehead—this is the most significant charm
2   the sacred thread of marriage around the neck
3   turmeric paste to anoint the body
4   fragrant flowers in the hair
5   perfumes on the body
6   betel leaves chewed in the mouth to sweeten the breath
7   a black beauty spot to ward off the evil eye
8   black kohl to rim the eyes
9   henna on the hands
10 red dye for the feet
11 a brightly colored sari
12 jeweled hairpins in the hair
13 jewels on the head—earrings, nose rings, and necklaces
14 jewels for the body, for example in the waistband
15 jewels for the arms—rings, bracelets, and bangles
16 jewels for the feet—toe rings and anklets

Balancing Your Chi Vibration

Chi is a dynamic vibration that circulates throughout the body and governs the quality of the life force. Our breathing, talking, sleeping, eating, and our ability to think, communicate, and be happy, all come from this vibration. To know ourselves, we must tune in to it. When our chi vibration is balanced, our organs and our internal circulation remain harmonious.

Energy Replenishment

The flow of chi inside the human body reflects the quality of energy that fuels it. Since chi is dynamic, the level and quality of energy is in a constant state of flux. Every moment of our lives, we are losing and simultaneously gaining energy. Whether there is a net gain or a net loss depends on what we are doing with our body. When there is excessive energy loss, the body becomes drained, weak, and vulnerable to illness and disease. This happens when physical and mental activity is not matched with enough intake of food, air, and rest.

If you are feeling drained, weak, and vulnerable your chi vibration is probably blocked and starved of fresh new energy. You should do something to revive the vibrancy of your life force.

Of the three kinds of energy input, it is rest that is the most vital, for when we sleep, our chi is replenished. Like a battery that is recharged, the body needs sleep for all its meridian points to receive energy from the Universe.

When the body does not get enough sleep, these vital points of the body simply cannot be properly recharged, and blocks start to form within the body that will ultimately affect the balanced flow of chi. Over time, these blocks harden and affect the vibrations of chi within. It is because of this that many Taoist masters stress the need to get a good night's sleep every night.

When you do not sleep well, the life force inside the body becomes seriously weakened. You will immediately lose the vibrancy that makes your body shine. Acupuncture and acupressure treatments can help dissolve the blockages in chi that result from lack of proper sleep, but no matter how excellent these cures are, they really are only temporary measures. It is more important for there

Sleep is the most vital of the three energy inputs; if you do not get enough sleep, your body's life force will weaken significantly.

A positive flow of chi energy encircles a happy, waltzing couple as they move across the floor.

to be a conscious effort to ensure sufficient energy intake to recharge the body chi.

In addition to rest, we must also breathe properly (which brings in air) and eat properly. Good breathing is deep breathing, and good foods are those that help the body get rid of toxins and other poisons.

Flow and Circulation

In addition to energy replenishment, there should also be an unimpeded flow of the life force within the body. The quality of the flow of chi inside the human body depends on the flow of oxygen and the flow of waste matter, both of which use the circulation of the bloodstream within the body. It is the bloodstream that brings air and nutrients to the body, and which also gets rid of wastes through the excretory system. When the circulation of blood is impeded, the body is immediately overwhelmed with problems. Cells die, organs are damaged, strength is sapped, disease sets in, tension mounts, enthusiasm wanes, and sadness creeps in. In short, the life force slows down.

Special exercises, food replenishment, breathing techniques, and meditation have been perfected to dissolve blocks in the flow of chi, and to improve the efficiency of organs and body cells—tai chi and pranayama (breathing exercises) are popular examples. They focus on dissolving blocks in the internal flow, giving total consideration to all the factors that affect the root cause of body ailments. The most vital is the focus on the circulation of energy, and especially circulation that engages the seven energy points of the human body.

The Seven Energy Points

The seven energy points correspond to the seven vital glands of the body. They are identified as:

The Sexual Glands

The sexual glands are the testes and prostate in the male and the ovaries in the female. These glands secrete the hormones that create sexual energy. The sexual glands of the human body are often referred to as the "stove" because they produce the fire energy to fuel the other six glands. The sexual urge is a powerful source of inner fire. Everyone needs a regular charge of this energy, so sex is a powerful way of replenishing this energy within us. Those who lack regular sex can pamper their bodies by having massages—especially pressure point massage—which directly aids the body in replenishing the energy. It is also possible to use meditation and visualization to regenerate the powerful inner fire.

The Adrenal Glands

The adrenal glands are on top of the kidneys. They support the kidneys' function, which is to purify the water system within the body. The element energy of this gland is water energy. Those who suffer from water retention should have their kidneys checked out. The Chinese use regular reflexology massage to cure kidney problems.

The Pancreas

The pancreas, located in the digestive system, supports the energy intake and levels within the body. An improperly functioning pancreas causes all the other glands to go out of balance. Once again, a reflexology massage is said to be excellent for restoring balance in this organ.

The Thymus Gland

According to Chinese medicine, the thymus gland, located near the heart, governs the efficiency of the heart and the circulatory system. When the thymus malfunctions, blood circulation becomes flawed. The best cure is pressure point massage and/or acupuncture. When the flow of blood is blocked, the chi within us also becomes blocked. An effective visualization cure is to meditate on a healing blue light emanating from the heart area.

The Thyroid Gland

The thyroid gland, which is near to the throat, controls growth. It is fueled by wood energy, and it governs the respiratory system. One of the best ways of sending healing energy to the throat gland is to picture a warm red light gently pulsating in the throat area. This is said to greatly enhance the growth chi created by the gland here.

The seven energy points of the body, which correspond to the seven vital glands of the human body.

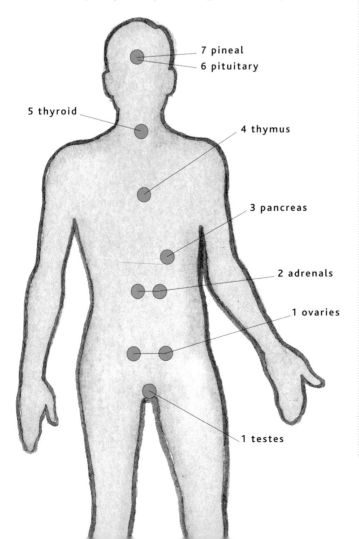

7 pineal
6 pituitary
5 thyroid
4 thymus
3 pancreas
2 adrenals
1 ovaries
1 testes

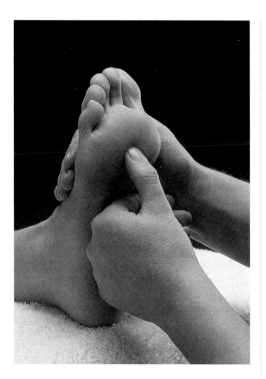

The Pituitary Gland

The pituitary gland, at the base of the brain, governs intelligence, wisdom, and memory. Visualize white light—pure, bright, and glowing—surrounding the head. This enhances clarity of thought and focus of concentration.

The Pineal Gland

The pineal gland, which is at the base of the brain, governs the spiritual dimensions of the body. It is associated with human intuition. This gland affects all other glands through its secretions.

Memorize the location of the seven vital glands, then think of each of them as vital vessels within you that are connected to each other by a labyrinth that carries the health-bringing chi. The vessels work together to ensure that no one ever runs short of energy. This, in turn, depends on the circulation system and energy replenishment.

The seven energy centers must also be kept unpolluted so that all of the toxins that enter the body system can be efficiently excreted.

The Five Elements and the Organs

The Chinese believe that the life force operates through the interplay of the five elements—fire, earth, metal, water, and wood—each of which is assigned to important body organs. The interplay of energy that takes place depends on the productive and destructive cycles of these five elements. Understanding these two cycles helps us to look after our bodies and stay healthy.

- Fire element: heart and small intestine
- Earth element: spleen and stomach
- Metal element: lungs and large intestine
- Water element: kidneys and bladder
- Wood element: liver and pancreas

Imbalanced energy within any organ sets off a chain reaction that results in the body malfunctioning. Many Chinese exercises, such as chi kung, are based on this view of internal body organs, energy centers, and circulatory flows. This way of explaining disease in the human body laid the foundations of Chinese traditional medicine.

Left: Having a regular reflexology massage can help repair a malfunctioning kidney.

Below: The best way to deal with blood circulation problems is to use acupuncture, which can restore the blood flow back to normal.

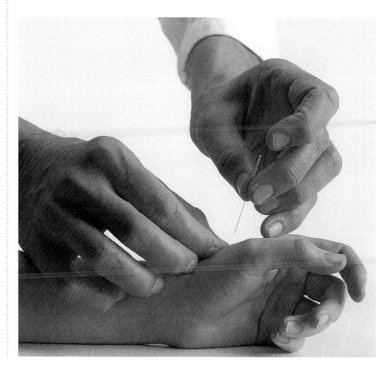

Thighs, Legs, and Buttocks
Reveal Success Potential

The balance between your thighs and buttocks and the appearance of your legs determines whether you will stride easily and confidently through life.

How do you move through life? Do you stride confidently as you navigate a pathway of success for yourself, or do you move uncertainly, unsure of yourself and of the way forward? The way you move determines your success potential, and how balanced you are manifests in the physical appearance of your legs, your thighs, and your buttocks.

Balanced thighs and buttocks that are neither too large nor too small is one of the indications of self-confidence and security. Well-balanced people usually move easily and exhibit slightly rounded behinds. Their legs also look solid and are seldom excessively long. Such types indicate that they are thinkers who are adept at coping with crisis situations. They are not likely to be easily fazed by obstacles, and they attain success in many different professions.

Balanced Lower Body

When the lower body is properly balanced, and when there is sparse hair on the legs, it is a clear indication that this person is exceptionally talented and success should come to him or her easily, especially in the early thirties.

Rounded Thighs and Buttocks

Thighs and buttocks that are very rounded indicate individuals who are determined and who can be uncompromising in matters involving ethical issues. Such people tend to be well-off and enjoy a good financial status. They are seldom among the seriously rich, but they do lead respectable lives. There will, however, be a certain dogmatism in their attitudes, and this will tend to hold them back.

When their legs are short and solid, however, their intellectual integrity will often see them through tough situations in life.

Flat Buttocks, Slim Thighs

Flat buttocks and slim thighs are an indication of high intelligence and lofty value systems. These people are usually impractical and can be rather naive. Women with slim thighs are believed to lack the matriarchal life force and thus could have difficulty having children.

In terms of success potential, people with a small lower body tend to be very adaptable. They are flexible about their choice of career and can find success in any field. They are usually open-minded about transfers to different assignments and countries, and tend to be quite adventurous. Such people usually have long legs, so they find success as athletes, farmers, or industrialists. If their legs are bony, however, the lack of flesh indicates a non-realization of their goals.

Broad Thighs, Ample Buttocks

Broad thighs and ample buttocks, on the other hand, indicate a warm, romantic, and caring person. In a man, it indicates a certain egotism and a self-centered approach to life. In a woman, it manifests as the earth mother type. This woman may have many children and enjoy looking after her family. These types have a tendency toward being rather calculating, but in a nice way and often for the benefit of the other person, since they are generally quite pleasant individuals.

Success comes to people of this type when the legs are straight, taut, and strong. Then they are able to accumulate wealth and property. When the legs are short, they indicate strong intelligence of the mind so they tend to be more calculating and analytical. Longer legs indicate prowess in the more physical areas of life.

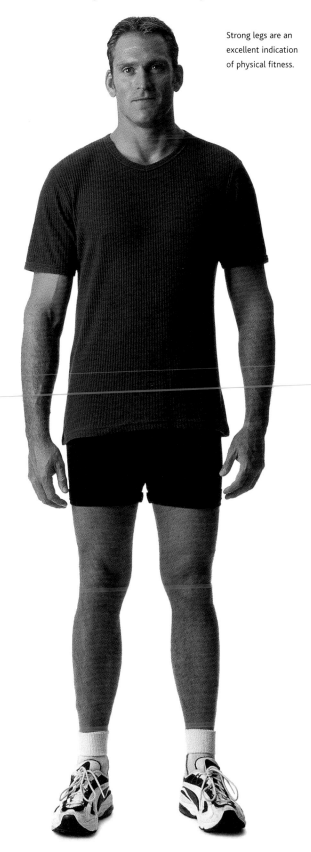

Strong legs are an excellent indication of physical fitness.

Auspicious Markings
on the Feet

The Chinese believe that secret markings on the feet are found only on exceptionally special people. These markings are usually auspicious and may resemble celestial creatures or other good-fortune symbols. Feet types also reveal much about people's quota of luck through their lives because much of the inner energies that sustain life have their seat in the soles of our feet.

Chinese Buddhists are ever mindful of the eight auspicious markings that were believed to have been found on the foot of the Buddha. When anyone is born with any of these lucky markings on the soles of their feet, they are believed to be extremely significant indications of great influence and power in later life. These auspicious images do not need to appear exactly as images. Often, merely a dark spot or a birthmark that suggests the objects is said to be an indication. Some of the auspicious markings on the feet are as follows.

These diagrams show some of the auspicious markings to be found on the feet. They are usually indicated as dark spots or birthmarks.

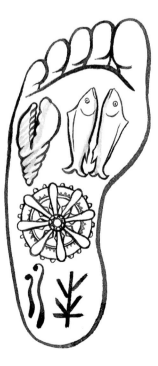
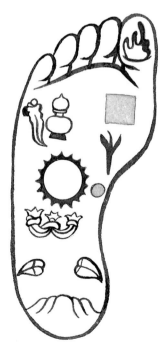

The Wheel

This can be with six, eight, or symbolically a thousand spokes. The wheel signifies someone of exceptional wisdom and nobility who will find recognition as a great philosopher and thinker. This shows up as a dark circle.

The Double Fish

This indicates abundance, wealth, and protection. Three lines form the mark of the fish. To be auspicious, there will be two such marks—a double fish marking. It is also auspicious on the hand.

The Conch

This is a sign of fame and popularity when found on the feet, and it indicates good fortune when traveling. It signifies someone close to the seat of power, wielding influence from behind the scenes. This shows up as an elongated shape.

The Trident

This is a mark of great career success indicating three types of luck—recognition, promotion, and money. On the feet, it suggests career success involving much travel. On the hand, it is also an indicator of career success, especially when found on the sun mount under the fourth finger.

An enlarged graphic representation of Buddha's feet, believed to have all the auspicious markings.

Three Cups

This sign is a divine version of the trident, usually found only on the feet of extremely special leaders or powerful people.

The Herb and Seeds

These are the signs of the healers. When markings on the feet look like herbs and seeds, it is an indication that the person has very special healing powers and would do well to work in the medical profession.

The Square

This is a mark of protection while traveling. A distinct mark is said to protect the person from all kinds of danger while outside the home.

Water

This is a sign of money luck. Several wavy lines on the feet are believed to indicate wealth flowing in from import and export businesses.

Fire

The fire sign symbolizes great fame and influence. Anyone with this marking on the feet will be extremely energetic and very powerful.

Tree

This indicates a person who is gifted with the ability to build empires. It also indicates a very good-hearted person. The tree looks like the trident except it has more branches.

The Vase

This indicates a life of great harmony and peace. As a mark on the feet, the vase also indicates wealth accumulation, which comes from all directions. This is a most auspicious sign indeed.

The Sun

This suggests an affluent and powerful life. Usually the sun sign is found on the soles of political and business leaders, kings, or great religious leaders. This shows up as a light circle.

MOLES ON THE FEET

Moles on the feet are an auspicious indication of authority and power. When the moles are light in color and protrude, they indicate a benevolent person of great compassion. When the mole is dark and black (whether protruding or not), it indicates a ruthless person.

The general appearance of the feet is also an indication of the person's attributes. Generally, the best kind of feet are always solid looking, never bony or thin and always well covered with flesh. Good-fortune feet are usually shapely and flexible and tend to be large, especially in a man. A short, fleshy big toe indicates good fortune.

The Chinese also believe that two other signs indicate a propensity toward prosperity. First, when there are numerous wrinkles on the heel, it indicates that the person will accumulate property and real estate. The second sign of success is when the feet have a high arch. This indicates upward mobility of the most special kind.

Ideally there should not be gaps between the toes, since this suggests money flowing outwards.

Character Clues from
Six Types of Hands

To the Chinese, the body extremities reveal much about the profile of our mind, body, and spirit. Thus, the outer appearance of hands, feet, and head is believed to reveal the essence of the inner consciousness and the destiny of the person. Chinese techniques of palm reading focus on the depth and color of hands as much as on their shape and lines.

Your hands communicate with your mind, body, and spirit all the time so the appearance, shape, lines, and markings on the palm offer remarkably accurate clues to your life's fortunes. Over time, the Chinese have developed guidelines and principles for analyzing the hands. They prefer fat, fleshy hands to thin, elongated, bony-looking hands. Dark-colored hands that suggest good circulation are preferred to light-colored hands. Thus you will notice that

To the Chinese, the hands reveal much about a person's life. The depth, color, shape, and lines of the hands are examined. In the same way as a rounded stomach is preferred, fleshy hands are more desirable.

wealthy Chinese matrons almost always have fat, fleshy hands, while beautiful second wives and mistresses usually possess long, elongated bony fingers. The Chinese divide hands into six types:

Medium-Sized Hands That Are Soft and Smooth with No Protruding Bones or Veins

These suggest an amiable, pleasant person who prefers a domesticated lifestyle to the glare of social climbing. A man with these hands is easily satisfied and not very ambitious. A woman with these hands will be gentle and caring and make a good wife and mother.

Medium-Sized Hands with Solid, Elastic Skin

These are also suggestive of a warm and caring person who will be popular among his peers and colleagues. This person is flexible and adaptable, and is career-minded although not very competitive. This type makes a good friend and can be counted upon to be loyal to his or her friends.

Dry-Looking Hands with Thin Fingers and Protruding Bones

These hands usually belong to a hard-working, self-reliant person who needs to put in a great deal of effort to achieve success. There is a tendency to be stubborn and dogmatic, and this can stand in the way of success. This type of person is usually uncommunicative and unhelpful, and possesses a certain coldness of attitude.

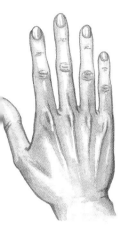

Large, Bony Hands with Gaps Between the Fingers

These are suggestive of people who are more physically inclined. They are generally mentally challenged people who work hard and long. Success and achievement will be in the fields of physical endeavor. People with hands like these tend not to save money. They will have financial concerns most of their life.

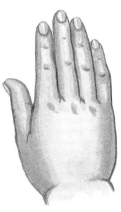

Big, Fat, Fleshy Hands That Are Soft, with Fingers Close Together, No Bones Showing

This type of hand usually belongs to highly affluent, successful, and creative people. They have attractive personalities and they enjoy good fortune. People with fat fingers, especially women, often enjoy a life of ease and experience great success in whatever they undertake.

Small, Thin Hands with Big Gaps in Between the Fingers

These are hands that belong to idealistic people who are rather unrealistic about life. It is hard to motivate them as they tend to float through life, often unable to stay long in one place or one job.

THE MEANINGS OF THE FINGERS

- *Flat-looking fingers usually suggest a life of hard work.*
- *Rounded fingers are considered an indication of intelligence.*
- *Fingers with bony joints are a sign of laziness and lack of success.*
- *Stiff fingers with hard nails indicate courage and a warrior's soul.*
- *Soft fingernails indicate a short life span, especially when the moon girdle is missing.*
- *Fingers of equal length and height indicate little chance of success.*
- *The thumb indicates one's parents luck. An upright thumb is most auspicious and beneficial as it suggests loving parents.*
- *The index finger governs power. When it is long and elegant, it indicates power and a long life. When short and fat, it suggests money but little influence. When damaged, it means serious illness.*
- *The middle finger is the dragon. This finger should be the longest for there to be good fortune and prosperity. When it is shorter than the palm, then luck is no more than mediocre.*
- *The ring finger should always be the shortest of the three central fingers. Otherwise there is a tendency toward vanity and weakness.*
- *The little finger indicates what happens in old age. A long little finger is a sign that old age is happy and abundant. A crooked little finger indicate sadness in old age.*

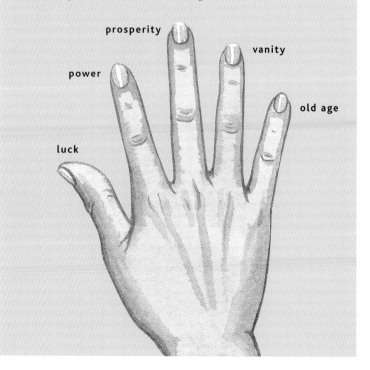

prosperity
vanity
power
old age
luck

Chinese Palmistry

In Chinese palmistry, fundamental signs on the hands—the palm palaces—are said to indicate good or bad fortune, and character. Specific rules for palm reading are passed on from grandmother to mother to daughter, and even today many people of Chinese origin, even those who are living outside China, are aware of these rules and can read palms.

When the three main lines of the hand—the heart, head, and life lines—are deep, clear, and have no interruptions it is a sign of a good life.

The principles that underlie hand analysis are related to the categorization of hands according to the five elements. All hands are classified according to the five elements—wood, fire, water, metal, and earth. The element of the hand should ideally "match" the element of one's physical shape. The way to determine the hand element that best describes you is to follow the three principal guidelines below and then look at the diagram of the eight trigrams, opposite, to make your analysis.

- First, a hand element that repeats your physical element is good.
- Second, a hand element that "produces your physical body element" is even better. A water hand would be great for a wood body; a wood hand would be great for a fire body; a fire hand would be excellent for an earth body; an earth hand is great for a metal body; and a metal hand is good for a water body.

These conclusions are based on the circular reproductive cycle of the five elements. In the same way, of course, you should also watch out for hands whose element clashes with the body element.

- Square palms with matching fingers belong to the metal element.
- Slender palms with long elegant fingers belong to the wood element.
- Round, fleshy palms with round fingers belong to the water element.
- Elongated palms with pointed fingers belong to the fire element.
- Thick, heavy palms with similar fingers belong to the earth element.

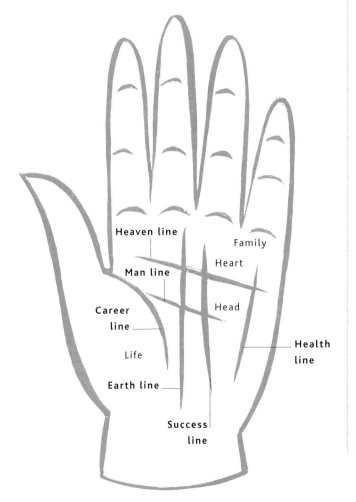

Heaven line

Family

Heart

Man line

Head

Career line

Life

Health line

Earth line

Success line

Palm Reading

The eight trigrams of the Pa Kua (derived from the *I Ching*) are superimposed onto the palm of the hand, offering clues to good and bad luck in different dimensions of one's life. This is indicated by the governing trigram in the different parts of the hand. When all eight trigrams show well-formed "mounts"—i.e., when you can "see" the appearance of raised flesh in these eight corners of the palm—it is a sure sign of high office and prosperity. You will have plenty of people working for you, and your life will be filled with power and influence.

Ming Tang

When the courtyard, or Ming Tang, looks bright and healthy, it suggests a good life filled with happy events—this is generally interpreted to mean many healthy and strong sons in the family.

Chien

When the place of the trigram Chien has a pronounced mount, it means that you will head a family whose fortunes will be good for five generations at least. You will benefit enormously from powerful friends and benefactors.

Kun

When the place of the Kun trigram has a pronounced mount, it suggests extreme good fortune for you if you are a woman. Kun is the trigram of the maternal, and earth is its element. It also signifies excellent marriage luck. If there is any positive marking here, such as the fish or the trident, the good luck is multiplied three times.

Li

When the place of the Li trigram is pronounced, raised, or has auspicious markings, it indicates great fame and recognition. This is also the mount of the dragon finger, so it is especially powerful.

Kan

When the mount in the Kan trigram is pronounced, it indicates that your family will be of great help to you, and you will enjoy tremendous good fortune in your work. Positive markings here, such as the fish sign, are especially auspicious and mean that your life improves as you grow older.

Ken

The trigram Ken refers to your relationship with siblings and your earlier life. When this mount is well pronounced, it suggests a very good start in life. Whether or not this early promise can be realized in your life will depend on the other markings found on the palm.

Below: Note how the hand is segmented here. The center is the courtyard, which is similar to the life palace of the face. The area in the center of the palm should always look bright and healthy.

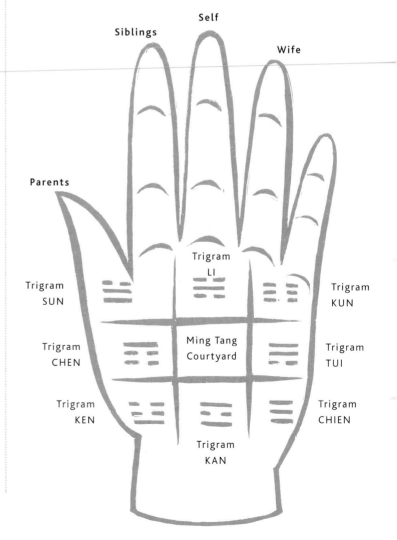

Self

Siblings

Wife

Parents

Trigram SUN

Trigram LI

Trigram KUN

Trigram CHEN

Ming Tang Courtyard

Trigram TUI

Trigram KEN

Trigram CHIEN

Trigram KAN

Part Three

DISCOVERING
YOUR SPIRIT

As we enter into the realm of the spiritual, of the inner levels of consciousness, and of the higher self, we reach out for psychic gifts and the God presence within us. The emphasis of our discovery journey now moves into the invisible spheres of cosmic energy fields that lie within us.

We investigate our chakra centers and examine the core of our psychic channels. These focal points of energy determine our higher and often hidden agendas at different stages of our life, and these agendas usually lie dormant within until they are awakened. When they do awaken, our interest in the spiritual higher self begins to stir.

When you energize the chakra axis of your intangible inner consciousness, you will be taking a quantum leap from physics to metaphysics, and you will begin to experience the full bliss of spiritual awakening.

Tuning Inwards

All the ancient wisdoms and spiritual traditions of the world place emphasis on the subtle life force that pervades the existence of human beings—an all-encompassing energy presence that resides deep inside us. The presence of this force affects every aspect and dimension of our life. It is called the spiritual essence of the self, and by tuning inwards, we can begin to connect with it.

Fu Hsi, the legendary emperor of China, said to be the founder of the Book of Changes known as the *I Ching*.

From journeying around the body, we now tune inwards to connect with the spiritual side of oneself. Think of your spirit as an invisible life force composed entirely of energy—without form or substance. This is the powerful wisdom source of your spirit, that which nourishes your body and your mind. When we knowingly tune inwards, the connection between body and spirit becomes something significant, marking something of a milestone in our spiritual awakening.

It is this awakening that accelerates the flow of energy and that fuses the chi of heaven, earth, and humankind. This is what the Chinese refer to as tien, ti, and ren—heaven, earth, and humankind. Many other spiritual traditions also describe this merging of body, mind, and spirit.

The Flow of Light

The manifestation of the life force (chi) is often defined as a flow of light. Thus, when the spiritual side of us is successfully engaged, we have access to the ability to manifest, or at least to cause into existence, the glory of light.

Ancient Chinese sages defined the universal spirit as a flow, a vibration, a movement that gives expression to the yang, and which eventually leads to the 5 elements, the 6 energies, the 8 trigrams, the 64 hexagrams, and ultimately to the 10,000 things. Lao Tzu expressed his philosophy in terms of the natural order, which brings harmony.

Within the human individual's body, there is yang movement going on all the time. Thus, when life courses through the heart and the blood

> To many spiritual traditions and even religions, light is the expression of the divine presence.

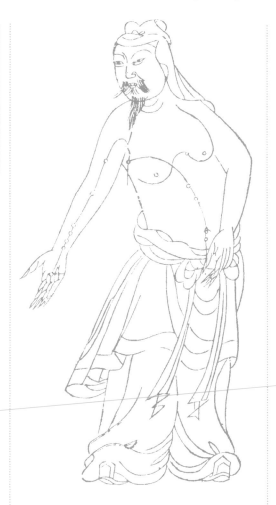

Traditional Chinese medicine believes energy lines, called meridians, flow through the human body directing chi.

vessels, streaming through the body, there is movement, and therefore there is also inner yang spirit energy. The vital points of the body stay connected via the meridians.

Inner and Outer Vibrations

When we vibrate in harmony with the environment, our bodies, minds, and spirits dance in rhythm with the energy around us. When discord sets in, the dance is finished and disharmony creeps in.

When we tune inwards, we generate acute sensitivity to these inner and outer vibrations. We begin to systematically tune in to these vibrations. Our mind and body develop new auditory sensitivities. Before long, these vibrations are "heard" with increasing clarity. Soon we realize that we vibrate differently with different people.

This inner wisdom tells us who and what excites us and makes us happy. It communicates by the way we resonate and manifest outward responses. When you become sensitive to your internal vibrations, you will instinctively respond in tune with them. Awareness is developed by making a conscious effort to focus the mind inwards to access the spiritual self.

The Inner Chi

Accessing the spiritual self involves a reaching inwards for the energy source within. It is a spectacularly sacred adventure. There are seven high-energy vortexes within the human body. Tuning

inwards through each and all of these seven centers of high energy, also thought of as doorways, has been acknowledged as among the best methods to open doorways into the spiritual self. Centralized chi centers, or chakra centers, are located along the central meridian of the body. We will refer to these seven spiritual gateways as the chakra centers of the human body.

All the wise men of antiquity refer to these seven pathways: Judaism refers to the seven heavens in the tiers of the Kabbalah; Christianity speaks of the seven sacraments; while Hinduism and Buddhism refer to the seven chakras. Moving from one chakra to the next brings you from one level sof spiritual consciousness to the next. It has been described as a transcendental experience.

Lighting Up the Chakras

The path of self-transformation involves a rite of passage that puts us in touch with our higher spiritual self. The ascent starts from the ground and proceeds upwards along the central meridian of the body. Thus, spiritual awareness begins from the base chakra at the feet, which makes contact with the earth energy, and moves along the body to the crown chakra at the top of the head.

A good way to learn visualization is by staring at a picture you want to remember, then closing your eyes and trying to recall it.

Lighting up the chakras does not imply floating in a dream world completely divorced from reality and ignoring the very real presence of the body and the mind. The first conceptual understanding is that spiritual awakening rarely occurs independently of the two other components of the self. In fact, this

Lighting up the chakras is a powerful way of opening yourself to spiritual realizations. Some call this accessing the wisdom of the higher self.

awakening is a coming together of the three aspects of the self so that the sum of the three parts takes on deeper meanings.

Second, lighting up the chakras implies a knowledge of mental imaging, the ability to close your eyes and create pictures in your mind—what is popularly known as mental visualization. This is because lighting up your chakras is a mental exercise. Everything is done in the mind. It is a directing of the mind to begin the process of lighting up the chakras. Not everyone is able to create images in the mind, let alone create these images with concentration and power. Those who are unfamiliar with the technique of creating pictures in the mind might want to spend some time practicing visualization.

ARE YOU A BASE CHAKRA PERSON?

When you are young, ambitious, and eager to conquer the world, try every new thing—break hearts, make a million dollars, sail to the ends of the earth, climb Mount Everest—it is the needs of the lower chakras that must be satisfied. It is only after the base chakras are sated that we start to question the meaning of life, the reason for our existence, the higher purpose that makes us what we are. This is probably why most people seek out their spiritual depth and focus on their higher chakras only when they have reached a certain level of success.

Take your time. Turn to the spiritual only when you are ready to do so. The higher self knows when you are ready and when you are not. It knows when the journey in search of your spiritual essence will yield results and when it will not.

Creative Visualization

Different people create mental pictures in different ways. There are no hard and fast rules, and it is true to say that every method works and there is no such thing as a right or wrong method. There is also no such thing as one method being better than another method. Another name for mental imaging is creative visualization. It is a technique that stresses the power of the mind and uses this power to create positive states of mind—exercising this positivity in areas from self-image to external situations or in relationships with other people.

In the past ten years, there have been some stunningly wonderful books written about the powerful technique of visualization. My personal favorite has always been Shakti Gawain's *Creative Visualization*. In the years since I first discovered this awesome little book, I have met up with highly realized spiritual masters from whom I have learned refinements of the methods of visualization. The most powerful meditators who use visualization are the Buddhist high lamas of the Mahayana tradition. These masters of the mind have an amazing capacity and ability to use their mind in ways that surpass my own feeble capabilities, but what little I have learned from my own spiritual guru has been so amazing that I have no doubts at all in my head about the power of visualization.

MENTAL IMAGING

There are a couple of easy methods you can use to practice visualization techniques. Think of mental imaging as simply remembering pictures you have seen. Stare at pictures you wish to remember and then close your eyes and make your mind bring the picture forward in front of you. I have discovered this to be the easiest way to learn visualization. Practice this until you develop an easy facility with the creation of mental pictures.

A second way of developing mental visualization skills is to watch a television series and then think of the moving images in your mind. Once again it is a matter of remembering images. You will find that the process of recall is easier when you are relaxed. The mind functions a great deal more efficiently when it is not under pressure, so take a few deep breaths to slow down your breathing before sitting down to do some visualization exercises.

LIGHTING UP YOUR CHAKRAS

Once you have developed an easy facility with the process of mental imaging, set aside a quiet time of the day to access your spiritual essence using this method. Dressed in loose clothing, sit quietly in a room where you will not be disturbed. Make sure you are comfortable. Close your eyes and breathe deeply for a few moments. Concentrate on stilling your mind. Then, when your breathing has attained a gentle rhythm, imagine yourself standing relaxed on solid ground on a high mountain. You can feel the earth beneath your feet, the air around you, and the sky above you. The sky is cloudless and very blue. The sun is shining gently, sending rays of yang energy into your body.

The First Chakra

Think of the seven chakra points on your body. Starting from the first or base chakra at the bottom of the spine, imagine a bright white light suddenly turned on there. Develop a warm sensation. Think thoughts of wholeness, and feel the nurturing energy of the ground under your feet.

The base chakra represents the material dimensions of your needs and is the beginning point of your awareness of yourself as an integration of mind, body, and spirit. It has both a positive and a negative expression, so think positive thoughts of purity, hope, perfection, and wholeness as you light it up.

The Second Chakra

Move to the second chakra. This chakra governs all the organs and systems in the body that deal with reproduction and the elimination of wastes. As you focus on this point, mentally turn on the light switch and light it up. Visualize the bright white light emanating powerful rays outwards.

The Third Chakra

Now move to the third chakra. This is the chakra of the solar plexus, and it focuses on the material needs associated with food. Once again, use your mind to light up your belly so that bright white light radiates outwards.

The Fourth Chakra

The fourth chakra is positioned at the heart. Here we enter the realm of our spiritual inner essence. We should turn on the heart chakra with a positive attitude. The heart energy centers on love, compassion, and selflessness. Visualize your heart filled with light as all darkness ceases to exist.

The Fifth Chakra

The fifth chakra is the throat chakra, and as you visualize it being turned on, generate an intense motivation to make your life meaningful. The throat chakra brings courage and determination

The positioning of the seven chakras. The seventh chakra is located at the crown of your head.

to your spiritual awakening. Visualize your throat completely lit up with light rays radiating outwards in all the ten directions.

The Sixth Chakra

The sixth chakra is located between the eyebrows. It is often known as the third eye and is connected to imagination, clarity of thought, intuition, and dreams. As you tune in to that spot between your brows, visualize a bright violet light suddenly lighting up your face.

The Seventh Chakra

Finally, turn your attention to the seventh chakra. It is the most vital pathway of all, for it is through this crown chakra that heaven and other divine energies enter our being. Visualize this chakra all lit up, creating a halo of light around your head.

Now all seven energy centers of your body are lit up with radiant white light. Visualize them linking like a strand of bright lights. Hold the picture of your lighted chakras for eight minutes if you can. Do not suddenly open your eyes. Instead, move from the crown chakra downwards, and turn off the light one chakra at a time. Visualize your chakras closing. Take a deep breath and open your eyes. You should feel refreshed and energized.

Sit in a quiet room wearing comfortable clothing and allow time for your thoughts to settle and calm before attempting visualization.

The visualization described on these pages is the foundation visualization for activating the chakras. It is advisable to practice with this basic process first before going further.

Always remember to turn out the lights and mentally close your chakras when you finish. This ensures that you do not inadvertently leave them open and vulnerable to the "winds." Taoist masters always warn that when you undertake meditations that involve visualization exercises, it is important to remember to retrace your steps before getting up from your seat or reopening your eyes.

Below is a chart showing the different attributes that are generally associated with each of the seven chakras. Use this table to fine-tune your daily visualization exercises.

UNDERSTANDING THE CHAKRAS

CHAKRA	7 CROWN	6 THIRD EYE	5 THROAT	4 HEART	3 SOLAR PLEXUS	2 SACRAL	1 BASE
PLACE	Top of the head	Between eyebrows	Throat	Chest	Stomach	Genitals	Base of spine
COLOR	White	Emerald green	Red	Blue	Purple	Violet	Yellow
LOTUS PETALS	972	96	16	12	10	6	4
MANTRA	OM	–	AH	HUM	SO	–	HA
GEMSTONE	Diamond	Emerald Diamond	Ruby Diamond	Sapphire Diamond	Topaz Diamond	Amethyst Diamond	Quartz crystal Diamond

Tapping in to Your Spiritual Chi

When the chi of your eyes is bright, your vision is clear,

When the chi of your ears is robust, your hearing is sharp,

When the chi of your mouth is strong, your speech is enticing,

When the chi of your mind is dazzling, your thinking penetrates the ten

directions and transcends into the higher realms.

The flow of chi should move like a meandering river of light through the chakras of your body, transcending mind, body, and spirit in a positive cycle. When the flow of chi is forced to a stop, it stagnates, and like a room deprived of fresh air, creates the conditions for disease and depression.

Spiritual chi is, thus, a precious commodity. We need to constantly replenish, feed, and empower it. This happens only when we tap in to it. It is the regular use of this higher energy within us that causes more of it to be created. Make it a daily habit to tune inwards so that your spiritual chi

To replenish your spiritual chi, learn to appreciate the natural world around you. Visit beautiful places that will uplift your spirit.

communicates with your mind at a conscious level. To be successful in tapping in to your spiritual chi, you must also nurture it. Feed the spirit within you by opening your eyes to the beauty of the world around you.

- Expose yourself to creativity—music, art, scenery, scents, clean air. Let your spirit absorb all that is beautiful in the physical world. Consciously visualize tapping into the auras and spirits of these beautiful things.

- Make a conscious effort to avoid spiritually unhealthy environments. Seek out people who

bring out the good in you, nurture your spirit, and open spiritual pathways for you.

- Avoid depressed and gloomy people, and most important, avoid people who feed on your chi and leave you drained each time you meet with them. When you go to crowded places such as shopping malls and football games, be prepared to feel drained. One way to prevent your energy or chi from being drained is to seal your chakras (see below).

Cleansing your Aura

In the evenings, and even late at night, create a visualization in your mind to ensure that while you are sleeping, none of your vitality can be taken from you. An easy method is to go to sleep with a glass of water mixed with rock salt next to you (sea salt is one form of rock salt). It will make you sleep well and will cleanse your aura of all the negative vibrations picked up during the day.

You can use pure sea salt to actually cleanse your aura. Place about four to eight ounces of rock salt into a bowl and dip both of your hands into it. Rub both hands vigorously in the salt until your palms tingle with the power of the sea crystals. Then, place the palms of your hands together above your head as if cradling it with your arms, with the inside of your palms about one inch above your head. Bring your palms down the body as if stroking it, moving from the top of the head down to the feet. As you do this, feel that you are brushing away all the negative vibrations that have somehow gotten stuck to your aura. Do this three times for the left and right sides, and then three times in front and three times at the back.

Shake your hands a few times in a flinging gesture to ensure that all vestiges of negativities are shaken off. Finally, wash your hands in salt, and then in soap, to cleanse your hands symbolically. Try this practice for a week and see how you feel.

To cleanse your aura, place a glass of water mixed with rock salt by your bed at night while you sleep, or rub pure sea salt into your hands and brush away all the negative vibrations.

SEALING YOUR CHAKRAS

Each morning when you awaken, spend a few moments centering yourself by breathing deeply before getting up. Stretch yourself like a cat and feel all the muscles of your body expand and then relax. Then, while still lying down, tune in to your seven chakras. Think of your chakras as orbs of light, pulsating with vitality and energy along the central vertical axis of your body. If you have time, pause at each chakra center for a few moments and imagine the center as an orb of intense white light. Then imagine millions of the tiniest strands of light emanating outwards to all parts of the body. Think that the light from your chakras is sending fresh, vital energy into your protective auras so that now you imagine yourself pulsating as a light-filled body.

Then specifically tune in to the crown chakra at the top of your head and visualize a white sun disk very bright above your chakra. Gently position this sun disk on top of your head, effectively creating an invisible force field. Next focus on your base chakra and, visualizing a white sun disk, position it to cover the base chakra.

Now visualize an invisible force field surrounding your whole body. Think "Nothing negative will be able to penetrate the force field I have created around my body."

Stay a few moments with this image in your mind before slowly opening your eyes and coming out of your visualization. Now you know the most basic secret of life: "Think, and it shall be so."

Opening Your Third Eye

The third eye is the key to inner and divine vision. It truly gives us the ability to understand the nature of reality and existence that is present in all of us. It is the third eye that communicates the visual manifestations of the highest realms of our highest mind, and opening it up leads to flashes of insight, clairvoyance, genius, and ultimate creativity.

Physically, the third eye is located on the forehead on the central axis between the eyebrows. Some say it is the "God spot" within the brain, and that when we succeed in "opening" it, we will be gifted with the insight to pierce the inner nature of every situation, every event, and every person. The third eye is a vertical eye, so it is unlike the two horizontal eyes we all see the world with. Different methods of opening the third eye range from concentrated meditation to symbolic rubbing. When the third eye opens, it does so very slowly, bringing great clarity of thought.

The third eye is located on the forehead on the central axis between the eyebrows.

❝ *I now rub my forehead out of habit. Each time I am stumped and feel the need for some divine guidance, even without thinking, I rub my third eye, probably in an unconscious act of communication with my highest self. I would hardly say that my third eye is completely open, but I am convinced that the conscious intention of wanting it to open has itself opened large pathways for me to enter into another dimension of existence. There is little doubt that my perception and perspective of everything has become clearer and definitely more focused. Through the third eye, I feel I have developed a meaningful blueprint for living life at a higher level of consciousness.*

❝ *I have also, since those early experimental days, come a fairly long way, simply because the thought consciousness that I send into the Cosmos through my daily meditative visualizations has certainly manifested stunning new inroads into a whole variety of spiritual dimensions that have left me rather breathless. It is as if I attract all the right people into my life now, people whose knowledge of other worlds and other dimensions of existence has obviously been accessed through their own insights gleaned through their third eyes. And so I am given many opportunities to learn and to understand. There are definitely other worlds out there of which we are, as yet, unaware.* 🙶

- Never dismiss the ideas that pop into your head seemingly from nowhere. They could be the start of something important.

- Never allow anyone to burst your bubble— follow through on your ideas no matter how silly they may seem to be. The early stages of any idea always seem silly.

- Never allow anyone to criticize your work until you have finished it. So-called well-meaning criticisms will reduce your work to nothing because they cannot see into your creative genius. Only *you* can, so keep working until all your ideas have poured forth.

- Never analyze an unusual idea until you have thought through the whole idea. Do not allow your lower mind to use intellect to override half-formed ideas of the creative mind.

- Trust your own instinct in every situation. When you meet someone whom you do not trust, even though there is no reason, follow that instinct. Alternatively, should you feel drawn to a person or to a place, then spend time with them or make that journey—you will benefit.

> There are no limits to what we can achieve, or to our ambitions. There are simply no limits to our life.

BUDDHAS WITH MANY EYES

It is possible that we have more than a third eye. One of the most beautiful Buddhas is called the Mother White Tara, and she is one of the goddesses of long life. She grants the blessings of good health and longevity. White Tara has seven eyes—three on her face, including the third eye, two on the inside palms of her hands, and two on the soles of her feet. One way of opening your third eye is to meditate on the image of the White Tara. In the illustration shown here, look closely at the third eye high in the center of her forehead.

Another Buddha is the thousand-armed manifestation of the Buddha of Compassion, known to the Chinese as the goddess of mercy, Kuan Yin. This manifestation of the goddess has a thousand eyes.

The Buddhists believe that by gazing at images of their favorite Buddhas and then visualizing them in their meditative practice as they chant their mantras and make their prostrations, they can create powerful pathways toward gaining wisdom realizations, one of which is the symbolic opening of the third eye. It is from these spiritual practices that the compassionate heart arises simultaneously with the wisdom of the higher self. Then the full grandeur of the mind combines naturally with the inner sense of the divine.

It is then that imagination becomes a conduit for the Holy Spirit to convey creative insights into our life. Intelligence as we know it at the mundane levels then becomes quite an infinite thing.

Signs of Personal Awakenings

How does the urge to become more spiritual begin? Are there needs that make themselves felt in the way we respond to events and people? Does the need for spiritual nurturing come to us in a flash of insight accompanied by a feeling of urgency? Or is personal awakening something that creeps up on a person, slowly growing to emerge into full bloom when signs of awakening appear?

A statue of the Buddha, who became enlightened and taught that spiritual awakening can be achieved in many different ways.

Perhaps you are ill and in pain. Someone suggests you surround your head and body in a golden healing glow of yellow light. So you close your eyes as you lie on your bed and you think first of your head, and then your body surrounded by a halo of golden-yellow radiance from which strands of shimmering light radiate outwards in all the ten directions. The rays then radiate back again with healing energy from the Cosmos. When you open your eyes, you feel better and the pain

has subsided. The next evening, you do this visualization again and once more you feel better. In your case, the illness triggers a transformation, and your small success leads you to search further.

> So trust your highest self and
>
> be your own highest guide.

Perhaps you are heartbroken and feeling helpless and alone. You sit by the window staring vacantly into the fields beyond, thinking random thoughts that make you feel like crying. You think of all the times when your partner had left signs that he or she had stopped caring, only you were too blind to see. You remember someone having once told you that the best way to repair a broken heart is to visualize a bright dazzling white light in the center of your heart. The light gently soothes you, and slowly it turns into light-blue light and you feel washed over with the healing rays of this blue light. The light is growing in intensity, and the blue gets deeper and deeper until it becomes the color of lapis lazuli and you are warmed by it. Eventually you feel so relaxed that you lie down and sleep like a baby. The next morning you awake, and the pain of heartbreak seems to have lessened. You close your eyes and invite the light into your heart once again. There is something inside you so strong that it has the power to transform negative feelings into positive ones.

Moments of awakening are almost always triggered by a small crisis. Random thoughts that crystallize from some experience could be telling you something you need to know. When you are ready, these insights will send you signals of an impending awakening to an awareness of another aspect of yourself. Every situation, every heartbreak, can teach us about ourselves.

SIGNS OF SPIRITUAL AWAKENING

When the signs of awakening begin to be attracted to your aura, you will discover that many things you were once ignorant or skeptical of now come to you like rain falling from heaven. For some, the signs of awakening may express themselves in the books they start to read, the programs they start to watch on television, or the spiritual friends they feel attracted to. Spiritual awakening comes in a million different ways. The Buddha taught 84,000 ways to attain enlightenment.

A falling leaf can set you thinking. Lying in the sunshine, sitting by a beach, climbing a mountain, cooking a meal, praying in a church, sitting in a puja, visiting holy places—anything and everything contains the spark of the divine waiting to ripen and to miraculously unfold in the presence of the person with the right affinity, the same frequency. Mine often come in the form of dreams.

It is important to stay open to the signs when they do come, but it is not necessary to rush into anything that seems spiritual. Do not be too eager to let someone else take charge of your spirit, and be wary of symbolically embracing every holy man that comes along.

- *There are simple, basic guidelines you can follow. True spirituality always creates loving energy. It is always positive and never negative. It never advocates violence or killing for whatever reason and it values life and living as the most precious things we have.*
- *Genuine spiritual masters never tell you, directly or indirectly, explicitly or implicitly, how special they are, how much "magic" they can perform, how they can save your soul, or how they can cure you. In short, they never make any claims to their own spirituality, let alone their divinity. You simply know.*

Contacting Your Higher Self

Your higher self can shine like the sun and glow like the moon. It can flow through an avalanche of wisdom—if only you know it. When you consciously access this wisdom that resides within you, all of your needs, desires, and wants will become clearer and better defined. For then you will be connecting with your inner higher self. You discover that all you need is already within you.

The higher self is your own good luck. It is the source of your confidence and belief in yourself. When you go within, you discover a persona inside who is always ready to be your friend, always on your side, and who understands you. Your doubts are given a hearing. Your fears are assuaged and your misgivings calmed. The higher self is an utterly magical dimension of your spirit. It can roar like a tiger and charge like an elephant—and it can be as gentle as an angel.

GIVE YOUR BODY AN OXYGEN BATH

To contact your higher self you need to develop a familiarity with the techniques of meditation and visualization. It is also advisable symbolically to cleanse the body of negatives. Prior to tuning inwards, go out into a garden or park and give yourself an oxygen bath.

In a relaxed standing position, gently take at least 20 gulps of air to oxygenate your body. Breathe in through your nostrils, using your diaphragm to take the breath right down into your stomach. Feel your abdomen expanding like a balloon. Then hold the breath gently. Now release it slowly and steadily through your mouth, starting at your abdomen, through your chest, and finally the last bit of air at the clavicle.

One powerful formula of yogic breathing is the 1-3-2 breathing formula, recommended by many sports coaches and fitness trainers. This formula is simple but very effective:

Breathe in to a count that you are comfortable with, for instance, say you start with a count of six.

So breathe in to a count of six, then hold the breath in the abdomen to a count of 3x6 = 18, and then breathe out to a count of 2x6 = 12. Repeat this in-breath, hold, out-breath for about 20 minutes. Make sure you breathe deeply and that you are in a place where there is fresh, clean air.

This oxygenating of your inner body has the effect of settling you and relaxing your muscles. Tension gets removed from the body when we take deep diaphragm breaths, so go outside and fill your insides with oxygen. Concentrate on the out-breath, as this is when the lymphatic nodes within you become energized. As you breathe out, you will feel yourself unwinding, and you should visualize all negativities, toxins, and doubts disappearing.

MEDITATIVE VISUALIZATION

Make yourself comfortable, anywhere you will not be disturbed. Take a few moments to compose yourself. Breathe gently and then close your eyes. Let your mind take you deep within yourself. Allow your mind to wander for a while.

Picture yourself going for a walk. Let your mind create the scenery and the time of day and year. How these mental manifestations of your higher self appear comes directly from your mind. Here are some visualizations that you might find useful while going for your mentally created walk—try practicing them.

As you round the bend of the footpath, you see before you a beautiful lake. The lake is crystal clear and the water is cool. Now as you gaze into the waters of the lake, you begin to see yourself reflected; and in the reflection in the water you watch, fascinated, as your higher self literally steps from your body, leaves it, and stays behind you, reflected in the lake.

As you walk, you begin to tire a little and want to take a rest. You decide to stop under a large tree whose spreading branches provide a cool shade. Soon you feel yourself dozing off, and slowly you become conscious of someone next to you. When you open your eyes, you are staring at your higher self. This higher self can be an older person you respect, such as your dad, your best friend, or your hero.

There are a thousand pathways that lead to the higher self, and you can choose a visualization that suits you. Connecting with the higher self requires a leap of faith that leads you into the magical realms of the spiritual inside you. In the beginning, you might be somewhat tentative, but if you let yourself go with the flow of your inner chi, what initially seemed farfetched and strange soon becomes so familiar that you wonder how you ever lived without the full involvement of your spiritual inner self.

The best place to give yourself an oxygen bath is outdoors in a garden or in a park, where the air is clean and fresh.

Learning to Meditate

The mind is like an ocean, forever at the mercy of shifting winds and swirling currents. Until the waves of idle thoughts subside, it is impossible to achieve the intuitive perception of inner spiritual wisdom that lies within. To subdue the swirling chaos that fills the mind, we need to engender calmness, a stillness. This can be achieved by practicing meditation.

Sitting

The meditation posture, cushion, and garments apply equally to all the contemplative traditions such as yoga, Taoist practices, and Buddhist meditation techniques. Religious meditations, however, tend to last longer, and the full lotus posture of the Buddhist yogics are excellent, but for the general practitioner, sitting in the lotus posture can prove to be quite a challenge. So sit in any position that makes you comfortable.

Breathing

Breathing techniques help induce a certain one-pointedness of mind. They also raise the internal energy of the body. The simplest methods favor the gentle spacing of in-breaths and out-breaths. Here the mind focuses on the breath as it moves in and out of the nostrils. The concentration helps the practitioner to quiet the mind.

For beginners, it is useful to add counting to the in-breath and out-breath. The need to keep counting prevents the mind from straying. Another way is to silently mouth the words "in" and "out" as the breath moves in and out. This is effective for preventing mental distraction. Breathing to your own unique rhythm is a very simple way of letting go of emotional blocks and other unsettling emotions. Use it to slow down the onset of anger

Drink strong Chinese tea to ensure you remain alert during meditation.

TEA

To ensure you do not fall asleep during meditation, drink strong tea before you start. The best tea to drink for meditation is Tit Koon Yam or the Iron Kuan Yin tea, available in Chinese supermarkets. These are named after the goddess of mercy. The tea is very strong, and you should get the best quality you can afford. Do not serve tea from an elaborately patterned teacup. Use a simple cup and teapot for this purpose. It is a good idea to brew the tea in advance and to keep it hot by putting the pot inside a thickly quilted basket specially made for this purpose. If your meditation sessions are long, have this tea set up conveniently nearby. Do not drink this tea at night as it will keep you alert and awake.

and frustration or to delay any quick reactions to surprises and difficult people.

Since true wisdom arises from a patient mind, this kind of sustained, mindful breathing takes you from stillness to spirituality and beyond. Try to lengthen your breath as you get better at your breathing. Remember that deep breathing that is evenly balanced holds the key to many wondrous experiences. At all times, you should remain very silent and tuned inwards.

Techniques that are more evolved than this and that go beyond simple breath-watching and breath control can be dangerous for the beginner who is not under the protection and guidance of a qualified master. My strong advice is to keep practicing your deep awareness breathing, and consciously visualize yourself meeting a fully qualified master.

Stillness

The purpose of working toward the creation of a quiet mind that is as motionless as the surface of the sea on a windless night is that the ordinary mind is an ocean of shifting currents and many winds. Perception of intuitive wisdom cannot possibly arise unless the waves subside and the thoughts can be brought under firm control.

An excellent way to still the mind is to focus on one object. This may be a physical object, a picture, an image, or a light. This also expands visualization capabilities, which will be useful for more advanced work later. Another way is to use mantras, which engage the sense of sound instead of sight—auditory perceptions often work faster at reaching the subconscious than visual perceptions.

Think of a bright lamp on a dark night casting its light on a vast expanse of desert. Feel the surrounding emptiness, and think of the warm comfort you get from the lamp. Focus on it with single-pointed concentration for some moments.

When you do this enough times, there soon comes that magical moment when awareness becomes nearly objectless. That is when the benefits of stillness blossom into intuitive wisdom.

Visions may occur that could engage your senses in either a positive or negative way. These experiences can develop into major distractions, so gently push them out of your mind. Concentrate on attaining the unwavering contemplation of the single object or phenomenon. Stillness opens the mind to the mysterious, which in turn leads you to a state of spiritual wisdom and enlightenment.

Stillness is achieved when the mind is able to cease thinking. It is not the result of trying—it just happens.

The Grounding Cord
and the Astral Cocoon

Our inner spiritual chi, which comes from the mind and spirit, is the core of our being. When we access it through inner focus and meditation, we are opening our chi to the Cosmos. We have powerful spirit guides and guardian angels that watch over our inner essence when we are meditating, but we should also protect ourselves with the grounding cord and the astral cocoon.

Advanced meditation masters always create a strong protective white light around the room where they conduct their meditation classes and sessions. This ensures that their sessions are not inadvertently disturbed by powerful manifestations from another dimension, or by wandering spirits who are attracted to the charged auric fields emanated by meditative thoughts.

Meditation often takes us into another dimension of existence where the mind's thoughts can often be so powerfully projected that they can

Meditating inside an astral cocoon ensures that your spirit is protected.

materialize as real physical entities. By preceding all your meditation sessions with visualizations of the grounding cord and the astral cocoon, you will ensure that while your spirit travels into the inner dimensions of your mind, the cord and the cocoon will protect your spirit from being affected, influenced, or stolen by unknown external forces. Remember that setting fixed ideas of what you will experience will impede your spiritual journey. Think of your spiritual meditations as journeys that have no known ending. Look on meditation merely as a

THE ASTRAL COCOON

Before focusing inwards, close your eyes gently and imagine an intense blue light at the center of your heart. As you concentrate on this blue light feel it slowly expanding outwards in the shape of an egg. Think of the blue light slowly getting larger and larger until eventually it completely surrounds your whole body. Every

part of you is inside this cocoon of intense blue light. Remember to breathe normally.

The blue light makes you invisible to everything outside of it. Once the cocoon of light is firmly established in your mind, slowly watch the blue light become white, transparent light. Now the cocoon has transformed into an invisible barrier and you are protected by it.

You are now ready to undertake all your meditations. When you have finished, slowly unwind the cocoon by imagining the light turning blue again. The blue light then absorbs slowly back into your heart, getting smaller and smaller until it is finally completely absorbed.

way of opening up the spiritual within the mind so that it brings a sense of clarity and power to the act of thinking. This is how we become more clear sighted, and certainly more empowered.

It is essential to guard against expectations of being "blissed-out" from the practice of spiritual meditation. Do not expect a sudden major revelation, it can take many weeks, even months, of practice before you begin to feel the cumulative effect of meditation. Be calm and cool toward any passing physical sensations, such as a tingling of the feet, a sudden perspiring sensation, shivering or trembling. Some people also experience "seeing" fearsome monsters in their minds—all these are passing experiences that can be ignored. The monsters are only representations of your own fears and worries—they cannot harm you and will soon pass. Stay detached and tell yourself that everything is manufactured by the mind, and it is only the mind that gives hallucinations their reality. Put your safeguards into place, and then let your mind take you where it will.

When you begin to practice meditation, do not expect major revelations, but be prepared for whatever may come. Even if you have negative visions, stay calm and they will gradually become harmless.

THE GROUNDING CORD

Before tuning inwards, light up your chakras and then focus on the base chakra. Close your eyes lightly and imagine a powerful tube of bright white light emanating from this base chakra then penetrating into the ground and going deep into the earth. Feel that it is your grounding cord, which keeps you anchored and centered. Turn your attention to the powerful energy of the earth whose strength you are now tapping in to. Feel that the great power of the planet has become part of you, connected to you by the invisible cord of light.

When you feel centered and strong, visualize yourself relaxed. Then turn your attention inwards, and watch the thoughts that flit through your conscious awareness. Do not react or try to change your thoughts. Just study the way your mind wanders, how it goes off at a tangent, and how it goes deeper into subjects. You will feel literally lost in your thoughts every now and again and will need to pull them back to reestablish connection with them.

When you have established easy familiarity with watching your thoughts, ask yourself: "Who is watching these thoughts? Who am I really?" When you repeat this question while meditating without really expecting an answer, it opens the mind to the spiritual answers that will one day come in a flash of insight.

The Cosmic Forces of Mandalas and Yantras

The cosmic spiritual forces of the mind can often be awakened when you are meditating on powerful esoteric images that symbolize the cosmic forces of divine beings or the celestial gods and goddesses of various spiritual traditions. The Hindus meditate on their yantra symbols, while Buddhists engage their meditations on deity mandalas.

There are advanced meditations taught by highly advanced yogics, spiritual teachers, and kung fu experts that make use of ritual symbols. These ritual symbols are said to be wonderful meditation aids, and those engaged in meditative visualization with them attain good progress in speaking directly to their unconscious and subconscious selves. What is produced by these symbolic, visualized meditations is a mystical sense of wholeness—a connection with the spiritual forces within.

Mandalas and yantras take the meditator on a wordless spiritual journey into the deepest recesses of the mind, providing the key to unlocking the mysteries of our minds. These mysteries are believed to contain all that the mind has experienced in past lives. The Hindus and Buddhists as well as the Chinese believe that the mind is a continuing momentum. This continuum never really dies. Instead it goes from one rebirth to the next, shedding one skin for the next, the quality of its rebirth depending on the karma it creates in each lifetime.

Thus, it is of a deeper spirituality that we speak when we engage the ritual symbols for meditational purposes. There are several differences between mandalas and yantras.

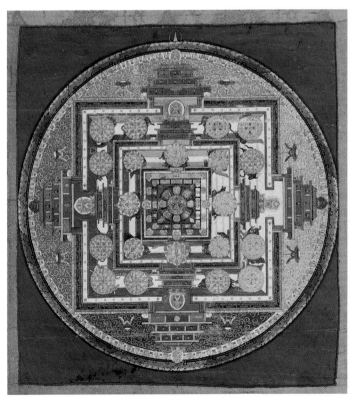

Buddhists use mandalas in their meditations. Each mandala symbolizes a particular divine being; over time, the meditator works to develop the qualities of that divine being.

Mandalas

Mandalas symbolize cosmic forces that take manifestation as celestial and divine beings—Buddhas and Bodhisattvas who are surrounded by their senior disciples and their attendants, all of whom represent separate aspects of their powers and qualities. The mandala signifies the realms of their fields of influence.

When we meditate on a mandala, we focus on the specific divine being within the mandala. Over time, it is believed, some form of transcendence and a merging of consciousness take place, so that the meditator actualizes the qualities of the divine being or Buddha inside the mandala. At a more advanced stage, this spiritual practice enables the practitioner to actualize as the Buddha himself. Thus, mandala meditations are regarded as being intensely spiritual.

Yantras

Yantras, on the other hand, focus on the symbolism of the divine trinities, and these are expressed in the form of geometrical triangles. The most famous of the yantras is the Yantra of the Illustrious One, which consists of nine triangles superimposed one over another and all converging on a central point. This is known as the Shri Yantra, and it symbolizes the cosmic field of creation in its state of creation. Everything is formless still, but the triangles signify the male, the female, and their union—the trinity concept of creation.

This is, of course, very similar to the Chinese idea of yin, yang, and wholeness. The Hindus believe that the Shri Yantra can also symbolize the god Shiva and the goddess Shakti, divine beings of the Hindu pantheon.

Meditating on the yantra is believed to take the mind back to the earliest origins, to the source of creation when man was formless. Both the mandala and the yantra are said to have the most amazing

powers to effect inner transformation. Whatever mandala or yantra you come into contact with, simply meditating on the symbols is usually sufficient to bring about a deep and lasting transformation. The images of these spiritual symbols speak directly to one's inner conscious mind—and then who knows what mysteries they will proceed to unlock?

> The images of these spiritual symbols speak directly to the inner conscious mind—who knows what mysteries they will unlock?

Hindus meditate on yantra symbols; this meditation is believed to take the meditator back to the earliest origins of creation.

Oracle Dreaming

The Tibetans say that placing some kushi grass under your pillow at night enhances your ability to recall prophetic dreams. Kushi grass is the long, dry grass that is often used to make brooms. The Chinese say that placing a statue or image of one of the Eight Taoist Immortals behind your bed as you sleep has the same effect. Keep a notebook by your bedside for recording dreams.

An illustration of the Eight Immortals of Taoist legend. Invite one of these immortals into your dreams to help you to develop the spiritual ability of oracle dreaming.

The Eight Immortals are superior beings of Taoist legend. They are said to have lived at various times, each having attained immortality under different circumstances by drinking nectar of the peach of immortality. The Immortals are revered as symbolic deities of longevity and good fortune. They are frequently depicted on Chinese porcelain—vases, urns, and plates—and are believed to bestow happiness and extreme good fortune when their images are displayed inside the home. They are shown singly or as a group of eight crossing the waters. Each Immortal is associated with a special symbol that enables them to manifest supernatural powers. They are therefore believed to possess the secrets of Taoist magic.

Each of the Eight Immortals represents some special wisdom that is helpful in coping with life's circumstance, and each expresses a significant ability or power. Two of these Immortals, Chung-Li Chuan and Kuo-Lao Chang, are said to possess the ability to bring news of good things that are about to happen, or they are able to warn you about impending disasters, in this way enabling you to take the necessary precautions.

The Power of Dreams

" *Nearly five years ago, I dreamed of white tigers. These magnificent creatures appeared in my dream as powerful, large animals. They were completely white, and I was very taken with the beauty of their muscular bodies and serene faces. One tiger jumped down from a tree, landing lightly very near my feet— he seemed like a big pussycat—and then, even as I admired the way he landed, I looked up and saw a second tiger.*

" *For weeks after that, I went around asking my Taoist friends if they could interpret the dream for me. Three months later, as I passed by my fax machine, a long fax came through for me. It was from a Tibetan High Lama asking me a list of questions about feng shui. It was amazing that the fax came just as I passed the machine, for I seldom look at my faxes. This time, however, I noted the sender, and on an impulse I replied immediately. An hour later, I was on my way to the airport and had forgotten the incident.*

" *Two months later, this same lama called me from Kathmandu and, to cut a long story short, he invited me to India. I accepted on an instinct, and it was in Bodhgaya where I met him that I saw my tigers. He had a beautiful thangka (a Tibetan Buddhist painting) that showed Buddha seated on a*

throne, and painted on the throne were two stunning white tigers, except they were not tigers at all but snow lions! Since then of course I have come to learn about the huge significance of snow lions in Tibetan Buddhism.

" *The dream, the fax I fortunately picked up, and the surprising phone call formed a precious pattern for me that led to a fabulous spiritual awakening. The white tigers heralded the coming of my precious guru into my life.* "

A snow lion; this animal plays a very significant role in Tibetan Buddhism.

Above: Shen Nong.
Below: Chuang Tzu.

IMAGES OF THE IMMORTALS

If you want to develop the spiritual ability of oracle dreaming, invite one of the Immortals into your dreams. Place their image (either as a porcelain statue or as a painting) high above the bed and also place some kushi grass under your pillow and under your bed. Before turning off the lights, meditate briefly on the question you would like answers to. If you are mentally connecting with Chung-Li Chuan, think of his image. He has a fat, exposed belly and carries a

magic fan, which he uses to cure sick people. He symbolizes good health and possesses curative powers. His presence in your dream is a signal that someone sick will recover. He is also believed to bring good health and longevity to residents. If you are connecting with Kuo-Lao Chung, note that he carries a bamboo tube. Chung possesses great wisdom, and he bestows wisdom on the family patriarch. He usually appears in dreams to bring news of good things or warnings of impending disasters.

Are You a Jesus Type or a Buddha Type?

Within the transcendental realm of the spirit, the divine within us manifests in many unexpected ways. It is virtually impossible to typecast the spiritual type, simply because when the divine reveals the real self, it is totally experiential. Our spiritual tendencies are unique to each one of us, yet in our hearts and minds, we know if we feel drawn to Jesus or to the Buddha.

To investigate which celestial being you identify with most, first gaze at an image of Jesus and meditate on it. Open your heart to signs and portents.

If one were prepared to do away with semantics and go only for meanings, then it would seem that all religious traditions teach pretty much the same thing—the need to develop a compassionate heart, live a virtuous life, and help others. At an intellectual level, there does not appear to be much difference between the major religions. All religious beliefs are founded on faith. Agnostics, atheists, and non-believers are generally sceptical of mysticisms that require a great leap of faith, and until they experience and accept the divine in some way or other, they will always feel alien to the culture of organized religions.

Whether you are a Jesus type or Buddha type seems to crystallize at the level of the heart, and the connection is usually emotional. To awaken to the instinctive connections we have with either of these great teachers, we need to awaken to the psychic and magical planes of existence within us.

Test yourself Answer the following questions after thinking them through to see if you are a Jesus type or a Buddha type. Take time to study the accompanying commentaries on the questions and then you might gain some insights into which type instinctively pulls at you.

1 Do you believe in a creator god?
Buddhists do not believe in a creator god—they believe that the Buddha nature lies dormant within every single human being, and that the seed of divinity that leads to enlightenment is imprinted within each one of us. Christians do believe in an omnipotent creator god.

2 Is your concept of time beginningless?

Christians think of the beginning in terms of the creation, with the first man on Earth being Adam. Buddhists believe there is no beginning, but that there will be an ending.

3 Do you believe faith is integral to religious life?

Christians have faith in Jesus, who they believe died on the cross to save humankind. Faith is an integral part of their religious belief.

4 Do you believe that it is right for people to question everything?

His Holiness the Dalai Lama repeatedly quotes Buddha, who advises that we should question and question until we are satisfied.

5 Do you prefer rules of proper behavior to be set out?

Both Christians and Buddhists have their respective codes that spell out virtuous behavior that is said to be most beneficial.

6 Should religious leaders be the most important people in your spiritual life?

Both Christians and Buddhists believe that our religious teachers should be respected. However, Buddhists usually see their spiritual leaders, and especially their teachers, as emanations of the enlightened one, as Living Buddhas.

7 When you look at the injustices of the world, do you find it hard to believe in the existence of a benevolent god?

Christians pray to a benevolent god for all their needs. Buddhists believe in karma and see all good and bad circumstances of their lives as being the result of good and bad karma that has accumulated since beginningless time.

8 When you think of the goal of your religious practices, is the thought of going to heaven after you die your most important motivation?

Christians speak of heaven and hell as the realms that we all go to when we die. Buddhists also have their pure realms, their paradise realms, but the ultimate goal is to become enlightened so that they are able to help others become awakened as well.

9 Do you feel that the only purpose of living is to benefit others?

Christians and Buddhists alike advocate helping others, but it seems that Buddhists make this the all-encompassing purpose of their lives.

10 Do you believe there are circumstances that justify violence?

Both faiths turn away from violence for whatever purpose at all.

It would seem then that the differences between the two types tend to be a question of emphasis and also of the degree of relevance placed on certain beliefs. So which type are you?

After meditating on an image of Jesus, select three images of the Buddha and gaze at them. Open your heart and mind to them and see what happens. Then you will know to whom you are drawn.

From Physics to Metaphysics

We are living in the period now of the kali yoga, the Age of Aquarius—a time when all things mystical and magical become increasingly commonplace as ancient yogics and shamans spill their secrets to a world hungry for knowledge. We have just come through a quantum leap from physics to metaphysics, and fresh perspectives on psychic magic constantly challenge our belief systems.

There has been an explosion of interest in magic and mysticism. Many ordinary people have experience of using tarot cards, as shown here.

In the unknown world of metaphysics, we are discovering new planes of existence, new dimensions of illusory worlds—all supposedly created and caused by the mind—completely far-fetched and yet seeming so real. The deepest and most advanced practitioners speak of acquiring amazing siddhic powers that enable them to perform mind-blowing feats of psychic magic.

The variety of magic put on display in the past few years has been astonishing. We have read of people developing the ability to walk on coals of fire. From India came news of holy men manifesting precious gems from thin air. It is said that a holy Indian master helped one of his disciples open the highly successful and famous chain of restaurants, Hard Rock Café, from cash realized from a single diamond materialized especially for the disciple from thin air—hence the name Hard Rock!

From the Philippines came stories of surgeons reaching their hands into human bodies to remove diseased organs, and from all over the world we hear of cures and miracles that defy conventional medicine. What we are seeing is a world of phenomenal mental powers, a flowering of a new and mystical science of the mind.

We are left to figure out if this leap into the realm of metaphysics performed by wise men and shamans alike has more to do with a form of science still unknown to humankind on a formalized basis, or with a supernatural power of some kind. Are the alternative techniques being thrust on us that seem so miraculous a new science that can be taught and used by everyone, or do they engage the human psyche at some esoteric, spiritual level?

Test yourself These questions will help you clarify your position regarding everything to do with magic and mysticism. The more intriguing you find these questions, the more interested you are in all things metaphysical.

1 Are you interested in developing your psychic powers?

2 Do you like using the *I Ching* and the tarot?

3 Do you like the idea of having your fortune read by a psychic?

4 Would you be prepared to have someone hypnotize you?

5 Have you ever tried astral travel?

6 Do you wish you were telepathic?

7 Would you travel to India to learn magic from a famous yogi?

8 Would you think of visiting an acupuncturist to treat your aching back?

9 Have you ever had an out-of-body experience?

10 Between being able to read thoughts and to hypnotize people, which skill would you prefer to develop?

11 Have you ever felt you were psychic?

12 Have you made a guess and found it true?

13 Do you see any difference between being awakened and being empowered?

14 Have you tried practicing exercises designed to develop mind power?

15 Do you believe in the power of visualization?

16 Would you ever use special powers to get even with people?

17 If you could make time stand still, can you think of three ways in which it would benefit you?

18 If you could materialize money from thin air, would it scare you?

19 Do you think having special powers has a cost?

20 Do you believe all of us have the potential to develop special powers?

Nowadays, many people in the Western world are prepared to undertake non-conventional treatments such as acupuncture. We also hear of many new kinds of cures and miracles from around the world that bring fresh perspectives on psychic magic to challenge our belief systems.

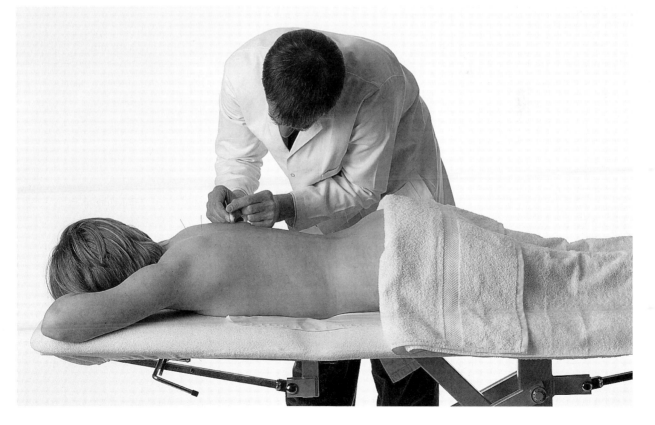

Tuning in to Your Siddhic Powers

Mystics and spiritualists alike will awaken their siddhic powers when they tread the spiritual road. These are powers that challenge the senses as much as the intellect—they are the stuff of eye-defying miracles, healing, telepathy, clairvoyance, mind-reading, and control of the body and mind. These siddhic powers are the side effects of intense spiritual practice at an advanced level.

Practitioners who raise siddhic powers within themselves rarely speak of their extraordinary ability. They never acknowledge that they possess such special powers.

What are siddhic powers, then? They are powers that become potent when the practitioner has reached a high level of spiritual meditative practice, so high that yogic powers have arisen giving them control over their body at both the conscious and subconscious levels, and at both the voluntary and involuntary levels. Merged with this awakening is the control of psychic vibrations within the psyche.

Siddhic powers are awe-inspiring. It is said that they are what enables the high lamas of Tibet to sit unwavering in the coldest of winters, kept warm only by their body heat. It is siddhic powers

> ## The spiritual road is strewn with wish-fulfilling special powers.

that give them the ability to be in several places at one time, that enable them to fast for years surviving only on water. It is only in recent times that knowledge of such powers has been revealed.

That they can be developed by humans is surely something phenomenal, but developing or having these abilities is not something that engages the mind only during one lifetime. Buddhist monks have confided that developing the mind occurs over many lifetimes.

First there is empowerment. Only when one practices with a proper motivation and a compassionate humility does the possibility of awakening occur. Thus, we should differentiate between empowerments and awakenings. Tuning in to the siddhic powers within us is a way of empowering ourselves.

Next comes the motivation for wanting this empowerment. The power may be used for good, such as in healing work, it can be used completely for personal gain, such as in commercializing one's ability to read fortunes and foretell events, or it can be used for evil, such as to control the minds of others in order to cheat or take advantage of them. How these siddhic powers are used is entirely a personal decision. What it does is make the most awesome use of the mind.

The main thing to note about the rise of siddhic powers is that it is completely individual. The Eastern mystics know this and have spent many years, even lifetimes, teaching about the safeguards that must accompany empowerment.

The temptation to use these powers for ill is phenomenal, and it is for this reason that many masters of the esoteric make their disciples spend years transforming their hearts and minds before teaching them spiritual practices that lead to siddhic empowerments.

It is dangerous to attempt to develop siddhic powers on one's own. To do so safely requires the supervision of a teacher, a fully qualified master of the paths that lead as much to empowerments as to awakenings. Genuine teachers are rare, and those who are genuine will put would-be disciples through many tests in order to gauge the motivation behind their urge to learn before even considering taking them on as students, let alone disciples. In almost every instance, the student must practice for many years to still the mind and bring it under total control.

Introducing siddhic powers in a mind that has not been calmed is like putting an elephant or horse in a china shop. Everything goes haywire, for the mind is not under control. Remember this if you are keen to travel further in your spiritual journey. The average mind is like a roaring sea filled with endless diversions and dangerous fears. Make real efforts to still the mind through constant meditative practice before attempting to make the leap into the illusory dimension.

A Tibetan mystic rests in seated meditation. It takes years of experience to develop siddhic powers.

Manifesting a Spiritual Teacher

We need a guru to guide us in our spiritual quest, to take us to levels and dimensions that would be difficult and even unsafe for us to tread alone. The teacher should be perfectly qualified, and it is only through sincere and persevering effort that we can succeed in manifesting this individual. When the teacher does manifest, be alert so you can recognize him or her.

Everyone's path is different, and mine came in 1997 when I had the great good fortune to meet, and the good karma to recognize, my most precious teacher, Lama Zopa Rinpoche, shown here meditating in the holy stupa of Bodhgaya, India.

DISCIPLINING THE BODY AND MIND

View your body and your mind as one. Make the body totally still and centered, and the mind will follow. Watch your thoughts and then gradually cease all thoughts.

Watch as the sense of self changes with each thought. Observe but stay detached as much as you can. Cessation of thought comes from persistent inner effort. Persistence through constant practice and non-attachment to the result is the best way to move forward. Keep at it and try different meditations to see which brings the better results.

YOGIC BREATH MEDITATION

Sitting in a relaxed posture, preferably the lotus posture, focus on the breath. Breathe normally until the mind becomes calm. Become aware of the in-breath and the out-breath, and of when you stop breathing between the in-breath and the out-breath. At that moment, move along with the breath. Call this moment of non-breath the holding breath. In that moment, think strongly, yet with no attachment to the outcome, that a teacher is manifesting soon into your life.

Note that the teacher seldom appears in a flash of magical light. Instead, a true and genuine teacher is usually so humble that when he or she enters your life you may not even be aware of it for a short period of time. So, it is necessary to be extremely sensitive to all the new people who touch your life, however briefly.

MILAREPA MEDITATION

Jetsun Milarepa is the most famous Buddhist saint in recent Tibetan history. To purify eons of negative karma, his master, Marpa, made him single-handedly construct a building seven times with his bare hands—six times it was rejected and he was made to tear it down. Milarepa lived the life of an ascetic in a cave. When pain racked his back, Milarepa practiced entering his pain and his suffering, observing both in total non-attachment. With a humble attitude, meditate on the pain of rejection and on the need for perseverance; this will attract the sort of vibrations that bring the most stunning guru. It is an intense, spiritual practice, and it can take years before the teacher comes.

MEDITATION OF THE SACRED DANCE

Barefooted and wearing loose clothing, play some Indian music. Cross your arms over your heart with each hand on the opposite shoulder. Extend your arms as you swirl around in a clockwise, then a counterclockwise, direction.

Raise your arms. Keep to the beat of the music and rotate with increasing speed. When you feel dizzy, cross your arms to steady yourself, then swirl again. Gather more speed and keep swirling until you finally drop to the ground. Think that you are transcending into the next dimension, and watch your teacher come to you.

CALLING THE GURU

Close your eyes and visualize yourself engulfed in a ball of intense spiritual energy. As you feel this energy becoming stronger, transcend into a different dimension and call for your guru of many lives past to find you. Many of us had gurus in past lives, who ensured we were reborn as humans. Do this meditation before sleeping so that in sleep, too, you will call for your guru.

Far left: This Tibetan thangka depicts Milarepa in his cave. His story teaches us to meditate on our problems or ailments with non-attachment.

Below: The god Shiva forms part of the later Hindu pantheon. He presides over personal destinies.

Part Four

DISCOVERING
YOUR POTENTIAL

The Chinese astrological charts reveal personality profiles that help us realize our potential. When you are able to view fate for what it is, manifestations from your karmic balance sheet that determine the positives and negatives of your life chart, you can then move into the tantalizing investigation of your own destiny.

How much control do we have over our destiny? Is our quality of life predetermined, or can it be transformed? We will investigate Chinese astrology and element analysis, lucky and unlucky directions using the Kua formula, and divination through the tea-leaf oracle.

We finally come full circle in this quest for self-discovery. By reaching into the upper chakras of our spiritual consciousness, we come to realize that knowing oneself intimately is the surest way of developing a true understanding and appreciation of others.

Astrology and Destiny

Chinese astrology charts destiny and personality profiles according to four pillars—the year, month, day, and hour pillars—from which are derived the eight characters. Each of these signifies one of the five elements, so destinies are interpreted according to a person's basket of eight elements. Accuracy of profiles and predictions is based on the astrologer's skill.

The two elements of the year of birth are described as the heavenly stems and earthly branches. There are ten stems comprising five elements with a positive (yang) or a negative (yin) aspect. There are 12 branches, corresponding to the 12 animals of the Chinese zodiac. Names given to the heavenly stems and the earthly branches describe each year, so year names are made up of the stem name and earth name. Chinese astrologers make reference to the year names of one's year of birth to tell which two year elements exert influences on your destiny.

The same analysis of stems and branches is extended to the month, day, and hour of birth, to get a more comprehensive natal chart of eight characters. This is perhaps the most famous system

of destiny charting used by Chinese astrologers and it is said to be extremely accurate in charting out periods of good and bad luck. Since calculating the natal chart requires the use of the thousand-year Chinese lunar calendar, this is not something that can be easily mastered. Detailed analysis is best left to professional astrologers.

The Annual Stems and Branches of Fortune

While it is not within the scope of this book to delve into destiny analysis, I can nevertheless use the year elements to discover the dominant

Ten Heavenly Stems	
CHIA	WOOD element
YI	WOOD element
PING	FIRE element
TING	FIRE element
MOU	EARTH element
CHI	EARTH element
KEN	METAL element
SIN	METAL element
ZEN	WATER element
KWAY	WATER element

Twelve Earth Branches		
TZU	Rat	WATER element
CHOU	Ox	EARTH element
YIN	Tiger	WOOD element
MAO	Rabbit	WOOD element
CHEN	Dragon	EARTH element
SZU	Snake	FIRE element
WU	Horse	FIRE element
WEI	Sheep	EARTH element
SHEN	Monkey	METAL element
YU	Rooster	METAL element
HSU	Dog	EARTH element
HAI	Boar	WATER element

The 12 earthly branches, which correspond to the 12 animal signs of the Chinese zodiac. Basic personality traits are initially assessed according to the year in the Chinese calendar in which a person was born.

characteristics and personalities of individuals. Comprehensive analyses are made by examining the interaction of the elements of the stems and branches for the year of birth. Basic personality traits are categorized initially according to the earthly branch (i.e., the animals) of the year of birth. For instance, if you were born in a year when the ruling branch is Tzu, then you are a Rat year person who will exhibit all of the characteristics that rule the Rat personality.

However, in the 60-year Chinese calendar cycle (see pages 183–4), the Rat year appears five times, each time with a different heavenly stem! So one can be a wood Rat, a fire Rat, an earth Rat, a metal Rat, or a water Rat. The attributes, temperaments, and personalities of these five rats will differ. The same is true for all 12 animals.

When looking for factors that describe and influence your destiny therefore, first investigate the earthly branch animal characteristics. This gives a generalized but complete first impression. Then extend to the heavenly stem and earthly branch element interaction.

To investigate further, examine the two characters that make up the name of the year. This addition of the heavenly stems brings the important dimension of element analysis to the personality and destiny reading.

The month and time of a person's birth can also be used to provide yet more clues to their character and destiny. This is easily done, and the relevant tables and information used for such an analysis are reproduced on the following pages. What has not been included, however, are the characters on stems and branches that apply to the day of birth. It would be simply impossible to provide every single possible combination for over 100 years!

The Chinese Horoscope Animals

The popular view of Chinese astrology is the categorization of years according to each of 12 animals. These animals, in order of appearance, are the Rat, the Ox, the Tiger, the Rabbit, the Dragon, the Snake, the Horse, the Sheep, the Monkey, the Rooster, the Dog, and the Boar.

There are special stories that explain why the Rat is the first animal of the Chinese Zodiac, and these usually make reference to his craftiness in achieving first place. The Rat, apparently, did not run all the way to beat the rest. Instead, he hitched a ride from the Ox, and just before the finishing line he merely jumped ahead and landed right in front of the Ox!

I prefer to view the selection of these 12 animals as reflecting the wisdom of the ancients, particularly as it applied to the mainly agricultural and superstitious society of ancient China. Thus, the Rat, being the all-important king during times of famine, comes first in the cycle because food is all-important for survival.

These animals in Chinese astrology have been in use since time was first officially recorded under the reign of the emperor Huang Ti—around the year 2637 B.C.—and they have thus been around for 47 centuries!

The cycle always starts with the Rat and ends with the Boar. The last century started with the Rat year, and this year—2003—is the year of the Sheep.

The lunar birth year tables that follow will enable anyone to determine their respective ruling animal or earthly branch. The cut-off annual dates for year beginnings and year ends enable conversion from Western dates of birth. The tables also contain the HS/EB element. This refers to the heavenly stem and earthly branch elements. These element combinations offer immediate clues on

compatibility and luck, based on cyclical element analysis. As well as looking up your own animal sign, try reading about friends, family members, or your partner. You will gain a better understanding of the people in your life.

Lunar Birth Tables

Use these tables to determine the animal sign that rules a person's year of birth. These animal signs represent the earthly branches of an individual's horoscope and offer wonderful insights into character and personality. After determining the relevant animal, refer to the sections that offer descriptions of men and women born under the respective animal signs.

Notice that each animal has a ruling element that does not change. Thus the Rat represents the water element, the Dragon is the earth element, the Tiger is wood, the Horse is fire, the Monkey is metal, and so forth. By themselves the elements do not mean very much. But when they are placed next to the element represented by the particular heavenly stem of the year of birth, these elements, or rather, the combination of the two elements, become additional indicators of characteristic tendencies, both positive and negative.

Thus, the next stage in the analysis is to discover, for example, what kind of Sheep one is dealing with, a water Sheep, a metal Sheep, or a fire Sheep, and so forth. You can use the tables to determine compatibility of people under different animal symbols, but always remember to analyze the elements as well.

EXAMPLE: According to the astrological affinity tables, the Dragon and the Dog are natural enemies. However, if you discover that one is a wood Dragon and the other is a fire Dog, the pairing of the two individuals might work, since wood produces fire. Thus, the heavenly stem might well prevail over the earthly branch.

Lunar Birth Tables, 1912 to 1948

Animal	Western Calendar Dates	Year Name	HS/EB Element
RAT (water)	Feb 18, 1912–Feb 5, 1913	Zen Tzu	water/water
OX (earth)	Feb 6, 1913–Jan 25, 1914	Kway Chou	water/earth
TIGER (wood)	Jan 26, 1914–Feb 13, 1915	Chia Yin	wood/wood
RABBIT (wood)	Feb 14, 1915–Feb 2, 1916	Yi Mao	wood/wood
DRAGON (earth)	Feb 3, 1916–Jan 22, 1917	Ping Ch'en	fire/earth
SNAKE (fire)	Jan 23, 1917–Feb 10, 1918	Ting Szu	fire/fire
HORSE (fire)	Feb 11, 1918–Jan 31, 1919	Mou Wu	earth/fire
SHEEP (earth)	Feb 1, 1919–Feb 19, 1920	Chi Wei	earth/earth
MONKEY (metal)	Feb 20, 1920–Feb 7, 1921	Ken Shen	metal/metal
ROOSTER (metal)	Feb 8, 1921–Jan 27, 1922	Sin Yu	metal/metal
DOG (earth)	Jan 28, 1922–Feb 15, 1923	Zen Hsu	water/earth
BOAR (water)	Feb 16, 1923–Feb 4, 1924	Kway Hai	water/water

- **Start of 60-Year Cycle**

Animal	Western Calendar Dates	Year Name	HS/EB Element
RAT (water)	Feb 5, 1924–Jan 23, 1925	Chia Tzu	wood/water
OX (earth)	Jan 24, 1925–Feb 12, 1926	Yi Chou	wood/earth
TIGER (wood)	Feb 13, 1926–Feb 1, 1927	Ping Yin	fire/wood
RABBIT (wood)	Feb 2, 1927–Jan 22, 1928	Ting Mao	fire/wood
DRAGON (earth)	Jan 23, 1928–Feb 9, 1929	Mou Ch'en	earth/earth
SNAKE (fire)	Feb 10, 1929–Jan 29, 1930	Chi Szu	earth/fire
HORSE (fire)	Jan 30, 1930–Feb 16, 1931	Ken Wu	metal/fire
SHEEP (earth)	Feb 17, 1931–Feb 5, 1932	Sin Wei	metal/earth
MONKEY (metal)	Feb 6, 1932–Jan 25, 1933	Zen Shen	water/metal
ROOSTER (metal)	Jan 26, 1933–Feb 13, 1934	Kway Yu	water/metal
DOG (earth)	Feb 14, 1934–Feb 3, 1935	Chia Hsu	wood/earth
BOAR (water)	Feb 4, 1935–Jan 23, 1936	Yi Hai	wood/water
RAT (water)	Jan 24, 1936–Feb 10, 1937	Ping Tzu	fire/water
OX (earth)	Feb 11, 1937–Jan 30, 1938	Ting Chou	fire/earth
TIGER (wood)	Jan 31, 1938–Feb 18, 1939	Mou Yin	earth/wood
RABBIT (wood)	Feb 19, 1939–Feb 7, 1940	Chi Mao	earth/wood
DRAGON (earth)	Feb 8, 1940–Jan 26, 1941	Ken Ch'en	metal/earth
SNAKE (fire)	Jan 27, 1941–Feb 14, 1942	Sin Szu	metal/fire
HORSE (fire)	Feb 15, 1942–Feb 4, 1943	Zen Wu	water/fire
SHEEP (earth)	Feb 5, 1943–Jan 24, 1944	Kway Wei	water/earth
MONKEY (metal)	Jan 25, 1944–Feb 12, 1945	Chia Shen	wood/metal
ROOSTER (metal)	Feb 13, 1945–Feb 1, 1946	Yi Yu	wood/metal
DOG (earth)	Feb 2, 1946–Jan 21, 1947	Ping Hsu	fire/earth
BOAR (water)	Jan 22, 1947–Feb 9, 1948	Ting Hai	fire/water

Lunar Birth Tables, 1948 to 1984

Animal	Western Calendar Dates	Year Name	HS/EB Element
RAT (water)	Feb 10, 1948–Jan 28, 1949	Mou Tzu	earth/water
OX (earth)	Jan 29, 1949–Feb 16, 1950	Chi Chou	earth/earth
TIGER (wood)	Feb 17, 1950–Feb 5, 1951	Ken Yin	metal/wood
RABBIT (wood)	Feb 6, 1951–Jan 26, 1952	Sin Mao	metal/wood
DRAGON (earth)	Jan 27, 1952–Feb 13, 1953	Zen Ch'en	water/earth
SNAKE (fire)	Feb 14, 1953–Feb 2, 1954	Kway Szu	water/fire
HORSE (fire)	Feb 3, 1954–Jan 23, 1955	Chia Wu	wood/fire
SHEEP (earth)	Jan 24, 1955–Feb 11, 1956	Yi Wei	wood/earth
MONKEY (metal)	Feb 12, 1956–Jan 30, 1957	Ping Shen	fire/metal
ROOSTER (metal)	Jan 31, 1957–Feb 17, 1958	Ting Yu	fire/metal
DOG (earth)	Feb 18, 1958–Feb 7, 1959	Mou Hsu	earth/earth
BOAR (water)	Feb 8, 1959–Jan 27, 1960	Chi Hai	earth/water
RAT (water)	Jan 28, 1960–Feb 14, 1961	Ken Tzu	metal/water
OX (earth)	Feb 15, 1961–Feb 4, 1962	Sin Chou	metal/earth
TIGER (wood)	Feb 5, 1962–Jan 24, 1963	Zen Yin	water/wood
RABBIT (wood)	Jan 25, 1963–Feb 12, 1964	Kway Mao	water/wood
DRAGON (earth)	Feb 13, 1964–Feb 1, 1965	Chia/Ch'en	wood/earth
SNAKE (fire)	Feb 2, 1965–Jan 20, 1966	Yi Szu	wood/fire
HORSE (fire)	Jan 21, 1966–Feb 8, 1967	Ping Wu	fire/fire
SHEEP (earth)	Feb 9, 1967–Jan 29, 1968	Ting Wei	fire/earth
MONKEY (metal)	Jan 30, 1968–Feb 16, 1969	Mou Shen	earth/metal
ROOSTER (metal)	Feb 17, 1969–Feb 5, 1970	Chi Yu	earth/metal
DOG (earth)	Feb 6, 1970–Jan 26, 1971	Ken Hsu	metal/earth
BOAR (water)	Jan 27, 1971–Feb 14, 1972	Sin Hai	metal/water
RAT (water)	Feb 15, 1972–Feb 2, 1973	Zen Tzu	water/water
OX (earth)	Feb 3, 1973–Jan 22, 1974	Kway Chou	water/earth
TIGER (wood)	Jan 23, 1974–Feb 10, 1975	Chia Yin	wood/wood
RABBIT (wood)	Feb 11, 1975–Jan 30, 1976	Yi Mao	wood/wood
DRAGON (earth)	Jan 31, 1976–Feb 17, 1977	Ping Ch'en	fire/earth
SNAKE (fire)	Feb 18, 1977–Feb 6, 1978	Ting Szu	fire/fire
HORSE (fire)	Feb 7, 1978–Jan 27, 1979	Mou Wu	earth/fire
SHEEP (earth)	Jan 28, 1979–Feb 15, 1980	Chi Wei	earth/earth
MONKEY (metal)	Feb 16, 1980–Feb 4, 1981	Ken Shen	metal/metal
ROOSTER (metal)	Feb 5, 1981–Jan 24, 1982	Sin Yu	metal/metal
DOG (earth)	Jan 25, 1982–Feb 12, 1983	Zen Hsu	water/earth
BOAR (water)	Feb 13, 1983–Feb 1, 1984	Kway Hai	water/water

Lunar Birth Tables, 1984 to 2020

Animal	Western Calendar Dates	Year Name	HS/EB Element
• **Start of 60-Year Cycle**			
RAT (water)	Feb 2, 1984–Feb 19, 1985	Chia Tzu	wood/water
OX (earth)	Feb 20, 1985–Feb 8, 1986	Yi Chou	wood/earth
TIGER (wood)	Feb 9, 1986–Jan 28, 1987	Ping Yin	fire/wood
RABBIT (wood)	Jan 29, 1987–Feb 16, 1988	Ting Mao	fire/wood
DRAGON (earth)	Feb 17, 1988–Feb 5, 1989	Mou Ch'en	earth/earth
SNAKE (fire)	Feb 6, 1989–Jan 26, 1990	Chi Szu	earth/fire
HORSE (fire)	Jan 27, 1990–Feb 14, 1991	Ken Wu	metal/fire
SHEEP (earth)	Feb 15, 1991–Feb 3, 1992	Sin Wei	metal/earth
MONKEY (metal)	Feb 4, 1992–Jan 22, 1993	Zen Shen	water/metal
ROOSTER metal)	Jan 23, 1993–Feb 9, 1994	Kway Yu	water/metal
DOG (earth)	Feb 10, 1994–Jan 30, 1995	Chia Hsu	wood/earth
BOAR (water)	Jan 31, 1995–Feb 18, 1996	Yi Hai	wood/water
RAT (water)	Feb 19, 1996–Feb 6, 1997	Ping Tzu	fire/water
OX (earth)	Feb 7, 1997–Jan 27, 1998	Ting Chou	fire/earth
TIGER (wood)	Jan 28, 1998–Feb 15, 1999	Mou Yin	earth/wood
RABBIT (wood)	Feb 16, 1999–Feb 4, 2000	Chi Mao	earth/wood
DRAGON (earth)	Feb 5, 2000–Jan 23, 2001	Ken Ch'en	metal/earth
SNAKE (fire)	Jan 24, 2001–Feb 11, 2002	Sin Szu	metal/fire
HORSE (fire)	Feb 12, 2002–Jan 31, 2003	Zen Wu	water/fire
SHEEP (earth)	Feb 1, 2003–Jan 21, 2004	Kway Wei	water/earth
MONKEY (metal)	Jan 22, 2004–Feb 8, 2005	Chia Shen	wood/metal
ROOSTER (metal)	Feb 9, 2005–Jan 28, 2006	Yi Yu	wood/metal
DOG (earth)	Jan 29, 2006–Feb 17, 2007	Ping Hsu	fire/earth
BOAR (water)	Feb 18, 2007–Feb 6, 2008	Ting Hai	fire/water
RAT (water)	Feb 7, 2008–Jan 26, 2009	Wu Cher	earth/water
OX (earth)	Jan 27, 2009–Feb 13, 2010	Chi Choh	earth/earth
TIGER (wood)	Feb 14, 2010–Feb 2, 2011	Ken Yin	metal/wood
RABBIT (wood)	Feb 3, 2011–Jan 22, 2012	Sin Mao	metal/wood
DRAGON (earth)	Jan 23, 2012–Feb 9, 2013	Zen Shen	water/earth
SNAKE (Fire)	Feb 10, 2013–Jan 30, 2014	Kway Tze	water/Fire
HORSE (fire)	Jan 31, 2014–Feb 18, 2015	Shia Wu	wood/fire
SHEEP (earth)	Feb 19, 2015–Feb 7, 2016	Yi Wei	wood/earth
MONKEY (metal)	Feb 8, 2016–Jan 27, 2017	Ping Sen	fire/metal
ROOSTER (metal)	Jan 28, 2017–Feb 15, 2018	Ting Yu	fire/metal
DOG (earth)	Feb 16, 2018–Feb 4, 2019	Wu Shih	earth/earth
BOAR (water)	Feb 5, 2019–Jan 24, 2020	Chi Hai	earth/water

Going Deeper: The Month Tables

If you wish, you can go deeper into the analysis by examining and comparing the month of birth as well. This does not require intensive examination of the heavenly stems and earthly branches of the exact lunar month. What is required is merely to determine in which season a person was born and then analyze the situation from there. In terms of relationship compatibility, this can also prove to be an excellent test of the match.

To undertake this analysis, determine the heavenly stem element of your year of birth. Next, determine whether you were born in a summer, fall, winter, or spring month. You will then be able to see from the chart reproduced here whether you are a strong or a weak representation of your element. The earth element has been excluded since earth is regarded as being equally strong or weak throughout the year, and this part of the analysis does not apply to those born in earth years.

The chart below gives an indication of the seasonal strength of the elements. The way to conduct the analysis is best shown via examples. Thus, if you are a wood person—if the heavenly stem element of your year of birth is wood—and you were born during the fall months—in the month of September or October—when it is cold,

and when plants usually wither, then it can be said that you are a very weak wood. If however you have some fire to warm you or bring you some sunlight, you will start to flourish, grow strong and thrive! Thus, for someone like you, a fire person—someone born in a year when the heavenly stem element is fire—would be wonderful, since that person would make you strong, look after you, and nurture you. The elements in this case will be exceedingly compatible for you, and work in your favor! Meanwhile, you will also be good for that person, since wood produces fire in the cycle of element relationships. Another source of fire is from wearing a lot of red, which represents fire—it will make you blossom and make your luck bloom!

Examining the Hour Tables

A further analysis based on a person's hour of birth can also be made. This provides additional clues to character and personality. Note that Chinese astrology divides a 24-hour day into 12 two-hour time slots, and assigns each of the animals to these time slots. Depending therefore on whether one is born in the hour of the Rat, or Boar, or any of the other animals, some of the characteristics of these animals will overlap in a personality reading. The hour tables are reproduced opposite.

SEASON	METAL	WOOD	WATER	FIRE
SPRING	dying	thrives/strong	weakening	born
SUMMER	born	in bloom	dies	thrives/strong
FALL	thrives/strong	dying/weak	born	weakening
WINTER	weakening	born	thrives/strong	dying

Another perspective of the hour analysis is to use the hour to detect nuances to personality characteristics. Thus, the nighttime Rat is always more curious, brave, and alert than his daytime sibling. The Ox, which sleeps at night and works hard during daylight hours, similarly demonstrates this trait. The Tiger hunts and prowls in the dark, and the night Tiger is more dangerous and ferocious. The Rabbit is most alert when born in the early hours of the morning. The Dragon is believed to come into his own during the mornings, while the Snake slithers most effectively into your heart and boudoir during the early evenings. The Horse is a daytime animal, while the Sheep is believed to think best during the early evening hours. The Monkey is at his most cunning during the afternoon hours. The Rooster reigns supreme when born in the early hours of dawn when his singing sounds the wake-up bell and calls successfully for the sun. The Dog's faithfulness shines forth during the night, while the Boar just goes to sleep at night.

Putting Things Together

Study the section on elements in Part Two thoroughly, since knowledge of the way elements interact according to their relationship cycles provides much of the explanations behind who you get along with and who you don't, who is good for you and who is not—this can all be explained in terms of the interactions of the elements that dominate your birth charts. If there is someone special you wish to investigate, you can also consult the *I Ching*. Use this wonderful divination tool to provide insights about the future potential of any of your relationships.

If your relationships always seem to go nowhere, or if you just have a hard time getting your love life together, you might want seriously to activate the relationship sector of your home using

The Hour Tables	
RAT HOUR	11.00 P.M. to 1.00 A.M.
OX HOUR	1.00 A.M. to 3.00 A.M.
TIGER HOUR	3.00 A.M. to 5.00 A.M.
RABBIT HOUR	5.00 A.M. to 7.00 A.M.
DRAGON HOUR	7.00 A.M. to 9.00 A.M.
SNAKE HOUR	9.00 A.M. to 11.00 A.M.
HORSE HOUR	11.00 A.M. to 1.00 P.M.
SHEEP HOUR	1.00 P.M. to 3.00 P.M.
MONKEY HOUR	3.00 P.M. to 5.00 P.M.
ROOSTER HOUR	5.00 P.M. to 7.00 P.M.
DOG HOUR	7.00 P.M. to 9.00 P.M.
BOAR HOUR	9.00 P.M. to 11.00 P.M.

feng shui tips. See my books *The Illustrated Encyclopedia of Feng Shui* and *Feng Shui Fundamentals, Love* to see how you can incorporate this ancient wisdom into your life.

Finally, remember that, to a large extent, although destiny as such cannot be changed, it can be improved. As I have stated throughout the book, learning about yourself can help you improve your life. Some things you cannot change—but all can be improved upon. The Chinese believe in the concept of tien, ti, and ren—heaven, earth, and human luck. While you cannot control heaven luck, earth and human luck is in your hands.

The Chinese Zodiac— Twelve Animal Signs

Check your animal sign from the lunar birth year tables, and find out more about yourself from the descriptions here that have been categorized according to gender and elements. Differences between men and women show up in the way key characteristics manifest themselves. These characteristics are also magnified or modified according to the stem elements.

The Spirited Rat Lady

Magnetic, vivacious, and dynamic—this is the Rat lady. Rarely beautiful in the classical sense, Rat women exude outward sophistication that hides an insecure and sometimes dogmatic nature. Rat women crave security—the type that comes from social acceptance. Marriage is seldom far from their mind. Rat women have few close friends, as they tend to be rather judgmental. Keeping up appearances is important to them. They are fundamentally honest, but they lack confidence. As a boss, a Rat woman is fiercely protective; and she is a loyal subordinate. As a wife, she supports her husband, but she is moody, requires reassurance, and could well drown you with her good intentions.

Singer Geri Halliwell, formerly with the pop music group the Spice Girls, has the lively personality of a Rat lady.

The **WOOD FEMALE RAT** is aware of her image, but she is more confident and enchanting than her sister Rats. She lets people know what she will not tolerate! To win her love, you must be prepared to adore her and massage her ego.

The **FIRE FEMALE RAT** is clever and devious. She knows what she wants and pursues it with ferocious determination. She succeeds in getting anyone or anything that she wants badly enough.

The **EARTH FEMALE RAT** tends to be self-centered but disciplined. She is sociable but cannot completely hide her feelings of superiority if she is higher up the social scale than you are. She is very family-oriented, with a hint of sexual adventurism.

The **METAL FEMALE RAT** needs public approval and works hard at feel-good causes. She is meticulous, hardworking, and sees projects through. She can be a little lacking in humor.

The **WATER FEMALE RAT** is feminine and soft. She is wiser and kinder than her sister Rats. All she wants is a comfortable life. The female water Rat harbors secret ambitions to bask in the reflected glory of a successful husband.

The Distinguished Gentleman Rat

Handsome, charming, and witty, the gentleman Rat has a most engaging personality. The key to winning the approval of a Rat male is to boost his ego. At their best, male Rats are interesting—they are full of creativity and oozing with confidence—but criticize them or disagree with them, and their negative side will begin to surface. When cornered, the Rat male becomes dangerous, even violent! If you can bring out their best side, Rat men make great partners and lovers.

Rat gentlemen are not generous by nature and are quite stingy with money. They are not great risk-takers but are restless and impulsive. Their need for approval can be so strong that they tend to cultivate splashy nonchalance when it comes to conspicuous spending.

Outwardly, Rat men appear cool and dignified. They carry themselves well and have a genuine talent for hiding nervousness, fear, or feelings of insecurity. Although they can be stubborn and dogmatic, they are also relentless and are not easily discouraged. When riled, Rat males react with determined ferocity. They hate being ordered around or made to feel small. Whether a boss, subordinate, or boyfriend, the Rat is won over by praise and flattery, not by criticism.

Rat men make excellent husbands. They are romantic and sentimental toward those they love, and they make caring and enjoyable lovers. If you win over their hearts, Rat men are generally honorable in their intentions. They take marriage very seriously, and you can also rest assured that they will stay faithful.

The WOOD MALE RAT is steadier, calmer, and more confident than all of the other Rats, and he is not as susceptible to flattery. That does not mean he does not also have a gigantic ego. His greater tolerance for criticism or disagreement merely takes second place to his fierce determination to be accepted in the company of those people he wishes to identify with!

The FIRE MALE RAT demonstrates greater intensity and brilliance than any of the other Rats. He is energetic, sharp, impatient, and highly strung. Fire male rats have a great fear of being alone. They fear rejection. If your boyfriend or boss is a fire Rat, do not be fooled by his charm and outward confidence.

The EARTH MALE RAT has enormous determination, being the most focused in his ambitions and goals. His willpower and strength are phenomenal, but he is also judgmental and can be self-righteous. He is soft-spoken, congenial, and is the most passionate of all the Rats.

The METAL MALE RAT is unabashedly socially ambitious. He uses his charm and good looks to cultivate influential friends. Metal male Rats can be possessive, dogmatic, and stubborn.

The WATER MALE RAT is the most relaxed and laid back of the Rats. Not as intense or as determined as the others, he is also not madly ambitious. The water Rat is satisfied with his lot in life but does enjoy himself—he loves good food, wine and elegant clothes, and he enjoys a good party.

The actor and director Kenneth Branagh exhibits the charming, confident, and creative characteristics of a Rat gentleman.

The Steely Female Ox

The Ox lady is quiet, conservative, and strong. Seldom sentimental and rarely romantic, she has an iron will and a great sense of responsibility. Ox women are self-disciplined and high-principled.

Think of women such as Margaret Thatcher and Barbara Bush, and you'll get a good idea of their personae. In public, they come across as stoical and possessed of a steely determination, taking their life, work, and even their hobbies seriously. As wives and mothers, family needs come before their own, and they take great delight in maintaining a happy home. They are virtuous and righteous, often to the extent of seeming intolerant. They hate idle gossip, cheating, and dishonesty. Ox women hold on to their high ground with great resilience!

Ox women are well dressed and well groomed. Their charm comes from their aura of strength and reliability. They are great at soothing and reassuring those around them and make perfect mates for those in need of strength. It is practical, sensible behavior that impresses the Ox lady, not flattery. Her sense of humor is limited. She does not like to be wrong and can be unforgiving when made to lose face, but she is someone you can definitely rely on!

Jodie Foster is a good example of a female Ox personality: she possesses steely determination at work, but always places her children's needs first.

The **WOOD FEMALE OX** is tough, strong, and domineering, capable of brushing aside weaker mates and taking full control. The wood element relentlessly compounds all of the attributes of the Ox character.

The **FIRE FEMALE OX** is less understated but definitely more impatient than her Ox sisters. The fire element introduces passion and excitement to an otherwise subdued and heavy-duty character. She is less restrained, and could be enticed to be more demonstrative of her feelings. She is more assertive than other Ox women and can voice her opinion strongly if pushed to do so.

The **EARTH FEMALE OX** is a self-possessed and very confident female. The earth Ox is glamorous and flamboyant. She pursues her goals with sheer determination and hard work, and is resilient in the face of adversity. Earth Ox women can be relentless and have great patience. They are also clever. Don't mess with them!

The **METAL FEMALE OX** comes across as the most charismatic of the Oxes (think of Princess Diana), but she is steely and tough. Prone to bouts of depression, she can nevertheless rise above these feelings and work hard at overcoming setbacks. The metal Ox can be generous to a fault, but do her wrong and she will never let up.

The **WATER FEMALE OX** is strong and fearless and has a long fuse. The water female Ox is gentler and probably kinder than her Ox sisters, but she is as tough underneath. She is also more understated and patient, exuding an outward calm that can be reassuring. She hides her thoughts superbly, and is usually reserved and secretly sentimental. If you cross her, or in any way betray her trust, she will get her revenge one day. A water Ox seldom forgets.

The Understated Ox Gentleman

He is the strong silent type, the sort who plans and plots his moves carefully, who thinks things through before speaking, and who is tough under the skin! He is sure of himself and clear about his ambitions. At his worst, he is quite ruthless, and even at his best, his sense of superiority shows through. Ox men are usually clever and often brilliant, and they usually rise to positions of leadership. Some of the last century's most feared men were Oxes—think of Adolf Hitler.

Ox men are seldom obvious or showy. They are not great conversationalists, preferring to observe from a distance and merge into the background, but engage them in conversation and you will find them enormously interesting and full of substance. Ox men read widely and have brilliant intellects.

Ox men are not particularly loving, neither are they especially sentimental. They dislike frivolity carried to excess, and are averse to obvious shows of grandeur. What they respond to is knowledge and a matching intellectual capability. They identify with those who express themselves with clarity. There is nothing vague about the Ox gentlemen, yet he is a man of few words. For him, actions speak louder than words.

The Ox male can be passionate, and he is capable of quite extraordinary loyalty and great love. His gifts of love are tangible and practical— such as a house, a car, or a piece of real estate! To win his friendship, let him know you respect and admire his intellect, and be very genuine. Refrain from being too obvious.

The WOOD MALE OX is ruthless to a fault. He is crafty and brilliant, and is thoroughly ambitious and unrelenting in the pursuit of his ambitions. Exceedingly eloquent and a gifted politician, the wood Ox tends to bring out passionate hatred in those who are stamped on by him. He can be authoritative and domineering, so you must be prepared to bend to his will!

The FIRE MALE OX is less ruthless than his Ox brothers; perhaps the passion of the fire element ignites the vigorous toughness of the Ox character. Nevertheless, he is impatient. He has great endurance and resilience.

The EARTH MALE OX is a perfectionist, and is unrelentingly ambitious, confident, and autocratic. He can be tender inside, but it takes digging to find it! He has strong endurance, and is meticulous and highly disciplined, pursuing his goals with single-minded resolve. Fiercely protective of those he loves, he can be rough on those who cross him.

The METAL MALE OX is very dogmatic in his approach to life. He tends to be stubborn and uncompromising, and is quite difficult to live with, being also critical and unimaginative. He is monstrously hardworking and expects all who work with him to demonstrate a similar level of industry and determination.

The WATER MALE OX works hard and pursues grand ambitions, but with less single-minded vigor than his Ox brothers. He is laid back, and tends to be more sensitive to alternative viewpoints. This is the most attractive of the Ox men. He will respond to affection, and can even be quite tender!

The actor Morgan Freeman is an Ox gentleman; true to type, he is confident, with clear ambitions.

The Mesmerizing Lady Tiger

Desirable, adventurous, and brave, the Tiger lady oozes sex appeal. Often brazen and impulsive, she dashes through life with fervent zeal, constantly looking out for new thrills and spills. Tiger women are ferociously exciting creatures—unshackled by rules and fiercely independent. Theirs is a passionate existence, and everything they do is lavishly heaped with emotion and enthusiasm. Their attitudes are often extreme—no half measures. They can be crafty and wily, but they can also be highly vulnerable. They can become victims of their own flamboyant passions. Easily bored, they move from one relationship to another, desperately seeking love. Plus, their innate honesty can blind them to potential dangers. When confronted with rejection, they stay crushed and broken—but only until the next great love of their life comes along!

Relatively speaking, Tiger women are good at making money, being both creative and imaginative. They are fun-loving and adore the good life, so may squander away cash.

The Tiger female prefers to be direct, and for her, *la grande passion* sounds as enticing as a marriage proposal. She makes a devoted wife and mother. She may be unconventional, but she is capable of great sacrifice for loved ones. Just do not expect great tenderness from her!

Desirable and possessing lots of sex appeal, the actress Penelope Cruz is a typical Tiger lady.

The **WOOD FEMALE TIGER** will never be a boring companion. This hyper-energetic lady is unconventional and full of fun. She is charming, temperamental, and flamboyant. If you want her, be manipulative. Flatter her, cajole her, appeal to her passionate nature—she'll lap it all up!

The **FIRE FEMALE TIGER** is not less vibrant or charismatic than her Tiger sisters, but she does mellow with age. She matures gracefully, but her sensual and passionate nature never quite cools. Fire-element Tigers are the most resilient, and for staying power, they are hard to beat.

The **EARTH FEMALE TIGER** has a calming influence, making her less headstrong and impetuous than other Tiger girls. She is passionate and adores the excitement of a love affair, although she is less carried away by the pleasures of the boudoir than her more gullible sisters! She has a stronger connection to home and family than other Tiger women and can be quite maternal.

The **METAL FEMALE TIGER** is a woman whose principles and convictions translate into meaningful action. She is also an optimist and has a very compassionate nature, but toward causes rather than people. She can be cold and chilly once love flies out the window, but she is magnetic and, once under her spell, it is hard to pull away.

The **WATER FEMALE TIGER** is the most appealing of the Tiger women because the water element adds great charm to her nature, transforming this passionate creature into someone loving and worthy of admiration and respect. Water Tigers are stable and serene, and hence they are more powerful. Beware of the explosive temper that lies underneath calm waters. Bask in her love and friendship, but play fair with her!

The Dazzling Tiger Man

Noble, action-oriented, and possessed of a magical aura of excitement, the Tiger man is hard to resist! Here is an energetic human dynamo who will sweep you off your feet with his tempestuous, gutsy, and passionate nature. His charm is legendary, and his eloquent gestures of love are irresistible. Tiger guys are hard to pin down, and are full of tantalizing grand plans to conquer the world! It is easy to get carried away by their sense of adventure, their obvious ambitions, and their super social graces. You sense they are the sort to get things done, to achieve great things, and you find their easy disdain for social snobbery refreshing and even enticing. Then, of course, there is their attractive air of hidden passion and sensuality.

But Tigers have lethal claws. They can be fierce, dramatic, stubborn, and vengeful as well. So dealing with Tiger men requires much emotional resilience. Vigorous in protecting his space, his ideas and his domain, the Tiger male can wear down anyone with his demands. Don't expect understanding from him. Engaging in a superficial friendship with a Tiger is easy, and even fun, but up close it's another story. The Tiger man will not think twice about walking out on a relationship. He loves change, and craves the excitement of new conquests and new homes! To get along with the Tiger, be as adventurous and as courageous as he is. Accept his all-or-nothing attitude. Share his majestic passions, his grand plans to transform the world, to make a billion dollars, and to reshape society!

The **WOOD MALE TIGER** loves change. Vital and energetic, he has grand plans and craves the excitement of testing innovative ideas. With him you will never be bored, but he could wear you out.

The **FIRE MALE TIGER** is the ultimate male chauvinist, dripping with macho sensuality and revolutionary ideas. Think Hugh Hefner, who changed an entire generation's attitude toward sexuality; and John Derek, the svengali of some of the world's most beautiful women.

The **EARTH MALE TIGER** is an expert at seduction. He loves the chase, but once successful he thinks nothing of walking away—often without a shred of remorse. Yet once snared, he is loyal and loving, though seldom faithful.

The **METAL TIGER MALE** is somber and conservative. He is less energetic and more thoughtful than the other Tiger males. The metal element lends him an air of thoughtfulness, which sits well on him, making him almost impossibly attractive!

The **WATER TIGER MALE** is lovable and loving, admired and respected by his peers. Success comes easily to him. He enjoys the kind of popularity his Tiger brothers find hard to come by. The water Tiger male is stable, diligent, and disciplined, keeping his passionate Tiger nature under tight control. He comes across as totally magnetic. To win him, you have to be beautiful, talented, sexy, and passionate!

Singer Robbie Williams is a Tiger man, an energetic action man who is difficult to resist. Tiger men require a partner who is as adventurous as they are.

The Virtuous Female Rabbit

The lady Rabbit is diplomatic, tactful, and works at being liked. Friendships are important to her, although the Rabbit woman rarely sticks her neck out for anyone. She colors her interactions with optimism and is eager to please. She is good at keeping up appearances and is discreet. Social acceptance is important to her; social climbing is her great skill. She is at her snobbish best as the wife of a successful man.

Appearing feminine, unassuming, and modest is the female Rabbit's forte. Her clothing is sedate and understated, her manners are impeccable, and she says the right thing at the right time. She is motivated by her instincts of self-preservation, is seldom outrageous, and never blatant or aggressive. This popular lady has a superb sense of prudence and intuition, and she conforms gracefully. She is an excellent listener; in her company you feel calm. She is probably the most materialistic of all the signs, and one of the most cautious.

The Rabbit lady will want a good marriage, a grand home, a successful husband, and a perfect family. She will rarely marry anyone with limited prospects. Rabbit women are rarely ambitious, but their husband and sons benefit from their networking skills and drive.

Actress Ingrid Bergman was born in the year of the Rabbit. Rabbit women are well mannered and sedate, and are excellent at keeping up appearances.

The WOOD FEMALE RABBIT is truly the solid-citizen type. Generous, altruistic, and immensely diplomatic, this lady is also very shrewd and clever, especially at camouflaging her true feelings and private ambitions. The wood element intensifies her sense of tradition. Appeal to her feel-good sensibilities if you want to get anywhere with her.

The FIRE FEMALE RABBIT seems more aloof, more reserved, and even more arrogant than other Rabbit females, but is also brilliant at stage-managing relationships. If you want to get along with her, don't play games—you will not win! She is the expert at subterfuge and getting her own way. She could smilingly demolish you, and you would not even know it!

The EARTH FEMALE RABBIT is the sexiest of all female Rabbits. She can love you and leave you. Candid in speech, the earth Rabbit lady uses her skills to personal advantage, without appearing to do so! She is charming in her approach. There is an understated and virtuous elegance in everything she does. Quite a lady!

The METAL FEMALE RABBIT is steely strong, using her considerable Rabbit-like skills to create a veneer of studied modesty and diplomacy. This lady seldom acts on impulse, deliberating her actions and words carefully. Don't try to pry her secrets from her. Accept her the way she is and you will get along famously.

The WATER FEMALE RABBIT is always proper and calm on the surface, yet may be fearful inside! Her sense of style and taste are more evident, but she is also less devious and clever than her Rabbit sisters. She will never upset her well-ordered existence; the symbols of security are crucial to her. She wants and needs looking after.

The Amiable Rabbit Man

Low-profile, tactful, and accommodating—these are some of the words that describe this easygoing, nice man! Always correct, well groomed, and well mannered, the Rabbit gentleman almost never offends anyone. He has honed the art of diplomacy to perfection, and it is very rare to hear him utter anything negative about anyone. He is seldom confrontational—he prefers to walk away from arguments or at the slightest hint of trouble.

The Rabbit male is very shrewd and is good at networking. For him, impressions count for more than substance, and he is much taken up with the trimmings of success—the right address, the right clothes, the right friends. Thus he carefully cultivates his image, and comes across as a polished and amiable person.

The Rabbit male knows how to accommodate and conform in the nicest way. He also knows how to lavish attention on people important to him. He is the ultimate survivor—smooth and suave and oozing charm, and always wearing a mask of amiability to hide his true intentions. This is a man who plans his moves and charts his course carefully. There is little room for spontaneity.

The **WOOD MALE RABBIT** is a real gentleman. Here is a man who represents all that is stable, correct, and rational. He is easy to get along with, kind, and provides more than adequately for those dear to him, but he needs to be in control. He will work at maintaining peace and harmony in the home, but he expects support and good behavior. Shame him, or make him lose face, and he will walk away without a trace of remorse!

The **FIRE MALE RABBIT** has a caustic sense of humor but an otherwise staid disposition. The fire Rabbit is more forthcoming than other Rabbits and although he is affable, he is also self-centered to the point of arrogance. He can be aloof and reserved. When successful, he is a snob, yet all the while continuing to be smoothly amiable to those who are important to him. This guy truly is great at practicing the virtues of hypocrisy—but of course he is a survivor!

The **EARTH MALE RABBIT** is more stylish than the rest. His keen intellect is camouflaged beneath a laid-back approach to life that can be deceptive. Underneath that smooth and pleasant exterior lurks a crafty mind that is sharp and knowledgeable. The earth male Rabbit cherishes conformity. Behave outside the norms of social decorum, and he will treat you with disdain.

The **METAL MALE RABBIT** is honorable, strong, and perceptive. He possesses steely determination and systematically implements well thought-out plans that map out his life and career. This is a man who can be very successful. He has good taste and an air of dignified good breeding. Stay loyal and true to him, and be scrupulously honest, and he will pull you up with him.

The **WATER MALE RABBIT** is faithful, charming, and always dignified, carrying himself with an air of refinement. This water gentleman has it all. Usually well educated and widely read, he is also an interesting conversationalist. He will work at getting ahead, and will have much to offer, but keeping up appearances is important to him.

Actor Brad Pitt is a Rabbit man. Rabbit men cultivate their image, and they come across as amiable and diplomatic.

The Charismatic Dragon Lady

She is so captivating and vibrant, so stunningly sexy, you cannot ignore her! The Dragon lady possesses tremendous personal magnetism and a brilliant intellect. There is an irresistible air of superiority about her. Her leadership qualities are universally acknowledged; her creativity and flair for making money are legendary. Success, good living, and wealth seem to come to her effortlessly. She is intimidating, and she carries it all off with easy nonchalance.

The Dragon lady is neither modest nor unassuming. She views the world as revolving around her, yet she is rarely boastful. She has class, good taste, and supreme confidence. The Dragon lady loves publicity and attention. She is vocal and independent. She will never play second fiddle to a man. Men are mesmerized by her and many pursue her. If you fall for a Dragon lady be prepared to face massive competition. She will flirt with you and entice you. Massage her ego shamelessly. Never hurt her pride. She does not take kindly to criticism, no matter how well intentioned. And do not gossip or whine. Don't try to be subtle. Laugh with her. Party with her. Hobnob with the beautiful people and invite her along. She adores the good life—champagne and caviar are her thing! Most of all, try to refrain from being possessive.

The actress Kate Winslet has the personal magnetism and vibrant sexuality that typify Dragon ladies. Dragon ladies have impeccable taste, and they enjoy the good life.

The **WOOD FEMALE DRAGON** comes across as warm, kind, and full of goodwill. She is clever but is nevertheless dramatic and extravagant. Encourage her exhibitionist tendencies and she will lavish attention on you. Help her when things go wrong; she cannot handle crises very well at all.

The **FIRE FEMALE DRAGON** is the most charismatic lady of the Chinese zodiac! She is endowed with a powerful intellect, is rampantly attractive, and totally mesmerizing. She is also vulnerable and easily hurt. She makes grand gestures and initiates massive projects, yet can get steered off course because of a fragile ego. She wants and needs support, but whoever provides it must stay behind the scenes. Like all Dragon women, she will not be shackled and enjoys independence of thought and action.

The **EARTH FEMALE DRAGON** is the most charming, but also the most vindictive and dangerous of the Dragons! Ego-driven and in constant need of praise and flattery, this lady wants power and recognition. She demands complete and utter loyalty. Cross her at your peril!

The **METAL FEMALE DRAGON** is supremely, achingly ambitious! Tough, steely, and ruthless, she is the epitome of the corporate big shot. She wants power, a lavish lifestyle with everyone deferring to her and adoring her . . . and she will get it all, by fair means or foul!

The **WATER FEMALE DRAGON** is extremely talented and creative, and often achieves success in the performing arts. She is less of a show-off, but she can be quite imperious. The water element cools much of her ardor, so she is less impulsive than her Dragon sisters and less prone to their sweeping, extravagant gestures.

The Impetuous Male Dragon

Dragon men are usually charismatic and dashing, running through life with massive doses of self-confidence. They have huge ambitions, and their dreams of success are usually larger than life. In their minds failure is never a possibility, so they implement plans, ideas, schemes, and other things with enthusiasm and great fervor.

Many formidable projects and deals of the Dragon man take root, grow, and flourish! Dragon men are wonderful performers and great exhibitionists. They face challenges head on, with courage and vigor, and even when situations sour, they rise to the occasion with great fortitude.

The confidence of the Dragon manifests in varying degrees of arrogant behavior, which can be obnoxious when in large doses! They often breeze through their relationships oblivious that they may be causing negative impressions. Dragon men can be tyrannical and despotic, although oftentimes their innate kindliness peeps through. They demand acknowledgment of their authority, being great snobs, and hence are terribly conscious of their job titles and social status.

Sometimes the self-centered arrogance of the Dragon male can be tiresome, but because he almost always delivers on everything promised, his ego is forgiven! In love this guy is notoriously unfaithful. To cope with the Dragon male, feed his need for recognition. Listen adoringly as he lectures you on his multitude of talents. To be fair, he is not just hot air. Dress magnificently when he takes you out. Remember, he loves to party.

The **WOOD MALE DRAGON** is the deep-thinking Dragon who directs his massive intellect toward creative and artistic pursuits with great success. Flamboyant and unconventional, he is the absolute master of the grand gesture.

The **FIRE MALE DRAGON** is feisty, magnetic and impressive. The fire Dragon's ardor and vigor drive him into schemes so grandiose and vast that they take your breath away! Yet his enthusiasm is also matched by a skill at successfully bringing his schemes to fruition.

The **EARTH MALE DRAGON** has an intensity that is hard to match. The earth element gives him resilience, and tons of charm. He will never lack for friends and supporters.

The **METAL MALE DRAGON** is tough and rough, and could even be ruthless. He has a huge temper, which can get out of control. However, there is a side to him that can be affable, gentle, and kind. It will take a special woman to bring this out. He can sometimes take a perverse pleasure in playing cat and mouse with those he loves.

The **WATER MALE DRAGON** is gentler, kinder, and more loving than the other Dragon types. The water element adds a soft touch to his fiery temperament so that friends and lovers benefit from his generosity. He is, however, less single-minded, and perhaps less confident than his Dragon siblings. To win him, actively boost his confidence and make him feel good and he will be indebted to you.

Actor Russell Crowe is a Dragon male. Dragon men are very ambitious and can sometimes be arrogant; they are notorious for being unfaithful in love.

The Tantalizing Snake Woman

Endowed with exceptional beauty, the Snake lady is cool, alluring, and dignified. She has impeccably good dress sense. Her excellent manners and sensitivity endear her to many. She has the good fortune of being unintentionally and innocently seductive, and is seldom short of admirers. Men fall passionately and irrevocably in love with her. She evokes uncontrolled jealousy, so deep friendships with women can be hard to come by.

The Snake slithers through life, blissfully unaware of her considerable charms, casting her serpentine spell with neither forethought nor malice. The Snake is simply the Chinese zodiac's symbol of feminine sexuality. Snake women are also exceedingly clever, capable of deep intellectual thought. If they pursue academic careers they will be successful. Snakes are wily, and are really good at evading truths. They also often skillfully color facts with tiny embellishments. The Snake temptress knows how to misrepresent in the nicest possible way.

They are meticulous in everything they do, in their work, social life, and dress. They have expensive tastes and are often narcissistic; their love of luxury is legendary. They adore opulence and are greedy for the good things in life. They are often lucky, usually marrying above their own class so money is always available.

Actress Kim Basinger's looks indicate she is a perfect Snake lady: alluring, dignified, and always meticulously dressed.

The **WOOD FEMALE SNAKE** is a dreamer, but she is also pragmatic in her work and career. Her burning urge is to attain fame and fortune, but she is vulnerable to rejection and irrational jealousies. She suffers from an acute fear of loneliness and craves popularity. She needs love and adoration in order to feel secure.

The **FIRE FEMALE SNAKE** is deep-thinking and masterful as she slithers her way into boudoirs and boardrooms. She has strong willpower and makes friends and allies easily. The fire Snake can be ruthless. She is elusive, and will stay devoted to you only if you stay true to her. Waver, and she will coolly slither out of your life.

The **EARTH FEMALE SNAKE** is the power-hungry one, whose head is full of glamorous dreams of power and wealth, fame and fortune. Amazingly intelligent and persevering, she attracts powerful mates who provide her with the lifestyle she craves. She has the drive to be very successful in her chosen field. She is also resilient and courageous, fighting back in times of adversity.

The **METAL FEMALE SNAKE** is a mighty, talented lady whose life often gets hit by major reversals of fortune, caused by the loss of loved ones or family fortunes, but they often rise again and go on to better things. The metal Snake is vulnerable to heartbreak, caused by an uncharacteristic naiveté, and tends to be a loner.

The **WATER FEMALE SNAKE** has a huge intellect, terrific determination, and the ability to achieve all she wants. She often becomes outstandingly successful in her chosen field, usually despite great odds. Vanity features strongly in her nature, but she also has a lot of common sense and often pulls through during tough times.

The Seductive Gentleman Snake

Strong, silent, and seductive, the male of the species is as irresistible as the female. His special appeal for women comes from his sunny disposition. He is never offensive or confrontational, seldom loses his temper, and is sensitive to others' feelings. The Snake gentleman is careful not to make waves. His approach to life is colored by his philandering ways and his success with women. He is inclined to be lazy, although he has the ability to pursue intellectual and other pursuits with great success—if he can discipline himself. Snakes make attractive mates, especially when they succeed in their careers.

Snake men are cautious and prudent, rarely making good entrepreneurs. They usually prefer compromise to risk-taking and lack the streak of ruthlessness required in managing large businesses. In the face of aggression, the Snake man tends to turn away from a fight. This is not a weakness, just the way he is. Indeed, most of the time he stays oblivious to aggression. He will not do anything that might upset his tranquil existence.

Snakes are thinkers more than doers. They cannot abide chaos and they dislike the frenzy of fast-paced activities, valuing predictability and routine. They hate surprises, especially nasty ones. Snake men are not good at handling rejection or setbacks, and although inside they are hurting like crazy, on the surface they stay cool.

The **WOOD MALE SNAKE** is an exquisite communicator, skilled at public speaking. This charming man, with his understated humor, is irresistible. He is resilient and pragmatic, and although he fears rejection and loneliness, his gregarious nature makes him a great social success.

The **FIRE MALE SNAKE** is brilliant and power hungry. Possessed of strong willpower and surrounded by many adoring cohorts, this guy makes and keeps friends very easily. He is also highly principled and has the courage of his convictions. He thinks deeply and though he finds it tough to be faithful, he nevertheless regards his wife and family with deep respect.

The **EARTH MALE SNAKE** is a gentle, delicate charmer whose dreams and fantasies protect his fragile ego from the harsh glare of reality. He lacks the perseverance and determination to transform his grand plans into reality, but he is usually able to attract and manipulate capable women who fall at his feet and will happily give him the support to see things through.

The **METAL MALE SNAKE** yearns for fame and widespread recognition, suffering delusions of grandeur and believing himself a creative genius. He is charming, and though he is very slow to trust those around him, they usually love him enough to play along, doing all the work, yet allowing him to take all of the credit! Lucky, lucky snake!

The **WATER MALE SNAKE** combines an almost genius-like ability at self-promotion with a huge dose of common sense. Water Snakes are so clever, and so focused on attaining the heights they set themselves, that they usually succeed. If you find a water Snake, stay with him. He is generous and quite prepared to share all that he has with those dear to him.

James Bond actor Pierce Brosnan is a Snake gentleman; they are characterized by their strong, seductive nature and success with women.

The Warmhearted Horse Lady

Proud, individualistic, and restless, the Horse lady has the natural self-assurance and unique confidence that come from a genuine belief in her own self-worth. Hers is the ultimate free spirit that should neither be broken nor confined. Anything that threatens her independence is regarded with suspicion. She is nobody's fool, but she is amazingly warmhearted, generous, and courageous.

Usually the Horse woman breaks free of the family at a young age. She will indulge her thirst for adventure by traveling to distant lands for new experiences. She is restless if not allowed to pursue this wanderlust. She needs to be surrounded by activity and enjoys championing causes, although these are usually short-lived. The Horse lady prides herself on being highly principled. Dishonesty is anathema to her. She is neither a fraud nor is she boastful, but she seldom compromises and can be idealistic. She does not require the outward trimmings of success, and is disdainful of lesser mortals who derive their self-worth from material accessories. More than being liked, she prefers respect. She is bossy, but seldom autocratic. Nor is she intolerant of other people's viewpoints. Once decided, she rarely changes her mind, so she can be dogmatic. Yet her strength, her perseverance in any given situation, and her interest when confronted with challenge enables her to have her way.

The model Cindy Crawford is a Horse lady. Horse ladies are naturally self-assured and confident. They can be bossy but will listen to the viewpoints of others.

The **WOOD FEMALE HORSE** is opinionated and judgmental. Highly sociable, she is a born over-achiever, and she can be self-centered. Headstrong and blessed with a multitude of talents, she runs riot, unfocused and without a real goal. Hence, she tends to suffer from burnout.

The **FIRE FEMALE HORSE** is like a volcano about to erupt, rebellious and headstrong. She is a mass of contradictions—naive and sophisticated, forthcoming and irrationally wild, greedy and generous. But many will find her exciting.

The **EARTH FEMALE HORSE** is far more good-natured and easygoing than her fire sister. She is also less impetuous, less hotheaded, less selfish, less excitable—and definitely more stable. She knows how to accept authority and play the game according to the rules. Consequently, she will be respected in her chosen career and well liked by her colleagues. She is sensible and faithful, but don't forget she's still a Horse, and if you want her, appeal to her sense of adventure.

The **METAL FEMALE HORSE** is a tame horse. She is law-abiding and serious. She does everything right, and is careful about hiding her true feelings. She seems to prefer a more ordered existence. Emotionally she is dignified and stable. If you love a metal Horse, be ready to allow for the occasional bursts of frenetic energy.

The **WATER FEMALE HORSE** is a winner of a woman! Generous, gregarious, confident, competent, adaptable, and usually successful in everything she undertakes, she can also seem aloof and reserved. She will not allow just anyone to get intimate with her, and true to her nature she abhors frauds and phonies. Patience is needed to understand her complex nature.

The Headstrong Male Horse

Independent, outspoken, and eloquent, the male of the Horse is the sporty type. He loves the outdoors and delights in fitness exercises and athletic pursuits. There is an air of suppressed restlessness, yet in public he maintains an almost elegant image of seriousness. The nonconformist underneath, however, creates an ambivalence of behavior, and he continually needs to find outlets for his impatient spirit.

He is pragmatic, respecting traditions and social conventions, yet he cannot deny his innate honest nature, eschewing subtlety and behind-the-scenes diplomacy. The Horse is not a politician. He speaks his mind, maintains a healthy ego and rejects dishonest behavior. The male Horse seldom lies, and he is direct and straightforward in all of his dealings. He does have the courage of his convictions, and although he lacks finesse and polish, he is nevertheless very reliable. Once he gives his word, you can depend on him to stay loyal to the work in hand.

He is a man of few words, and sometimes appears shy and modest, but he is attracted to glamour and finds sophisticated women with painted fingernails and long hair quite irresistible. Horse males are attractive because they come across as macho and strong. When in love, they are capable of doing crazy things and going all the way. They do not just like the women in their lives. They fall madly in love and often carry a torch for the same woman for years. When occasionally they succumb to a one-night affair, they are riddled with guilt and often confess to their infidelity.

The WOOD MALE HORSE has a pretty high opinion of himself. Yet he is a man of substance, demonstrating talent in a variety of fields. He is also bold, foolhardy, and intolerant of stupidity.

Often his uncompromising attitude causes him to self-destruct, and his insensitivity could sabotage his chances of success.

The FIRE MALE HORSE is fiery, touchy, and temperamental. Proud and opinionated, he is hard to understand and seems easily upset. This free spirit is liable to spin out of control at the slightest hint of disagreement, and personal relationships often suffer, yet he is an exciting and wildly attractive man.

The EARTH MALE HORSE is much more good-natured and easygoing. Often clever, he is also a survivor and holds his own counsel, even when cornered. He is the sort who will give in, in order to live and fight another day.

The METAL MALE HORSE walks tall and dignified. He is emotionally stable, a bit of a snob, and ambitious. He conforms to society's norms and is very good at hiding his feelings. Because he keeps things bottled up inside, he could explode and suffer from nervous collapse.

The WATER MALE HORSE is confident, adaptable, relaxed, and laid back. As a result, he finds success in his pursuits, and enjoys the material fruits of his success. The water Horse makes a wonderfully warm and fun-loving mate. He is reliable, honest, highly principled, and quite the best kind of friend. He may appear aloof, but he has a heart of gold.

The actor Harrison Ford is a Horse. Horse gentlemen are respectable and straight talking. They are macho and strong, and fall madly in love with women.

The Gentle Female Sheep

This lady comes across as gentle, dreamy, and pliable. She is willing to please and is the first to commiserate when your plans go awry. Sheep ladies almost always avoid confrontation, preferring to let others have their way rather than get into an argument. They display this same attitude in other areas of their life. They prefer to let others lead, decide, and take the responsibility.

Sheep women are rarely ambitious in their corporate career, but they are not weak. They overpower with their special brand of passive non-resistance. They never directly humiliate their enemies. Their way is to manipulate behind the scenes, and they are subtle and patient. Sheep women make dangerous enemies. They confound even their worst adversaries by seeming innocent.

Sheep ladies are long-suffering. Their inner fortitude sets them apart from those who give in to fatigue and obstacles. On the surface they seem to follow dull routines, yet they are, in fact, infuriatingly spontaneous, giving in to whims and seeming easily distracted. When they stand you up, rather than apologize directly, they are likely to shower you with gifts. It is all part of their charm—they break your heart without the slightest intention of doing so. They often appear extremely surprised when they let you down because they never intended to hurt you at all! There is something ethereal and very beautiful about the Sheep lady. Sweet-natured and always ready to oblige, she responds to gentle persuasion.

The **WOOD FEMALE SHEEP** is a whimsical, seemingly "dumb blonde" whose gentle smile hides a tough interior. She is an expert at worming her way into the affections of those who can be useful to her. She does not mind living off the generosity of others.

The **FIRE FEMALE SHEEP** adds passion and excitement to an otherwise controlled nature. She is exceedingly dramatic, especially when things go wrong. She needs the solid and dependable support of a strong mate to bring out her refined nature. She needs security, yet can be annoyingly careless with money, squandering her resources.

The **EARTH FEMALE SHEEP** is the ultimate femme fatale, a lady who works (often very successfully) at being the favored love of a rich and successful man. She can rely on the support and largesse of others, yet she is often also able to keep her self-respect intact.

The **METAL FEMALE SHEEP** comes across as a total pushover, innocent, simple, and apparently bird-brained. It is easy to underestimate her. The metal element lends her a toughness of spirit and a hard heart. She is expert at subterfuge, and is a master puller-of-strings behind the scenes! She is proud and sensitive. Be wary—don't hurt her.

The **WATER FEMALE SHEEP** is the sex siren of the Sheep species! This is a powerfully attractive lady, whose irresistible charm and skills in the art of flattery get her everywhere. She is a great social success. She maintains her reserve and has her own agenda, and it is not easy getting close to her.

Actress Nicole Kidman was born in the year of the Sheep. Sheep women are ethereal and beautiful and never threatening. They are not weak, but they do prefer others to take responsibility.

The Romantic Male Sheep

Cunning, manipulative, and unpredictable, the male Sheep is probably the Chinese zodiac's most crafty politician. Not for him the obvious show of strength or the dramatic display of resources. He plays his cards very close to his chest, cultivating an image of dignified rectitude. He comes across as placid, unruffled, and seemingly vague.

Inside, however, he is hatching one great scheme after another. Extremely ambitious, he wants power, influence, and wealth, but he is careful never to let the world know of his ambitious schemes. His strategy is almost always subterranean. In business, he builds layers of protective structures that shield him from having to deal directly with anyone, and he stalks the competition patiently, cautiously. As a boss, he is never patently autocratic, but he will not tolerate insubordination or criticism. Unless you have already won his respect, don't try to influence him—better to enjoy his benevolence. In politics, he can be ruthless and quite devoid of scruples.

For the male Sheep, there is no such thing as friendship or goodwill. When crossed, he will not forgive or forget, and he makes a fearful adversary. His methods are never brash or foolhardy. He is insidious and totally unpredictable. He will never let his guard down. In love, he is adventurous and imaginative and quite the romantic. If he wants you, he will get you, annihilating the competition with his characteristic and quiet perseverance.

The **WOOD MALE SHEEP** is a less serious, more amenable Sheep. He is not as ambitious as his Sheep siblings, nor does he have the same steely determination, but he is as wily and clever. His forte lies in his immense social success.

The **FIRE MALE SHEEP** is quite irresistible. Such a sensitive and romantic gentleman! He has an air of quiet dignity and calm refinement that sets him apart from others, and he is blessed with a persuasive countenance that makes him extremely influential. The fire Sheep is, thus, easily successful at whatever he chooses to do. He has charisma and is often incredibly lucky.

The **EARTH MALE SHEEP** may not be as eloquent or as hardworking as the others, but he has the uncanny ability of attracting the most wonderful coterie of friends and acquaintances. His success comes from a vivid imagination and a brilliant ability to get along with everyone.

The **METAL MALE SHEEP** is a gentleman who will charm you with his bohemian outlook and often disheveled appearance. Casual and easygoing, he is kind and thoughtful, and is always eager to please—but don't be fooled. The metal element gives him a steely and determined outlook. He can be temperamental and moody, and he is also quite capable of combative behavior.

The **WATER MALE SHEEP** is the most outstanding of the Sheep men! Clever, intuitive, and intensely charming, he is a survivor and will rise to great heights, no matter what his background or circumstances. He looks innocent and simple, almost childishly lovable, but he is a completely ruthless and ambitious manipulator.

The owner of Microsoft, Bill Gates, is a male Sheep. The male Sheep is a master of cunning strategy and is extremely ambitious.

The Delightful Monkey Lady

Unconventional, gracious, and hospitable, the Monkey lady is a delightful and entertaining friend. Extremely generous, she tends to be a sweet busybody who solves everyone's problems. She is seldom boring, always full of gossip and anecdotes, yet never intentionally malicious. Monkey ladies have opinions about everything and everyone, but hers is a fun-filled attitude where everyone is viewed as an ally and a chum. She is tolerant of other people's shortcomings and rarely overly critical or judgmental. No matter how you offend her, she will not hold a grudge against you.

She has a beautiful sense of humor and can laugh at herself. She is a good sport and a loyal friend. Her spirited approach stops short of sarcasm, and her jokes are rarely at anyone else's expense.

However, she is hard to pin down. She tends to be disorganized and is not good at keeping to schedules. She is not a great planner or plotter, yet has a natural flair for cunning. She can be slippery and is hugely quick-witted, especially if she feels threatened. Any attempt to confine her will make her take off. The Monkey lady cannot abide anything that is likely to constrain her independence.

This lady has a fantastic memory for details. She is meticulous in her work and is excellent as an editor or accountant. Yet she can expend enormous energy on small, unimportant things.

Oscar-winning star Halle Berry is a Monkey lady. Monkey ladies have a great sense of humor and are full of fun.

The **WOOD FEMALE MONKEY** epitomizes all that is stunning about the species. The busy wood Monkey has many commitments to friends and business associates. Here is an enormously entertaining and good-natured social creature— a social-climbing phenomenon who will always be surrounded by people.

The **FIRE FEMALE MONKEY** is such a glamorous and stunning female! The fire element lends extra drive to an already smoldering character. She is dominating and hugely imaginative. Her energy levels are high, and, for her, the thrill of the chase is what makes life exciting. Here is a trendsetter par excellence, a free spirit consumed by a fierce passion for life.

The **EARTH FEMALE MONKEY** is definitely a sentimental and more serious female, respected for her wisdom and insights. It is easy to like and respect her, for she is jolly and inspirational and achingly romantic. She is also a perfectionist, and can be excessively intense.

The **METAL FEMALE MONKEY** is the tough one, being feisty and hostile. The metal element lends her a determined and strong personality. She is also cunning and crafty when put on the defensive. There is an air of tragedy about her, and when despair sets in, which is not uncommon, she gets caught in a spiral of depression.

The **WATER FEMALE MONKEY** is both beautiful and talented. Elizabeth Taylor is a celebrated water Monkey. Unselfish and totally supportive of her man, here is a witty, clever, and resourceful lady Monkey, a glorious survivor who meets with disappointment and yet is able to pick herself up again and again. She is strong yet gentle, seductive yet vulnerable.

The Impudent Male Monkey

Here is the most extravagant suitor of the Chinese zodiac! He will woo you with diamonds and sapphires, serve you the best champagnes, take you to the most expensive dining rooms of the world, and fly you first class-everywhere! Monkey men are so generous that they will give you everything they own, but they will never give themselves. Monkey men guard their independence jealously.

The outrageous Monkey gentleman loves the sound of his own voice and is happiest when he has an attentive audience. Prone to spending sprees and impulsive binges, he will happily lend money to a friend in need, but will balk at extending his own palm out for help. He would rather suffer in silence than lose face by admitting that he has any financial or personal difficulty.

The Monkey is unrelentingly obvious. He wants only to be well thought of and to be liked by everyone. He is also quite funny, never taking himself too seriously. In business, he is a fantastic risk-taker, often getting himself into a bind as a result. Being a Monkey, he also has the supreme ability to wriggle out of difficult situations and tight spots. Indeed, he can be very crafty and wily, and he survives as much by his wit as by his unerring charm, which never fails him.

The Monkey male often has a boyish appeal that attracts the maternal instinct in women and the paternal instinct in men. People like him a great deal because, at face value, he almost always comes across as extremely trustworthy and seemingly deserving of help.

The **WOOD MALE MONKEY** is a man who is literally oozing with good intentions. He is the ultimate social climber, and he possesses the consummate skill of being able to move gracefully through a roomful of strangers with total ease.

He comes across as superficial, mainly because most of the time he is. The wood Monkey is not one for intimate friendships.

The **FIRE MALE MONKEY** has drive and ambition and a more focused outlook. He is a self-starter whose enormous energy and fertile imagination can propel him into the stratosphere. He can be driven to excess as he climbs the ladder of opportunity. Be wary—he can be ruthless.

The **EARTH MALE MONKEY** is perceptive and calm. He is scholarly and thoughtful, and makes an excellent teacher, being ingenious and creative in the way he presents things. He is popular, with an attractive sense of humor. His sentimental view of the world makes his approach to love and romance attractive to women.

The **METAL MALE MONKEY** can be resentful of other people's success, and sibling rivalry could bring out the fighter in him. He can be a formidable adversary. This man has a winning demeanor that often hides dark motives.

The **WATER MALE MONKEY** is clever and witty. He is fun, gregarious, spirited, and affable. This man is highly popular, being generous both in spirit and in kind. The water Monkey is helpful and supportive. He tends to be wildly sexy, and is often attracted to temperamental, fiery females.

Actor Michael Douglas is a Monkey gentleman. Being a Monkey, he is quite crafty but has a boyish charm. He is funny and loves to have an appreciative audience.

The Purposeful Rooster Lady

The Rooster lady is a resourceful, practical woman whose organizational talents are legendary, and who is forthright and frank. She is supremely confident, unbowed by convention and comfortable with prestige and power. The Rooster lady is loyal and will go to great lengths to protect her roost. She rules her roost with a heavy hand, expecting her attitudes and her feelings to be reciprocated. Roosters love deeply, and when disappointed develop a protective shield against those who have hurt them.

The Rooster lady rarely wears her heart on her sleeve, preferring to suffer in silence. She takes life seriously and is disdainful of impressive rhetoric not backed by substance. She hates snobs and social climbers. When challenged, she often adopts a confrontational approach. Roosters can come across as forbidding and hard. Don't corner her. When her back is to the wall, she will lash out in a cruel manner.

Inside, however, she is as kind as can be, seldom bearing grudges. She is sentimental when touched by love or when she meets someone she vastly respects. Professionally, the Rooster woman is multitalented. She pursues a course of self-sufficiency and independence resolutely, often placing her work above her family. She appreciates tangible things such as cars, yachts, and real estate. She tends to attract weaker men, but it is the strong she will die for!

The **WOOD FEMALE ROOSTER** is a strong, persevering female. She is an efficiency expert, great at expressing social niceties, and quite adept at diplomacy. She seldom reveals her true feelings.

The **FIRE FEMALE ROOSTER** thrives on arguments, taking joy in demolishing lesser mortals. Complex and passionate, the fire element lights up the Rooster's temperamental nature. She is also impulsive and headstrong—often her own worst enemy. Yet she can be emotionally fragile. She needs and wants close friends, and is a great pal.

The **EARTH FEMALE ROOSTER** is an elegant fowl indeed. Quick-witted and clever, hers is a penetrating mind that sifts the chaff to find the substance. Nothing fools her. Her powerful memory is awesome, and her knowledge of all things is intimidating. She will shine and shine in a structured corporate environment.

The **METAL FEMALE ROOSTER** is the ultimate performer. She thinks she is always on show, and blows her own trumpet a lot, not because she needs to impress others, but because of her naturally boastful nature.

The **WATER FEMALE ROOSTER** is multitalented, adaptable, and terrifically attractive. She works hard at everything she takes on, and makes a fabulous boss—a truly benevolent despot. She often makes it to great heights of success late in life. She has secret ambitions to be as rich as Croesus—although wealth seldom comes easy to her—she needs to work for it. Water Roosters have a seductive streak that makes them quite irresistible.

The actress Catherine Zeta-Jones is a Rooster lady. Rooster women are confident, and they like to rule the roost! They are very talented, and they often prioritize work over family.

The Resilient Male Rooster

This macho and masterful male is the epitome of the person who values outward appearances. He truly enjoys strutting his stuff! There is a studied elegance in the way he stands and carries himself, and in the way he reacts to situations.

Rooster males are productive and surprisingly creative. They are capable of superb analysis and have tremendous organizational skills. They make great CEOs of large corporations. Rooster bosses are methodical, responsible, and play by the rules of the game. Power sits easily on them, as does the odd subterfuge, although they are not schemers by nature. Rooster males are direct and transparent. They are loudly righteous about their honesty, which can be a weakness. This tendency to be outspoken gets them into conflicts, but they are resilient and can successfully pick themselves up when bruised and in difficulty.

The Rooster male is unrelenting when it comes to breaking hearts. He is a passionate and skillful lover, but with this man it is mainly physical. When you are ill or unavailable, you can expect him to fly the roost in search of gratification elsewhere. Unless you are clever enough, and sufficiently strong emotionally, think twice before hitching yourself to him. Having said that, Rooster men will seldom permanently desert their family. While you cannot expect any emotional support from him, he is a good provider.

The **WOOD MALE ROOSTER** is singularly image-oriented. Face is vital to this man's makeup, and he will go to great lengths to maintain appearances. He is an outspoken man, but will rarely reveal his true feelings. He is sociable, amiable, and makes a sincere friend.

The **FIRE MALE ROOSTER** is bad-tempered; the fire element manifests itself in a tyrannical rage if this man is crossed. His inflated ego constantly needs stroking. If he is able to settle down, this Rooster can be a great friend.

The **EARTH MALE ROOSTER** has a penetrating wit, a great intellect, and the gift of the gab. He is direct, focused, and makes a great team player. He can usually be found working with people in large corporations or on committees. Neither too impulsive nor too overenthusiastic, this male is also less showy than his more flamboyant siblings.

The **METAL MALE ROOSTER** has charm and bottled-up vigor. Women find him intensely attractive, and men seek out his company. The metal Rooster is often the soul of the party, holding forth eloquently. He adores being surrounded by people and loves an audience; to please him pay him lots of attention. With his skill at giving performances, he is extremely suited to the theater. A great guy!

The **WATER MALE ROOSTER** is often conservative and old-fashioned and is less rigid and forthright than the others. He is gregarious, eager for companionship, and full of good intentions. He suffers from feelings of inferiority, which can impair his chances of success at work or in love. If he can overcome this, he is a joy to know.

The actor Christian Slater was born in the year of the Rooster. Rooster men are macho and masterful; they are both creative and methodical in their working lives.

The Generous Dog Lady

Agreeable, self-effacing, and shy, the Dog female comes across as quiet and introspective. Often a loner, always low-profile, and not very sociable, she drowns herself in work and is most comfortable engaged in some charitable and noble purpose. She is generous with her time. Often naive, to her everything in life is serious; there is little room for frivolous pursuits. She is sober and careful, punctilious and correct. As a result, she seldom takes risks. Despite the tendency toward negativity, however, the Dog lady is genuinely nice and touchingly candid. It would be difficult to find a more loyal or helpful ally. It is just tiresome that she can be so self-righteous.

This lady is always worrying, fearful, and panicky. When in the company of courageous and foolhardy people, she tends to come across as a dreadful wet blanket. She requires emotional support and tender loving care. It is easy to take advantage of her easy, trusting nature. Often she knows it, and she will find herself a powerful mate to protect her from the big, bad world. Emotionally, the Dog woman develops maturity late in life, and when she does, she might well devote herself to a cause that means a great deal to her. Her pessimism, however, can be all-pervasive, and most Dog women simply cannot shake it off. As a result, many of them end up alone, as spinsters or favorite aunts.

The **WOOD FEMALE DOG** is profoundly affectionate, a real sweetheart—warm, caring, and totally reliable—but she is not a pushover. She is basically a giver, mainly to those she cares for and to causes she believes in. She is not motivated by material gain, nor by recognition. She has to believe in what she does.

The **FIRE FEMALE DOG** is modest and idealistic, and her sincerity and earnestness endear her to many. She is an eloquent, persuasive, and influential spokesperson for her favorite causes. When success eludes her, she can spiral into a vortex of addictive behavior and suppressed rage. She feels things much too deeply and must relax.

The **EARTH FEMALE DOG** is reserved, secretive, and uncomfortable with crowds. She can be hypersensitive, and her view of the world is colored by a belief that things always go wrong. She tries to be adaptable but responds positively only to someone strong and loving.

The **METAL FEMALE DOG** has a bark and a bite! She is the dame with the confidence to accomplish great things—climb Mount Fuji, find a cure for Aids, revolutionize the education system. The metal element adds sparkle to her idealism and will spur her into action.

The **WATER FEMALE DOG** is very beautiful, with an air of aloofness. She is hard to know, and is aggressive, but not vicious. As a friend, she is as loyal as all Dogs, but it is not easy getting close to her. If you manage to break through, however, she will overwhelm you with affection.

Singer Madonna is a Dog woman. Dog women make loyal and candid friends. They tend to take their work seriously, and they are generous with their time.

The Faithful Male Dog

Affectionate, faithful, and loyal, the male of the Dog clan wears a sober, droopy countenance that reflects his pessimistic view of life. He whines and growls about a multitude of wrongs, injustices, and tragedies that befall humankind, yet he seldom does much about it. The male Dog lacks courage and is usually averse to risk-taking. He is fearful and nervous, sometimes verging on paranoia. There is also a defeated look about him, as if the burdens of the world are just too much to bear.

However, despite his initial negative appearance, the male Dog has many positive attributes. He can be fastidious and industrious. He can rise to great heights when motivated, although this is often the exception rather than the rule. Once he reaches a plateau in his career, he is content to spend his days researching, analyzing, and criticizing the ills of humankind. What is important to him? Justice! The environment! Human rights! Global warming! The rainforests of the world! Yet he is no visionary. He supports all of these causes from the armchair, and while he will pontificate, loudly and with a certain eloquence to all who will listen, he will not stick his neck out or take risks for the cause.

He is loyal and a great chum; a devoted friend. At a personal level he is the ultimate giver. He could easily overwhelm you with his acts of benevolence. He is appreciative of every little kindness, meticulously indebted for every small favor, and profuse in his gratitude. He fears rejection with a passion and works at all his friendships. In any relationship, he is comfortable only when he is the giver.

The **WOOD MALE DOG** is your best friend, complete ally, and loyal chum. He is the faithful subordinate and the trustworthy partner. He can be relied upon absolutely, but he abhors all things underhanded. Play fair and straight with him and he will reward you with long-term service and loyalty. His climb to the top will be achieved through industry and conviction.

The **FIRE MALE DOG** is an uncompromising champion of the underdog. Well meaning and feisty, his idealism is often naive and quixotic. Yet he plods along, unfazed by cynicism or opposition. Cool his passions by redirecting his energies toward other causes.

The **EARTH MALE DOG** needs solitude and peace. When his well-meaning attempts to take on good causes rebound, he is physically sickened. A typical Dog's tale indeed.

The **METAL MALE DOG** is the Dog who has the bite as well as the bark. He is the cleverest and most likely to succeed among the Dogs. He has the confidence, strength, and perseverance to marry his idealism with action. He is a great conversationalist and a superb mixer.

The **WATER MALE DOG** is affable, a really good friend. His intentions can border on being meddlesome, and he is frequently taken advantage of. He is extremely handsome, but lacks courage and self-esteem. Water Dogs are impetuous. Theirs is a false bravado. They need strong mates. Motivate him with a sense of self-worth and he will sparkle. Otherwise he could sink down into a well of pessimism.

Prince William is a Dog man. Dog men are affectionate and very loyal, and in their relationships, they are the givers.

The Sensitive Boar Woman

These lovely ladies of the Chinese zodiac make the best girlfriends! They will be delightfully compassionate, affectionate, and supportive of all your hair-brained schemes, and instantly forgiving when you wrong them. Little wonder they are well liked and popular. The Boar lady nurtures her friends, plying them with gifts and obliging them with favors, even at some sacrifice. It seems part of their nature to be caring. They tend, however, to be gullible, falling prey to unscrupulous cads.

Particularly in matters of the heart, boars tend to take a fantasy view of romance, dreaming of the dashing prince in shining armor, and being stubbornly naive, refusing to see anything but goodness in the men they love. They appear to be in love with love, and this artlessness can cause them to fall for the wrong sorts of men. When they are wronged, however, they are seldom vengeful.

Boars have a passion for food. They also love opulence and luxury, and are frequently blessed with a good deal of money luck (they either inherit or marry into money). Most Boars have the wherewithal to indulge their sumptuous tastes. Boars are comfortable at dinner parties, either as guests or as the hostess. Boar women are also incurable name-droppers.

Boars are possessive. If there is one thing they take umbrage with, it is if you try to steal their friends or boyfriends. They can become petty and competitive. Yet even then, they are guileless, and will seldom demonstrate bitchy behavior. Boars really do shy away from confrontation and quarrels. At worst, they will drop you from their guest list and, quite literally, cease being your friend.

The WOOD FEMALE BOAR is considerate, compassionate, and kindhearted. She gives of herself to friends and colleagues with a great outpouring of kindness. She can be excruciatingly shy and self-effacing. She is home-based, and in love is timid, seldom taking the initiative.

The FIRE FEMALE BOAR is the aggressive Boar. She is energetic, obstinate, and has rigid ideas about how things are done. The fire Boar is a fervent idealist and loves taking up arms on behalf of some seeming social injustice. She loves being the power behind a successful partnership.

The EARTH FEMALE BOAR always starts with the best of intentions, and with an idealistic view of how relationships (and the state of their world) ought to be, but when upset by reality, she will rave and make your life miserable.

The METAL FEMALE BOAR is honest and forthright and has impressive personal integrity. She strenuously avoids confrontations and prefers to reach quiet consensus than argue. In a stalemate, she will give in and back off gracefully.

The WATER FEMALE BOAR is levelheaded, sane, and has excellent manners. She is neither sophisticated nor does she yearn for a particularly materialistic lifestyle. Water Boars need friends, and although she is seldom gushing about those she cares for, she is always loyal.

Sarah Ferguson was born in the year of the Boar. Boar women take a fantasy view of romance and can be rather naive. They love to indulge in good food.

The Perceptive Male Boar

This perceptive gentleman inspires good feelings in others. Everyone likes him because he is sensitive. He is also delightfully self-effacing, always giving way and never being aggressive. At his most extreme, the Boar man appears meek and slightly apologetic, but his good nature is sometimes laced with sarcasm. Like his female counterpart, the male Boar loves opulence. When surrounded by the security that luxury represents, the Boar man's confidence soars, and it is this sense of well-being that brings out the best in him.

When things don't work out his way, the Boar male finds it hard to cope. His tendency is to turn on himself. He will blame and flagellate himself, feeling guilty and depressed at his own stupidity. Yet he seldom learns from his mistakes. The Boar male is not trusting of anyone and everyone, and in love he is slow to enter into a relationship. He is successful with the opposite sex, and he plays his game slowly and steadily. To win this amiable character, mother him mercilessly. He just adores being smothered and indulged, being treated like a child again.

Professionally, the Boar is industrious and productive—an excellent employee. Contrary to the popular view, the Boar is not lazy. In business he tends to be lucky, and although his naiveté makes him vulnerable to unscrupulous types, he usually pulls through, and has little difficulty making money. He has good taste in personal grooming as well as in the design of his work and living spaces.

The WOOD MALE BOAR is bashful and needs to be encouraged to take the initiative in friendships and relationships. He avoids occasions where he is required to make idle conversation—parties and social gatherings are not his style! This man is distinctly uncomfortable with emotional outbursts. Be gentle with him.

The FIRE MALE BOAR is more forthcoming and energetic than the other Boar types. The fire element imbues him with spirit and courage. He tends to be self-centered and opinionated, and can be stubborn and recalcitrant. Fire Boars make excellent powers behind the throne, and can be counted upon for loyal and faithful support.

The EARTH MALE BOAR doesn't know the meaning of subtlety. Sometimes his lack of sophistication makes him appear like a country bumpkin, but he plods on, oblivious to criticism. He is the sort who can take jokes directed at him, but he usually has the last laugh, because success comes easily to him.

The METAL MALE BOAR is a nice, rational man whose life is well ordered. He is conventional and unadventurous. His is a practical and pragmatic view of life and he can also be dogmatic. Usually reserved and retiring, he shuns the spotlight. Mother him if you want to, but don't push him to do what he doesn't want to do. He will resist.

The WATER MALE BOAR is a clever and patient diplomat who works systematically from behind the scenes. He is idealistic and a visionary. His ambitions are not to do with personal or material gains; he wants a better world! Think of Henry Kissinger and you get a feel for what this man is like.

Director Steven Spielberg is a gentleman Boar. The Boar man tends to be lucky in business but becomes depressed if things do not work out well.

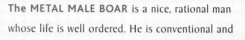

Calculating Your Kua Number

There is a powerful feng shui formula that can be used to determine if you are a West group or East group person, and from there to identify your lucky and unlucky directions. The calculations are based on your birth date and your gender. The formula offers a personalized method of determining your auspicious and inauspicious directions.

To find out if you are an East or West group person, you need to know your Kua number. This is based on the year of your birth and your gender. To discover this, check the tables in the three following pages.

First, look down the table to find your relevant year of birth, paying special attention to the starting date of each year. On each line you will see the animal followed by the year element, followed by the Kua numbers for males and females. For instance, if you were born in March 1941, you are a Snake—if you are male your Kua number is 5 and if you are female your Kua is 1. East group people have Kua numbers 1, 3, 4, 9. West group people have Kua numbers 2, 5, 6, 7, 8. East group people: East group directions are lucky; West group directions are unlucky. West group people: West group directions are lucky; East group directions are unlucky. Try to tap your lucky directions at all times.

This diagram shows your lucky directions, depending on whether you are an East or a West group person. Ensure you face your lucky directions as much as possible to bring you good luck.

EAST GROUP
SOUTH
SOUTHEAST
EAST
NORTH

WEST GROUP
SOUTHWEST
WEST
NORTHWEST
NORTHEAST

KUA NUMBERS
1 3 4 9

KUA NUMBERS
2 5 6 7 8

Kua Numbers Direct from the Chinese Lunar Calendar

ANIMAL		WESTERN CALENDAR DATES	HEAVENLY STEM ELEMENT
	Male Kua number Female Kua number		
RAT (water)	m7 f8	Feb 18, 1912–Feb 5, 1913	water
OX (earth)	m6 f9	Feb 6, 1913–Jan 25, 1914	water
TIGER (wood)	m5 f1	Jan 26, 1914–Feb 13, 1915	wood
RABBIT (wood)	m4 f2	Feb 14, 1915–Feb 2, 1916	wood
DRAGON (earth)	m3 f3	Feb 3, 1916–Jan 22, 1917	fire
SNAKE (fire)	m2 f4	Jan 23, 1917–Feb 10, 1918	fire
HORSE (fire)	m1 f5	Feb 11, 1918–Jan 31, 1919	earth
SHEEP (earth)	m9 f6	Feb 1, 1919–Feb 19, 1920	earth
MONKEY (metal)	m8 f7	Feb 20, 1920–Feb 7, 1921	metal
ROOSTER (metal)	m7 f8	Feb 8, 1921–Jan 27, 1922	metal
DOG (earth)	m6 f9	Jan 28, 1922–Feb 15, 1923	water
BOAR (water)	m5 f1	Feb 16, 1923–Feb 4, 1924	water

• Start of 60-year cycle

RAT (water)	m4 f2	Feb 5, 1924–Jan 23, 1925	wood
OX (earth)	m3 f3	Jan 24, 1925–Feb 12, 1926	wood
TIGER (wood)	m2 f4	Feb 13, 1926–Feb 1, 1927	fire
RABBIT (wood)	m1 f5	Feb 2, 1927–Jan 22, 1928	fire
DRAGON (earth)	m9 f6	Jan 23, 1928–Feb 9, 1929	earth
SNAKE (fire)	m8 f7	Feb 10, 1929–Jan 29, 1930	earth
HORSE (fire)	m7 f8	Jan 30, 1930–Feb 16, 1931	metal
SHEEP (earth)	m6 f9	Feb 17, 1931–Feb 5, 1932	metal
MONKEY (metal)	m5 f1	Feb 6, 1932–Jan 25, 1933	water
ROOSTER (metal)	m4 f2	Jan 26, 1933–Feb 13, 1934	water
DOG (earth)	m3 f3	Feb 14, 1934–Feb 3, 1935	wood
BOAR (water)	m2 f4	Feb 4, 1935–Jan 23, 1936	wood
RAT (water)	m1 f5	Jan 24, 1936–Feb 10, 1937	fire
OX (earth)	m9 f6	Feb 11, 1937–Jan 30, 1938	fire
TIGER (wood)	m8 f7	Jan 31, 1938–Feb 18, 1939	earth
RABBIT (wood)	m7 f8	Feb 19, 1939–Feb 7, 1940	earth
DRAGON (earth)	m6 f9	Feb 8, 1940–Jan 26, 1941	metal
SNAKE (fire)	m5 f1	Jan 27, 1941–Feb 14, 1942	metal

HORSE (fire)	m4 f2	Feb 15, 1942—Feb 4, 1943	water
SHEEP (earth)	m3 f3	Feb 5, 1943—Jan 24, 1944	water
MONKEY (metal)	m2 f4	Jan 25, 1944—Feb 12, 1945	wood
ROOSTER (metal)	m1 f5	Feb 13, 1945—Feb 1, 1946	wood
DOG (earth)	m9 f6	Feb 2, 1946—Jan 21, 1947	fire
BOAR (water)	m8 f7	Jan 22, 1947—Feb 9, 1948	fire
RAT (water)	m7 f8	Feb 10, 1948—Jan 28, 1949	earth
OX (earth)	m6 f9	Jan 29, 1949—Feb 16, 1950	earth
TIGER (wood)	m5 f1	Feb 17, 1950—Feb 5, 1951	metal
RABBIT (wood)	m4 f2	Feb 6, 1951—Jan 26, 1952	metal
DRAGON (earth)	m3 f3	Jan 27, 1952—Feb 13, 1953	water
SNAKE (fire)	m2 f4	Feb 14, 1953—Feb 2, 1954	water
HORSE (fire)	m1 f5	Feb 3, 1954—Jan 23, 1955	wood
SHEEP (earth)	m9 f6	Jan 24, 1955—Feb 11, 1956	wood
MONKEY (metal)	m8 f7	Feb 12, 1956—Jan 30, 1957	fire
ROOSTER (metal)	m7 f8	Jan 31, 1957—Feb 17, 1958	fire
DOG (earth)	m6 f9	Feb 18, 1958—Feb 7, 1959	earth
BOAR (water)	m5 f1	Feb 8, 1959—Jan 27, 1960	earth
RAT (water)	m4 f2	Jan 28, 1960—Feb 14, 1961	metal
OX (earth)	m3 f3	Feb 15, 1961—Feb 4, 1962	metal
TIGER (wood)	m2 f4	Feb 5, 1962—Jan 24, 1963	water
RABBIT (wood)	m1 f5	Jan 25, 1963—Feb 12, 1964	water
DRAGON (earth)	m9 f6	Feb 13, 1964—Feb 1, 1965	wood
SNAKE (fire)	m8 f7	Feb 2, 1965—Jan 20, 1966	wood
HORSE (fire)	m7 f8	Jan 21, 1966—Feb 8, 1967	fire
SHEEP (earth)	m6 f9	Feb 9, 1967—Jan 29, 1968	fire
MONKEY (metal)	m5 f1	Jan 30, 1968—Feb 16, 1969	earth
ROOSTER (metal)	m4 f2	Feb 17, 1969—Feb 5, 1970	earth
DOG (earth)	m3 f3	Feb 6, 1970—Jan 26, 1971	metal
BOAR (water)	m2 f4	Jan 27, 1971—Feb 14, 1972	metal
RAT (water)	m1 f5	Feb 15, 1972—Feb 2, 1973	water
OX (earth)	m9 f6	Feb 3, 1973—Jan 22, 1974	water
TIGER (wood)	m8 f7	Jan 23, 1974—Feb 10, 1975	wood
RABBIT (wood)	m7 f8	Feb 11, 1975—Jan 30, 1976	wood
DRAGON (earth)	m6 f9	Jan 31, 1976—Feb 17, 1977	fire
SNAKE (fire)	m5 f1	Feb 18, 1977—Feb 6, 1978	fire

HORSE (fire)	m4 f2	Feb 7, 1978–Jan 27, 1979	earth
SHEEP (earth)	m3 f3	Jan 28, 1979–Feb 15, 1980	earth
MONKEY (metal)	m2 f4	Feb 16, 1980–Feb 4, 1981	metal
ROOSTER (metal)	m1 f5	Feb 5, 1981–Jan 24, 1982	metal
DOG (earth)	m9 f6	Jan 25, 1982–Feb 12, 1983	water
BOAR (water)	m8 f7	Feb 13, 1983–Feb 1, 1984	water
RAT (water)	m7 f8	Feb 2, 1984–Feb 19, 1985	wood
OX (earth)	m6 f9	Feb 20, 1985–Feb 8, 1986	wood
TIGER (wood)	m5 f1	Feb 9, 1986–Jan 28, 1987	fire
RABBIT (wood)	m4 f2	Jan 29, 1987–Feb 16, 1988	fire
DRAGON (earth)	m3 f3	Feb 17, 1988–Feb 5, 1989	earth
SNAKE (fire)	m2 f4	Feb 6, 1989–Jan 26, 1990	earth
HORSE (fire)	m1 f5	Jan 27, 1990–Feb 14, 1991	metal
SHEEP (earth)	m9 f6	Feb 15, 1991–Feb 3, 1992	metal
MONKEY (metal)	m8 f7	Feb 4, 1992–Jan 22, 1993	water
ROOSTER metal)	m7 f8	Jan 23, 1993–Feb 9, 1994	water
DOG (earth)	m6 f9	Feb 10, 1994–Jan 30, 1995	wood
BOAR (water)	m5 f1	Jan 31, 1995–Feb 18, 1996	wood
RAT (water)	m4 f2	Feb 19, 1996–Feb 6, 1997	fire
OX (earth)	m3 f3	Feb 7, 1997–Jan 27, 1998	fire
TIGER (wood)	m2 f4	Jan 28, 1998–Feb 15, 1999	earth
RABBIT (wood)	m1 f5	Feb 16, 1999–Feb 4, 2000	earth
DRAGON (earth)	m9 f6	Feb 5, 2000–Jan 23, 2001	metal
SNAKE (fire)	m8 f7	Jan 24, 2001–Feb 11, 2002	metal
HORSE (fire)	m7 f8	Feb 12, 2002–Jan 31, 2003	water
SHEEP (earth)	m6 f9	Feb 1, 2003–Jan 21, 2004	water
MONKEY (metal)	m5 f1	Jan 22, 2004–Feb 8, 2005	wood
ROOSTER (metal)	m4 f2	Feb 9, 2005–Jan 28, 2006	wood
DOG (earth)	m3 f3	Jan 29, 2006–Feb 17, 2007	fire
BOAR (water)	m2 f4	Feb 18, 2007–Feb 6, 2008	fire

Notes:

The element next to the animal is the earthly branch element. The letters and numbers that follow this refers to the Kua number; m = male and f = female.

Personal Directions of Fortune and Misfortune

From the Kua formula you can easily determine your lucky and unlucky directions, which are further broken down into specific types of good and bad luck. Note that each of the eight main directions of the compass represents either a specific type of good luck, or a specific type of bad luck. Each of the Kua numbers indicates the specific types of good and bad luck.

Here are the reference tables of lucky and unlucky directions based on the Kua numbers. Study the directions and the specific good and bad luck of each direction for each of the Kua numbers.

Use this knowledge to determine the best orientation of locations and objects in your house, from the main and secondary doors and the sleeping and working directions and locations to the eating and travel directions and much more besides. For more, consult my feng shui books. Use the tables to determine which specific direction you should activate for specific types of good luck. Once you know what your unlucky directions are, you will be able to tell whether a particular house will be good for you simply by checking the orientation of the main front door.

The reference of tables of lucky and unlucky directions based on the Kua numbers

KUA no.	1	2	3	4	5 (male)	5 (fem)	6	7	8	9
BEST	SE	NE	S	N	NE	SW	W	NW	SW	E
HEALTH	E	W	N	S	W	NW	NE	SW	NW	SE
LOVE	S	NW	SE	E	NW	W	SW	NE	W	N
GROWTH	N	SW	E	SE	SW	NE	NW	W	NE	S
Unlucky	W	E	SW	NW	E	S	SE	N	S	NE
Five ghosts	NE	SE	NW	SW	SE	N	E	S	N	W
Six killings	NW	S	NE	W	S	E	N	SE	E	SW
Total loss	SW	N	W	NE	N	SE	S	E	SE	NW

KUA no.	1	2	3	4	5 (male)	5 (fem)	6	7	8	9
Your direction	N	SW	E	SE	SW	NE	NW	W	NE	S
Your self element	water	earth	wood	wood	earth	earth	metal	metal	earth	fire
Your trigram	KAN	KUN	CHEN	SUN	KUN	KEN	CHIEN	TUI	KEN	LI
Yin or yang	yin	yin	yang	yin	yin	yang	yang	yin	yang	yang
Colors good for you	Black blue	Ocher red	Green blue	Green blue	Ocher red	Ocher red	White metal	White metal	Ocher red	Red green
Shapes good for you	Wavy round	Square pointed triangle	Rectangle wavy	Rectangle wavy	Square pointed triangle	Square pointed triangle	Round square	Round square	Square pointed triangle	Pointed triangle
Directions good for you	East group	West group	East group	East group	West group	West group	West group	West group	West group	East group

You can use the tables to determine your best sleeping direction. Depending on what kind of luck you wish to activate, let your head point toward the direction most appropriate to your particular aspiration. If you wish to activate family or romance luck, you want to start a family, or if your marriage is not going quite right, then you should sleep with your head pointed toward your love direction.

You can use this Kua formula of directions and orientations to activate particular aspirations. If you wish for success at work, if you want a promotion, or if you want to make your company more profitable, then sit at your work desk facing your best direction. If you are having health problems, constantly succumb to viruses, or simply cannot rest well at nights, then you should try to sleep with your head pointed to your health direction and you should eat facing your health direction. If you wish to study better, then you should sit at your desk facing your personal growth direction, and try to take your exams facing this direction. If you cannot tap in to this direction, then try to sit facing at least one of your four lucky directions.

If you are unable to sleep, sit, or work facing the direction you want, try to tap at least one of your four auspicious directions. This is to ensure that you do not face any one of your inauspicious directions, two of which can be deadly indeed. The six killings direction and the total loss direction are considered harmful and malevolent. Remember, no one has perfect feng shui or can tap all their best directions perfectly. There is no such thing as a perfectly feng shuied house. All we can do is get some advantage from good feng shui directions.

From the Kua number, you can also derive your self element and your trigram. These details will help you to enhance the feng shui of your personal body space as well as your living space.

Tea-Leaf Oracle

For more than a thousand years, tea-drinking has given great pleasure to the Chinese—it is the drink most lavishly praised, even above wine. Tea symbolizes earthly purity, so the preparation of tea calls for the most stringent standards of cleanliness. Drinking tea is associated with a special preparation ritual, which allows the mind to settle and become mellow. When one wishes to consult the tea-leaf oracle, drinking tea takes on connotations beyond assuaging thirst.

MAKE THE TEA

Two teapots are required, one for preparing the tea and keeping the tea leaves moist but not soaked in water, and the other to contain the freshly brewed tea. The water used must be properly boiled and teacups are warmed before use. Teapots should have a texture that allows the tea to "breathe." New teapots must be "seasoned" with tea leaves soaked in water boiled to high temperatures prior to their first use. This will get rid of any lingering odors, which can affect the accuracy of the oracle.

1   *Pour boiling water into an empty teapot to warm the pot. Make certain that all the bubbles have settled.*

2   *Empty the teapot and put in the tea leaves. As you do so, think of the question you wish to ask. The teapot should be filled up to about halfway with tea leaves. Ensure you do not block the spout, which is inauspicious.*

3   *Pour the boiled water into the teapot until the water overflows. Quickly pour away the water to "cleanse" the tea leaves.*

4   *Pour boiling water into the teapot along the edge of the pot once again until it overflows. Replace the lid and give the lid and the whole teapot a dash of boiling water as well.*

5   *All of the tea and some of the tea leaves can now be transferred into a second, more lavishly decorated teapot.*

6   *Pour the tea into three cups, allowing the leaves to also fall into the cups. Allow the tea to cool for a while and as you wait, close your eyes lightly and think of the question you wish to ask the oracle.*

7   *When the tea has cooled a little, drink the first cup in one continuous gulp, until only the leaves are left stuck to the bottom of the teacup. Do the same with the second and third cups.*

INTERPRETING THE SYMBOLS

- Shapes that are sharp or that represent weapons, arrows, and pointed objects denote danger and threats.
- Enclosed shapes, like a full square or circle, signify being hemmed in, a prison-like situation, a loss of freedom or independence.
- A bow and arrow shape indicates jealousy and spitefulness.
- Three solid lines or three broken lines are auspicious indications, the former for the man in the family and the latter for the woman, the mother figure. Three broken lines can also indicate the possibility of marriage.
- Numbers that total six or eight are auspicious.
- Numbers that total two or five indicate illness.
- Numbers that total three indicate court cases.
- Numbers that total four are an indication of forthcoming literary or educational success.
- Seeds indicate new beginnings.
- Trees and plants indicate growth, friends, and auspicious developments.
- Mansions and houses indicate security and protection.
- Flowers, bouquets, and bushes suggest celebrations, joyousness, and prosperity. A full bouquet could also indicate marriage.
- Sailing ships mean coming wealth.
- Airplanes mean forthcoming travel.
- Balloons and kites indicate a wish fulfilled.
- Birds often indicate new opportunities, although it depends on whether the bird is looking up (good) or down (bad). The more plumage indicated, the better.
- Trigrams and three-pointed symbols are auspicious. A fork indicates an important trade-off confronting you soon.
- Combs and comets indicate betrayals and deceit.
- Crosses indicate troubles, obstacles, and impending loss.
- Fish and bats are excellent indications of increasing incomes.
- Flags indicate victory of some sort, while umbrellas and turtles indicate protection from some accident.
- Full arches signify a marriage, while a half-arch indicates danger.
- Horseshoes and horses indicate that good luck and money are coming.
- A leaf, a shell, or a letter indicate significant news coming—often news about a rise in station or a promotion.

8 Study the tea leaves left over in the teacup very carefully. Perform the reading in order of the three cups so that you can get a chronology of the oracle prediction. The first cup describes the near-term situation, the second cup describes the medium-term situation, and the third cup describes the ultimate situation.

Check against the dictionary of meanings and indications given on this page. If you cannot see any equivalents, drink another three cups to see whether some outcomes may be more forthcoming. You do not need to be psychic to use the tea-leaf oracle—what is required is focused concentration. You do, however, need to have an "eye" for seeing symbols, patterns, images, and shapes in the tea leaves. The more you practice, the better you will be. Do not doubt the intuitive links and leaps you make between what you see in the leaves and events currently happening in your life. After a while, you will come to know when your intuition is seriously telling you something and when it is not.

Heart

Arch

Arrow

Boat

Trigram

Cross

Kite

Index

Acknowledgments

I thank my dear friends at Ebury—Amelia, Judith, and Denise—for sharing my excitement and enthusiasm for this book. Also Grace, and the team at Bridgewater Book Company, for all their effort working on the illustrations, editorial, and design of this book, making it come alive and vibrate in sync with the text. A manuscript is truly only one part of what makes a good book. It is your treatment of it that has made this book so special. Thank you.

VISIT LILLIAN TOO's Websites on the Internet as follows:

www.lillian-too.com
www.wofs.com
www.fsmegamall.com

You can write to Lillian at:
ltoo@wofs.com

picture credits

AKG, London 58, 59, 148, 166, 177tl.

BRIDGEMAN ART LIBRARY / Collection of the Earl of Leicester, Holkham Hall, Norfolk 65tl / V&A Museum, London 60.

CORBIS 29 / Asian Art & Archaeology, Inc 77 / Christies Images 65br, 132 / Cinema Photo 194 / Sheldon Collins 133tr / Dean Congor 61 / Maduff Everton 74 / Rufus F Folkks 190, 192, 195, 196, 202, 206, 207 / Mitchell Gerber 201, 205, 210 / Lynn Goldsmith 189 /Richard Hamilton Smith 37 / Historical Picture Archive 65tr / Angelo Hornak 177br / Dave G.Houser 141 / Christine Kolisch 157 / Chris Lisle 175 /Ali Meyer 64 / Ethan Miller 203 / Photo B.D.V 198 / Roger Ressmeyer 28, 129 / Leonard de Selva 133bl / Morse Shai 200 / Paul A. Souders 159/ Michael S. Yamashita 75.

CORBIS SYGMA 204/ Beirne Brendan 193, 209 / Robert Eric 199 / Trapper Frank 191, 211 / Szenes Jason 188 / Schwartzwald Lawrence 208 / Thierry Orban 13 / Hellestad Rune 197.

GETTY IMAGES / Chris Cole 138 / Larry Dale Gordon 134 / Alain Daussin 36 / G & M David de Lossy 55 / Stuart Dee 142 / Michael Krasowitz 70 / David Lees 79 / Jean Mahaux 44 / Kaz Mori 52 / Mark Romanelli 47 / Adam Smith 67 / V.C.L 23 / Andy Whale 104.

NASA 63.

We hope you enjoyed this Hay House book. If you would like to receive a free catalog featuring additional Hay House books and products, or if you would like information about the Hay Foundation, please contact:

HAY HOUSE

Hay House, Inc., P.O. Box 5100, Carlsbad, CA 92018-5100

(760) 431-7695 or (800) 654-5126 • (760) 431-6948 (fax) or (800) 650-5115 (fax) • www.hayhouse.com

Distributed in Canada by: Raincoast, 9050 Shaughnessy St., Vancouver, B.C., Canada V6P 6E5